European Casebook on

Principles of Marketing

The European Casebook Series on Management

Series Editor: Paul Stonham, EAP European School of Management, Oxford

Competing Through Services: Strategy and Implementation, Vandermerwe / Lovelock with Taishoff

European Casebook on Business Alliances, Greenwood

European Casebook on Business Ethics, Harvey / Van Luijk / Steinmann

European Casebook on Competing through Information Technology: Strategy and Implementation, Jelassi

European Casebook on Cooperative Strategies, Roos

European Casebook on Entrepreneurship and New Ventures, Molian / Leleux

European Casebook on Finance, Stonham / Redhead

European Casebook on Human Resource and Change Management, Hiltrop / Sparrow

European Casebook on Industrial and Trade Policy, Cadot / Gabel / Story / Webber

European Casebook on Managing Industrial and Business-to-Business Marketing, Jenster

European Casebook on Principles of Marketing, Saker / Smith

European Casebook on

Principles of Marketing

Edited by

Jim Saker
and
Gareth Smith

Loughborough University Business School

Prentice Hall

London   New York   Toronto   Sydney   Tokyo   Singapore
Madrid   Mexico City   Munich   Paris

First published 1997 by
Prentice Hall Europe
Campus 400, Maylands Avenue
Hemel Hempstead
Hertfordshire, HP2 7EZ
A division of
Simon & Schuster International Group

Typeset in Palatino and Times
by Hands Fotoset, Leicester

Printed and bound in Great Britain by
Hartnolls Limited, Bodmin, Cornwall

Library of Congress Cataloging-in-Publication Data

European casebook on principles of marketing / edited by Jim Saker and
    Gareth Smith.
        p.   cm.— (The European casebook series on management)
    Includes index.
    ISBN 0-13-227653-4
    1. Marketing—Europe—Case studies.   I. Saker, Jim.   II. Smith,
    Gareth.   III. Series: European casebook series in management.
    HF5415.12.E8E957   1997
    658.8'0094—dc20
                                                                        96–16019
                                                                        CIP

British Library Cataloguing in Publication Data

A catalogue record for this book is available from
The British Library

ISBN 0-13-227653-4

---

1 2 3 4 5   01 00 99 98 97

Contents

vi Contents

Series Editorial

The idea of a series of European Casebooks on Management arose from discussions during the annual case writing competition organized by the European Foundation for Management Development (EFMD) in Brussels. The case writing competition itself was set up to encourage the production of more case studies in management with a specifically European content, to meet the growing demand in European business schools and training programmes of corporations. Begun in 1989, the competition has now established itself as a major focus of interest for case study writers.

However, knowing that many European cases were being produced outside the context of the competition, it was decided to extend the search for cases more widely. The project was taken up by Prentice Hall International in 1991, who undertook to publish the series, and appointed a Series Editor to manage the academic aspects of the collection of volumes.

From the inception of the project, the EAP European School of Management, a *grande école* of the Paris Chamber of Commerce and Industry, agreed to finance the costs of the Series Editor, and Prentice Hall funded secretarial assistance. As well as its financial support, EAP is well positioned to supply an appropriate academic infrastructure to the editorial management of the Series. From its headquarters in Paris, it maintains establishments in Berlin, Madrid and Oxford, and its masters' level students train in three countries. EAP is one of the leaders in European multicultural management education and, of course, a major user of case studies with a European focus in its courses.

Early market research showed a strong and largely unsatisfied demand for case studies in European management at a time when interest in the completion of the Single European Market was at its height. Calls for case study writers and for volume editors met a good response, and the major fields of management were quickly covered as well as several important specialized areas not originally considered.

There is an increasing number of titles available in this Series of European Casebooks on Management on a wide range of topics including Business Alliances, Business Ethics, Competing Through Services, Cooperative Strategies, Entrepreneurship and New Ventures, Finance, Human Resource Management, Managing Industrial and Business-to-Business Marketing, Industrial and Trade Policy, Information Technology, International Business, Leadership, and Industrial Trade Policy. A full list of current titles is available from the publisher's UK address shown on page iv.

The case studies are intended to draw on the main developments and changes in their respective fields of management in recent years, focusing on managerial issues in corporations trading in or with the European Union. Although the principal concentration is on the non-governmental sector, the experience of governments and governmental agencies is included in some of the volumes to the extent that they affect the corporate sector. In the light of the title of the Series, cases dealing with European cross-border involvements have been given priority in inclusion, but material that relates to national experience or is conceptual or global in nature has been considered relevant if it satisfies the criteria for good cases.

A driving motive for developing the Series of European Casebooks on Management has been the wish to encourage the production of cases with a specifically European dimension. Not only have the regulatory background, institutional framework and behavioural traits of cases developed in the American business schools like Harvard always been barriers to their use in European management education, but the developing European Union has emphasized aspects of corporate development and strategy completely ignored in most American cases. With the build-up of cross-border business activity in Europe have come difficulties in cultural adjustment. The growing legislation of the European Commission in its '1992 programme' has imposed constraints and given freedoms not known in an American context, in such fields as technology, patents, competition, take-overs and mergers, freedom of establishment and workers' rights. There was clearly a need for case studies which took account of the rapid changes occurring in the European Union and which analysed corporations' responses to them. It is recognized in the kind of terminology which is now much more current in management thinking: 'European management', 'Euromanagers' and 'Pan-Europeanization' no longer raise eyebrows even if not everyone believes these are totally valid terms.

In selecting cases for their volumes, the Editors and the Series Editor asked the leading question again and again – what is a good case? It was not sufficient to take the accepted Harvard view. Cases are critically important to teaching at the Harvard Business School and have been since they were first produced in 1910. For example, in 1986 Benson Shapiro said that 'one must understand the fundamentals of course design, because each case must fit into the rubric of the course'. Shapiro also said the case writer should 'Ensure the case includes a balanced conflict'. In 1955, Robert Davies, also of Harvard, wrote that 'There are two kinds of cases . . . the *issue case* in which the writer poses a particular problem and the reader prepares a recommendation designed to overcome the problem, and an *appraisal case* in which the writer describes a management decision already made and the reader evaluates this decision'. Generally, cases now being written in Europe are less rigid and constrained. They reflect the multifunctional and multicultural aspects of modern European business. They are pedagogical, but less tied to functional disciplines than the Harvard cases described by Shapiro, and this again is probably because the boundaries of the functional disciplines themselves, like marketing and finance, are becoming less distinct. However, according to Paul Lawrence, in 1953, many of the 'good' points of Harvard case study teaching are nonetheless incorporated into European case writing: the emphasis on complex, real-life situations, the degree of interest aroused, the use of 'springboard cases', and the need for good reporting.

The essentials of 'good' case writing in European management have been discussed extensively by the judges of the annual case writing competition organized by EFMD. They can be summarized as follows from the main points of a presentation by Robert Collins of IMD Lausanne at the annual conference workshop and prize-giving in Jouy-en-Josas, Paris, in September 1993.

Although writing case studies in management involves an element of opportunistic, investigative journalism, the pedagogical needs of students should be paramount. The case writer should be objective; there is no place for personal opinion or advocacy – the case writer or teacher is neither judge nor jury.

As far as the audience for cases is concerned, the case must be interesting. The setting or topic should be attractive and the case raise compelling issues. A decision-forcing case is more likely to turn students on than a descriptive or expository one – but the snag is that students do not generally like open-ended and vague cases. The case should be transferable – across faculty members, programmes and institutions.

In terms of product quality, the case should exceed audience expectations of both performance and conformance. The length of a case is important – it should give optimal time for reading and analysis, and the quality and quantity of data should be right. Assimilation is made easier when the case focuses on characters or issues, is structured, has internally consistent data, avoids jargon and is written in high-quality prose. It should be remembered that inexperienced students have a low tolerance of ambiguity and of data/information.

Writing a good case involves creating a favourable climate among all the stakeholders in a company. They will not assist if there is not confidence, discretion and cooperation. In a company there are archetypal executives who must all be managed, for example, the 'champion' may steer the case writer through the company (but only when he or she is on hand); the 'guerilla' will appear to help, but snipe from out of sight; the 'security guard' will consider everything classified and not for discussion. The reality for a case writer on site in a company is that not everyone will love you.

The teacher can maximize the benefits of a good case. Opportunities for customization and experimentation should always be sought – among different sets of participants, programmes and in-team teaching. A good teacher can exploit the richness of a case and the acuity of the participants.

Clearly, the case method is not the only pedagogical method of teaching management. Charles Croué of the École Supérieure de Commerce de Tours believes it is the most revolutionary, because unlike teacher-centred or self-tutoring methods, it is an active and interactive method.

The method encourages students to organize their work, to exchange different points of view in complex discussions, to find compromise by negotiating, and to improve their skills at oral presentation. They learn to compare different solutions and to synthesize information and decisions. They can observe the relationships between different disciplines of management – like marketing and strategy – and understand the difference between theory and practice. In the case-study method they do all this in a situation of reality, solving a real management problem. All of these skills prepare students well for manager status.

The case method has three main distinguishing characteristics which set it aside from other teaching methods. It is *cooperative* – students work in groups, they exchange information, and it improves their communicative abilities. It is *dynamic* – students are stimulated from passivity to effort. And it is *democratic* – teachers and students have equal roles; there are no preset solutions, and ideas are freely exchanged.

Finally, the case method is well suited to the changing nature of management and business at the present time. The current environment is moving very quickly: case studies can 'catch' new events and issues as they happen (likewise, they may quickly date). They lend themselves well to performance measurement, as the managerial qualities of the students improve. The current wish for 'action-learning' is satisfied, and cases can be delivered using multiple media like videos and computers.

The present volume, by Jim Saker and Gareth Smith, is the first in the European Casebooks on Management Series which covers the general field of marketing.

There are at least two features of this volume of special interest. The first is that the cases are very up-to-date, all written after 1990 and most in the past couple of years. Few subjects move so rapidly as marketing, in theory and in practice, so cases which are contemporary are especially appropriate. They are also product- and corporate-based with names like Polo Mints, Nivea Sun, Carlsberg Ice Beer, Virgin Atlantic, ABB Transportation and IKEA. Contemporaneity and familiarity are features of case studies particularly appealing to students.

Secondly, the cases reflect a wide range of marketing themes and issues, and hence the title, *European Casebook on Principles of Marketing*. This casebook is tied in to the widely-used textbook by Kotler, Armstrong, Saunders and Wong, *Principles of Marketing* (The European edition, 1995), also published by Prentice Hall. In fact, the authors of the casebook specifically show how the cases and the text of Kotler *et al* can be linked in a powerful combination of learning experience.

Jim Saker and Gareth Smith also contribute a detailed analysis of the methodology and benefit of using marketing case studies, including an extensive marketing audit which is necessary to make informed decisions in cases as well as in the real world. They provide a step-by-step problem-solving process for case study work including SWOT analysis, objectives setting, gap analysis, and strategy generation and choice. Students using this book are provided with a scientific, logical and analytical framework for their work. There is no doubt *European Casebook on Principles of Marketing* is a rich complement to Kotler *et al*'s new European edition of *Principles of Marketing*, as well as a learning experience in its own right.

Paul Stonham, Series Editor,
EAP, European School of Management, Oxford

About the Authors

Patrick Barwise is Professor of Management and Marketing, and Director, Centre for Marketing, at London Business School, England.

Richard Blundel is senior lecturer in business management at Harper Adams College, Shropshire, England, and a tutor for the Open University Business School, England.

Margaret Bruce is senior lecturer in marketing and design management at Manchester School of Management, UMIST, England.

Vitaly Cherenkov is Professor of International Marketing at St Petersburg University of Economics and Finance, Russia.

Brenda Cullen is a lecturer in the Department of Marketing, Graduate School of Business, University College Dublin, Ireland.

Pantéa Denoyelle is a research associate at INSEAD, France.

Mike Elsas was formerly a research assistant at the UFSIA Center for Business Administration, University of Antwerp, and is now Physical Distribution Manager with a major Belgian transportation concern.

Ilya Girson is director of the MA in Marketing programme at the University of Westminster, London, England.

Bruce Hardie is Assistant Professor of Marketing at London Business School, England.

Frans A. Kense is Professor of Industrial Marketing and Printing Management at Tilburg Polytechnic, Holland.

Sabine Kuester is Assistant Professor of Marketing at Groupe Ecole Supérieure des Sciences Economiques et Commerciales, France (ESSEC).

Barny Morris is a research assistant in marketing and design management at Manchester School of Management, UMIST, England.

Timo Ranta is a PhD student at the Helsinki School of Economics and Business Administration, Finland.

John Saunders is the National Westminster Bank Professor of Marketing and Director of Loughborough University Business School, England.

Gareth Smith is Senior Lecturer in Marketing, Loughborough University Business School, England.

Tiziano Vescovi is Professor of Business Management at the University Ca'Foscari of Venice, and is head of the Marketing Department at CUOA Business School, Vicenza, Italy.

Walter van Waterschoot is Professor of Marketing at the Saint Ignatius Faculty of Applied Economics (UFSIA), University of Antwerp, Belgium.

Maureen Whitehead is the Marks & Spencer Fellow in International Retailing at Manchester Metropolitan University, England.

Ian Wilson is Senior Lecturer in Marketing, Staffordshire University, England.

Liesbeth Wuyts was formerly a research assistant at the UFSIA Centre for Business Administration, University of Antwerp, Belgium.

INTRODUCTION

Using Marketing Cases

A Cautionary Tale

A newly qualified graduate with a business degree from an eminent university was a little nervous on his first day in his new job. He was now well versed in all the latest management theories yet there was still something nagging at the back of his mind. He met up with the MD who asked him what area of the business appealed to him. The new employee dismissed finance because he was not fond of numbers; personnel because of his difficulties with people; operations because he did not like the noise and the grime, and marketing because he did not like selling. When asked what area he would like to work in he asked tentatively if there were any openings in the company's case study department.

The moral of this little tale is that studying business using cases does not inevitably produce well trained managers who are capable of transferring their learning quickly and efficiently to the real world. The reason for making this point right at the beginning of a casebook in marketing is to highlight the need for a more sophisticated approach to using cases than has been the norm in the past. The skills which may be developed within the case need first to be understood and then carefully developed to enhance their eventual transfer to actual problems when the student takes up managerial responsibilities. This simple assertion justifies the inclusion of a chapter devoted to the case method itself. We need to know more about cases to get the best out of them. In the process of getting the most out of them our business skills will improve. As our business skills improve so will the ability and confidence to transfer these skills to the real world when the time is right.

Why a Book of Marketing Cases?

There is a basic problem with a casebook. When you read a textbook you get what you seek, namely knowledge. When you read a casebook you also obtain knowledge but it typically is of limited intrinsic value as it relates only to one company's experiences at one point in time. Seen from this angle, the gathering of knowledge about a case is not an end in its own right. Instead it is a necessary base of information which then allows other types of complex learning to take place. It is the purpose of this introductory chapter to understand all the potential uses and limitations of the case method. This is critical for both student and case leader alike. Without a clear view of the required outcomes from the case method, students will find the method intimidating and eventually frustrating; frustrating because progress is not easy to gauge. Unlike a lecture, you do not end up with pages of notes which clearly signify a body of knowledge learned. The reason for this is that a skill is only seen when it is being used. When you stop, there is no clear physical record of progress. This inevitably impacts on the case leader who is also under pressure. He/she needs to understand the potential and limits of the case method to produce a useful learning experience for the student. This chapter therefore seeks to help both the student and the novice case leader alike. It starts, like all good stories, at the beginning.

Back to Basics: What are Cases and Why do We use Them?

The term 'case study' at its most basic simply refers to a description of a situation which exists or existed within an organization. Cases are therefore stories (usually real-life ones) about things which happened in a business. The story may be short or long; complex or simple; tightly focused or wide-ranging and including irrelevant information alongside the relevant. The reason generally put forward for studying cases is to develop skills which are impossible to achieve using more traditional methods (for example the lecture or tutorial). By detailed study of a case it is possible to develop analytical skills, and those of problem solving and decision making.

At its most basic, the activity which we call management is really about applied problem solving. Managers are paid high salaries to deal with the problems facing their organization. The extent to which they do this better than chance is a matter of training. Clearly, in as much as cases can teach such a complex and (literally) valuable skill it is an indispensable part of any aspirant manager's education.

An additional benefit often cited is that by using cases you may learn from your mistakes in a much less costly way than in a real business situation, If you make a poor decision in a case analysis your pride may be hurt or, if it is being assessed, a poor grade achieved. A poor decision in the real world may cost you your reputation, promotion prospects, even your job. As such, cases act as a lower risk, half-way house between an academic course and real-world problem solving.

The Cases Used in this Casebook

Cases come in all shapes and sizes. Most of the cases in this book are what may be called complex, open-ended cases. These cases, sometimes referred to as Harvard-style, are typically between ten and twenty pages in length and are intended for use on postgraduate and undergraduate/higher-level programmes of study. We have also included a few more narrowly focused cases which exemplify a particular practice. Thus, for example, the Sport-Trax Ltd case deals with a company trying to sell a 400 metre running track to Loughborough University. The case focuses primarily on selling skills and how organizational buying behaviour operates. The remaining complex, open-ended cases tend not to focus on one or two issues but include a whole raft of complicated ideas and information, covering a wide range of issues. With such cases a major skill is the ability to identify what is and what is not relevant. In such a way skills of analysis and distillation of the major issue from the more trivial are practised.

Historical Development of Cases

The current use of cases has developed over time and from areas outside management education. The new military academics at Sandhurst (founded in 1799), West Point (1802) and the Kriegsakademie (1810) used the campaigns of Frederick the Great and Napoleon as case studies. Interestingly, such cases were apparently learned as examples of good strategy. However, Napoleonic strategy proved to be notably unsuccessful when used in the American Civil War, as did the early use of mass head-on attacks in the First World War. Both strategies failed to take account of new developments in weaponry, such as the machine gun, with catastrophic results.

Cases moved from this initial military base to the commercial world when the Harvard Law School began to use the method at the beginning of the twentieth century. The Harvard Business School noted that it was losing students to the Law School and offered a case-taught course as early as 1908. Business cases really took off in 1920 when research money was put aside for developing case study material. Since then, cases have been used widely in the USA and more recently in Europe. The latter has been aided by the growth of cases available from the European Case Clearing House and the constant stream of cases from prestigious universities such as INSEAD. Also, casebooks have begun to develop which tie directly into textbooks – in much the same way, this book links with the new European version of the Kotler *et al.* (1995) *Principles of Marketing* (published by Prentice Hall). Now cases are used on all higher education and post-experience courses in business in Europe.

Cases have moved on from their earliest military usage. Now they are used to develop problem solving, not to provide right answers. They are also recognized as giving relevance to a course as well as generating enthusiasm via interesting, up-to-date cases.

Case Studies – A Qualified Success

It might be thought from the growth of case usage that the earlier problems faced by the military had been ironed out. This would be an overstatement of the truth. The overall balance of research into the effectiveness of the case method in developing student skills is positive (Smith, 1987). Research which has looked at the progress of case-taught programmes compared with lecture-taught programmes has shown that there are greater improvements in problem solving ability on the case-taught courses. However, there have also been a small number of articles which are rather critical. One famous piece of research at the Harvard Business School concluded that when the actual business success of one thousand of their graduates was compared with their academic success using cases (whilst studying for their MBA) there was little or no correlation. What was happening was the cases were being learned in such a way as the student could earn good marks without acquiring the skill to transfer this learning to different situations, particularly new situations in the real world of business later on. This clearly produces the need for cases to be better understood by user (student) and facilitator (lecturer) alike. Understanding the problems associated with the case method will allow both sides to appraise the learning that is taking place within the case *and* the problems of using these new skills in differing non-case situations.

Cases and the Ladder of Learning

When you are studying on any course at a higher level (e.g. a BTEC qualification or a degree) you do not learn at just one level. It is possible to view learning as a ladder or hierarchy of learning levels, some steps of which are easily gained, while others are much harder to reach. Below is an overview of the different types of learning that may be achieved using cases.

Knowledge Acquisition

As mentioned earlier, the knowledge obtained from a case is to be treated with caution. The case being studied may not be an example of good practice. Indeed, the case may have been chosen because it shows bad practice, where an organization fails to deal with a problem faced. This means that the student should not take things at face value.

A major strength of cases is the important role of reflection in the learning process. When a case is 'finished' it is important to spend time thinking about what was learned. What were the useful things the organization did? What were its mistakes? What would you do in their position and what not? The case leader may lead this process or you may ask for advice. At the very least you ought to write down for every case studied what you learned – both good and bad – about marketing and wider organizational practice from the case.

Knowledge Retention

Previous research has claimed that cases are a good way of learning because students retain what they have learned. The reason for this is that cases tend to be interesting and highly relevant to students. The cases chosen for this book are, it is hoped, a good example of this. Also, cases act to reinforce the learning that has already taken place in the lecture or through guided reading.

Knowledge Application

Following on from the previous point, cases are useful vehicles for reintroducing what has been learned in the lecture period. This is why many marketing courses integrate closely the lecture with the use of a related, and therefore relevant, case study. This book is no exception, and a little later (page 19, Exhibit 3) there is a matrix which shows clearly just which case covers which part of the Kotler *et al.* textbook. That the case works in this way is supported by commonsense logic. For example, consider that you have just learned about consumer buyer behaviour and then study a case where an organization successfully (or unsuccessfully) applies this insight to its own business. Chances are you will reinforce both the original knowledge on buyer behaviour and add new knowledge of how theory and practice go together.

Problem Solving

This is not one type of learning but an amalgamation of a number of different skills which go to make up problem solving ability. As such, it is a complex skill to learn and a primary reason why cases are studied in the first place. Paradoxically, despite its complexity we all have the ability to solve problems. Children all go through the process of trying to arrange a game of football or hide and seek. They start by setting an objective which is to play the game and enjoy it. Next they analyse the current position – usually there are too few playmates, or too many, or there are no goalposts. They intuitively consider ways of overcoming these problems: ringing up friends, organizing several teams or using reserves when there are too many. Then they implement, using pullovers as goalposts or deciding on captains to choose sides. Finally the game is started and the problem is resolved. All these steps are part of the problem solving process which the case study seeks to develop. Why, if we can solve problems as children, do we need to practise problem solving much later in life whilst on a college course? The answer is a simple one: complexity. Whereas organizing a game is a relatively sophisticated activity, it is carried out in a relatively simple environment where others understand what you are trying to do and there is nothing that will change radically (except perhaps the weather). In a business context many/most things are unknown or uncertain; many more people are involved and they may not want to 'play your game'. Also, over the timescale of the problem many things are likely to change and affect the equation.

Because this is the most important skill learned from most cases it is necessary to develop our understanding further. For now it is enough to know that the case helps us to practise the following:

1. Objective-setting – what does the organization studied wish to achieve?
2. Analysis – what sort of position is the organization in at the moment?
3. Gap analysis – what is the gap between where the organization wishes to be (its objectives) and where it is now (as shown from analysis)?
4. Strategy generation – how might the organization bridge the gap/ overcome obstacles to achieve its objectives?
5. Strategy choice – of all the options considered, which one or ones are the best to move it towards its desired objectives?
6. Implementation – in detail, what will the chosen strategy entail? Who will do what, when, where and at what cost?
7. Control – using the detailed plan of action, is everything going as it should, and if not, what will we do to get things back on track?

It is worth noting that although cases develop complex problem solving skills it is easier to apply problem solving skills to the case than to a real-life situation simply because you know that this is expected of you. There is an unwritten but clear understanding that a problem lies within the case that needs solving. In business this is not always the case. Many businesspeople have failed to address problems because they were too busy doing other things (like running the business day to day) or because the problem itself was too intractable to identify its causes.

Cases, on the other hand, although complex, are still simplifications of reality. Within a case all the information that you need or are going to get is provided. In reality this information may be spread all over the organization. Another difference is that in businesses it is recognizing that a problem exists and is in a particular area which is probably the major skill. This is done for you in case work. Good case studying is about applying solid logic to analysing a problem. Good management is not only this but also the proactive skill of defining the real nature and parameters of the problem in the first instance.

Finally, but of at least equal importance, is the ability to make recommended changes work. This is a critical skill for marketers, as it is for all management. Clearly it is one thing to recommend a strategy but something else to implement it and make it work. Cases tend not to allow for the impact of recommendations to be followed through, and so this skill is more difficult to test via cases.

Behavioural Skills

Individual Skills

The case approach has the benefit of developing interpersonal skills in addition to those skills previously outlined. Cases can involve one-to-one justification of views between a student and the case facilitator. In a large group this exercise may entail individual presentations or, more likely, questions cast around the group by the case facilitator. The latter is the Harvard style of casework and claims to develop the confidence and experience of defending one's views against attack – clearly a useful business/ adversarial skill for use in a wide variety of contexts where one has to make one's position clear and defend it against others.

Group Skills

Increasingly, 'new wave' organizations emphasize cooperation over competition, in internal dealings at least. With the growth of the idea of relationship marketing, external cooperation with preferred suppliers becomes the norm. Cases are particularly relevant to cooperative working as they usually involve syndicate group work, which allows for group skills to be practised. This ought not to be viewed as an extension of the adversarial skill into a group context where defending one's own ideas is practised. There clearly will be times when a fundamental view will need to be defended, even if it is a minority view in the group. Einstein is reported to have said that being in a minority of one does not mean that you are wrong.

However, it is true that an individual who considers only his or her own views as relevant will either end up domineering or be cast off by the rest of the group. Neither option is desirable. Group work is the main work-form in most organizations. The ability to contribute and influence groups is thus a critical skill and one which requires the development of sensitivity and awareness of the views of others. If aware of this, the case provides a great opportunity to develop the skill of knowing when to compromise and when to stand out against the majority.

Values and Attitudes

Linked to the group processes involved in cases, it is worth noting that such activity can powerfully influence your values and attitudes to well-held principles. A classic, real-life case occurred a few years ago when a chauvinistic male was placed in a syndicate group along with a number of assertive (not aggressive) women. Initially a lot of conflict was generated before a *modus operandi* was worked out between them. In the process all parties learned a good deal about their own prejudices and also how to deal with prejudice itself.

Ethical issues may also be highlighted within a case and a person's implicit attitudes and values uncovered and questioned. Should the company offer bribes to get business when such is the widespread cultural practice of the competition?

This section has sought to identify the wide range of learning which can go on within cases generally and within the cases in this book in particular. The next section considers the differing ways in which cases may be used and the ways in which you should prepare for each.

Case Processes

Cases can be handled in the classroom situation in a variety of ways. It is possible to identify three broad approaches:

1. Open-ended case analysis.
2. Closed-ended case analysis.
3. Implicit structure analysis.

Open-ended Case Analysis

Many lecturers who use cases were themselves taught using this approach. The method is the most open and least directive of the case learning styles.

Often, no question or guidance on how to address the case is given. The benefit of this approach is that it does test, as much as is possible within the case approach, the student's ability to distinguish the important from the unimportant issues. In fact, the unwritten question is 'what are the main issues in the case and how would you deal with them?' This is the approach which is closest to the real world of problem solving, where often no direction is available to the manager save what he or she provides. As such, it is perhaps the most difficult approach and should be used with postgraduate/ postexperience students or those undergraduates who are already skilled and confident with cases.

The downside of this approach is that it does not provide much by way of guidance or support for the student. Also, as no structure is imposed then the actual case sessions themselves can be difficult to direct. From the student's point of view this may lead to a feeling of uncertainty both on how to best analyse the case and what has been learned having done so. This approach therefore puts a great burden on the case leader to show the reasons for the lack of structure and to summarize the main learning points covered.

In practice, research into the open-ended approach suggests that the sessions are more structured than even the case leaders thought. The case leaders said that their role was to achieve the following:

1. Minimum reliance on the instructor.
2. Maximum involvement of the students.
3. Appreciation that no right or wrong answers exist.
4. Only logical problem solving is encouraged.

Impartial observation of case sessions revealed that case leaders provided subtle, and sometimes not so subtle hints about the right way to handle things: asking questions in a particular area does direct thinking. Also, when students are not responsive to general questions, more directive ones tend to follow. As students often do not wish to take risks by expressing views on open-ended questions they may learn to wait until 'easier', more specific questions are provided by the leader.

Perhaps more worrying was the finding that case leaders apparently become wedded to certain solutions to cases rather than staying open-minded. This is a particular danger if the case has been used many times – a not unusual situation. Such bias is potentially damaging to the process as it teaches students that there is a right answer which the facilitator knows. When a student's own views on a case differ from those of the leader the student's confidence both in their own case ability and eventually in the case method generally is reduced.

Closed-ended Case Analysis

Closed-ended analysis is the opposite of the previous approach, in that specific questions are posed for the student to use to develop their analysis of the case. Through the questions direction is given telling students what areas to consider and what not, and thereby what is important in the case and what not. Whilst limiting the problem definition element of the problem solving process, this approach does allow for more focused and therefore potentially deeper analysis of specified parts of a case. It is particularly useful at the earlier part of a case course or where a case is so complex that it needs a narrowing of focus. In both situations it is also a useful way of building up a student's confidence in cases.

Implicit Structure Analysis

Implicit structure analysis is used where it is deemed important for the student to be free to define the nature of the problem within the case whilst also having access to an acceptable structure to follow. This does not mean that all students will come up with the same view on the case because the same structure is used. The structure suggested in this chapter is a flexible one which will allow for different outcomes and recommendations. It is, moreover, useful to be able to compare the position arrived at by you and your group with that of other groups.

Such a structure needs to be robust enough to be used on all kinds of case. Typically, in the area of marketing the structure given is that of the problem solving process outlined earlier but tailored to include specialized marketing activities. A widely used approach is that which follows the marketing planning process. The next section expands on this process, showing how marketing ideas from your taught programme can be integrated.

Analysing the Case and Understanding the Problems Therein

You should remember that most cases are not floating in a vacuum. More typically they will have been chosen for a particular reason. Usually this reason will be to cover a big issue or several big issues covered by the marketing course. It would be a naive student who did not take account of this information at the outset. At this stage it is useful to ask yourself what exactly you know about the general area being covered. It might even be useful to review your notes at this early stage. Chances are your notes will not be full enough and further reading around the area is encouraged.

Now read the case itself. An approach which is often recommended is to scan the case first just to get a flavour and to highlight the area covered and big issues therein. Then a more detailed reading may be followed by a third reading when you start to make notes to flag the big issues. One technique is to use the SWOT method at this stage. Issues are thus classified as either Strengths or Weaknesses, Opportunities or Threats. Many students make SWOT notes in the margins. This is useful not only if you intend to do a formal SWOT of the case but also if you wish to gain an initial feel of the balance between the positive and negative elements of the case. Another approach to help at this analysis stage is to apply a marketing audit checklist to the case (possibly using an easily accessible one like Kotler's – a simplified version is supplied in Exhibit 1). The checklist will identify gaps in your information as well as aid the SWOT analysis.

What is a marketing audit? It is a systematic way of analysing the current marketing capability of any organization. It is the equivalent of a general analysing the situation before embarking on a battle. He needs to know about his own army. Are they well armed and trained or more akin to Wellington's view that his soldiers were the 'scum of the earth'? He also said, 'I don't know what they do to the enemy but by God they frighten me'.

In addition to your own troops and resources you need to know about the enemy's army – the competition. During the Battle of Trafalgar, Nelson was able to use the greater seamanship of his sailors and accuracy of his gunners (strengths) to overcome the French who, despite having larger ships and numerical superiority, were out-manoeuvred and outgunned (weaknesses).

Carrying the analogy further, to fight a battle you also need to have knowledge of the battlefield you are fighting on. Do you have the high ground? Is the land flat to allow for the use of tanks or is it like Afghanistan where the mountainous terrain prevented the Soviets using their tanks to full effect? The business parallel is the marketplace and the customers being 'fought over'.

Beyond the battlefield it is necessary to know the prevailing weather conditions. Hitler's failure in Russia was as much due to the Russian winter as to any other factor. Is the weather therefore in our favour or not? The general ignores such influences at his peril. In the business world the equivalent of the weather is the PEST (Political, Economic, Social and Technological influences) analysis (see Exhibit 1, p. 15). The areas covered by the PEST analysis are considered more fully below. Suffice to say here that PEST factors are like the weather in being uncontrollable and in having to be worked with and around rather than altered. Consider the much-quoted feel-good factor with its impact on the level of consumer spending. It may be critical to a new product launch but cannot be influenced by the business.

The marketing manager is therefore similar to the general in that he/she also has to do battle in the marketplace if not on a battlefield. Exhibit 1 gives

Exhibit 1   *Elements of a marketing audit*

Internal Audit

Own organisational capabilities – analogy: your army

Existing objectives and strategy
Marketing organization
- Structure
- Efficiency
- Appropriateness to strategy

Marketing systems
- Marketing information systems (Mk.I.S)
- Marketing planning process
- New product development system

Marketing mix audit
- Products, price promotion, distribution, people (physical evidence and process also for services)

Marketing productivity audit
- Profitability by products
- Source of sales analysis
- Cost effectiveness of marketing activity

General internal audit questions:
Ask of the internal audit:
- What is done currently?
- Is this logical, sensible?
- Are we strong or weak in these areas?

Typical internal audit questions:
- Is the marketing structure flexible enough to change rapidly?
- Are the products at different stages of the product life cycles?
- Are the prices logical given the quality of the products?
- Are all products equally profitable?

External Audit

Customer/market audit – analogy: the battlefield

Customer audit
- Who are they?
- Why do they buy?
- What products do they buy?
- How do they buy?
- What do they want from the products bought?

Market audit
- Market structure: size, segmentation practices, targeting practices
- Market dynamics: what is growing, what is changing

Typical customer audit questions:
- What is the decision making unit like for business to business sales?
- Is price, after-sales service, confidence or delivery more important?
- Do sales occur more at one time than another (e.g. August for cars)?

Typical market audit questions:
- Is most competitive activity aimed at the larger customers?
- Are niche markets well supplied?
- Which segments are growing; declining?

Competitive audit – analogy: the enemy

Key players
Competitor: internal audit
- Competitor objectives and strategies
- Competitor marketing organisation
- Competitor marketing systems
- Competitor marketing mixes
- Competitor productivity
SWOT analysis of the competition
- Using the internal audit (above)

Typical competitor audit questions:
- What would the competition do if we reduced price?
- What is the weakest competitor to target?
- What is our competitive advantage over our competition?

Exhibit 1 *Continued*

Macro environment audit – analogy: prevailing weather conditions

Political and legal factors	*Typical PEST questions:*
Economic factors	● Politics/legal: deregulation and
Social factors	denationalization
Technological factors	● Economics: inflation, currency
	movements
	● Social: one-parent families, more
	women workers
	● Technological: new products/markets
	from microchips, biotechnology, etc.

---

examples of the range of marketing audit information needed to make informed decisions both in cases as well as in reality. As with reality, not all the information will be of equal importance or even available within a case. Students must learn to deal with this ambiguity and frustration. Business decisions are rarely taken with all the needed information available, so it is useful to get used to decision making where risk and uncertainty exist.

In addition to the marketing audit elements it is important not to forget that marketing problems are in fact business problems which cannot be isolated from the wider organizational position. As such, it is necessary also to consider the financial position of the case company and its organizational structure. Does it have spare capacity, money for investment or signs of entrepreneurial spirit? These are not marketing issues but they will impact on marketing activity. They need to be considered along with the marketing audit in your analysis. You will therefore have the opportunity to integrate things learned from finance, organizational behaviour and quantitative methods, using all relevant sources to improve your analysis.

Objectives and Gap Analysis

It is not possible to analyse a case properly without some idea of what the organization wishes to achieve. Sometimes within the case there is a clear statement of what is required. This may be couched in terms of sales growth, market share improvement or the successful introduction of a new product or a new market information system. Such a statement is necessary to give a context to the analysis: you need to know what is wanted before you can start to think more deeply on ways of attaining it. Unfortunately, some cases do not make clear what is required and it is left to the student to decide what they think is required. This can be daunting. If the company itself does not know then how should we? Unfortunately in case analysis, as in the real world, things tend not to be fair. A major skill is to consider a situation and then decide what success would mean. A simple way of thinking this through is to ask three questions:

1. What would be a conservative level of achievement?
2. What would be a radical level of achievement?
3. What constitutes a medium performance, perhaps on a par with the rest of the industry?

This can translate into any area. It applies to sales improvement (same as in the past may be the conservative objective) as well as to developing a new product (within eighteen months within budget and achieving a 20 per cent market share in the first year after launch may be a radical set of objectives). In many ways, where no guidance is given it is as well to remember that the more radical the objective the more radical (and risky) is likely to be the strategy to achieve it. Conversely, a conservative objective within a case may be less risky but will it really satisfy the performance wishes of shareholders or put a brake on competitive activity?

Gap analysis is a narrowing down of the case from masses of data which develop from the audit to a single page (maximum) statement of the key issues and the size of the gap between what the company wants and what it currently has. This gap statement is not always seen as necessary by some case leaders. We tend to differ because we think that a good analysis is completed only after a period of reflection and distillation of what the mass of analysis really means. Going forward to the next stage whilst still confused as to the meaning of the previous one seems a victory of hope over realism. General Eisenhower is reputed to have required all plans (including analysis) to be reduced to a single sheet of paper containing the critical issues. His view, as ours, was that when dealing with a complex problem you must be sure that you can see the wood for the trees; know the detail but clearly see the bigger issues involved.

Strategy Generation and Strategy Choice

When you are clear on the nature of the problem and the gap to be bridged, the next stage is simplified if not made simple. First, it is critical that creativity is used at this point to think up as many strategies as possible for bridging the gap. Choosing the obvious one or the first one considered is dangerous and to a large extent makes the previous analysis unnecessary. If any way will do, why not just choose one and get on with it? If any way would do why do we need to pay managers their large salaries to make such choices? Clearly, there are good and bad solutions to any problem and there is no guarantee that the obvious or first solution is the best one. Good strategies come from the logical evaluation of their merits when compared with others. You need other strategies therefore to prove that the one chosen is the best. This may seem a small point but it should be remembered that there may not be a very strong strategy available. It is only by seeing that it is better than others is it shown to be the right one. The process of considering other options and rejecting them therefore strengthens the option finally chosen. (This process may be done effectively in any case presentation by including the rejected strategies in an appendix with a brief commentary as to their inferiority to the one chosen.)

The list of all possible strategies clearly cannot be provided here. Instead it is useful to consider what strategy ought to deal with. Strategy ought to deal with things which will affect the medium- and long-term future of the case. For example, a strategic issue would be the overall weighting of expenditure between advertising, selling and sales promotion (the promotional mix). A short-term (tactical and not strategic) issue would be ensuring a chosen type of promotion is used to its fullest potential. Strategic issues try to ensure that you *do the right things* over time to bridge the problem gap. Tactical or short-term issues concentrate more on *doing things right* regardless of whether they are the right things to be done in the first place. Strategy is the *direction* whilst tactics are the *detail*.

Implementation and Control

The final phase of the problem solving process is to identify exactly how the chosen strategy will be carried out. One-year marketing plans will contain this sort of information. Activities which will achieve the overall strategy will be highlighted along with who has the delegated responsibility to carry through the activity. In addition, timescales and budgets are required to guide the individuals involved and to allow for control of the activities. After a period, say a month, it would be possible to check that progress has been made as agreed. If progress is not as agreed or if too much/too little money has been spent, senior management may call those responsible to explain the deviation. In this way the plan/strategy is controlled and slippage minimized. A diagrammatic version of the overall problem solving process for case study work is set out in Exhibit 2.

Content Covered by the Cases

The cases provided in this book have been chosen because they have the following features:

1. They are contemporary.
2. They are typically based on companies either well known to the student or which the student will find intrinsically interesting.

Exhibit 2   *Problem solving process for case study work*

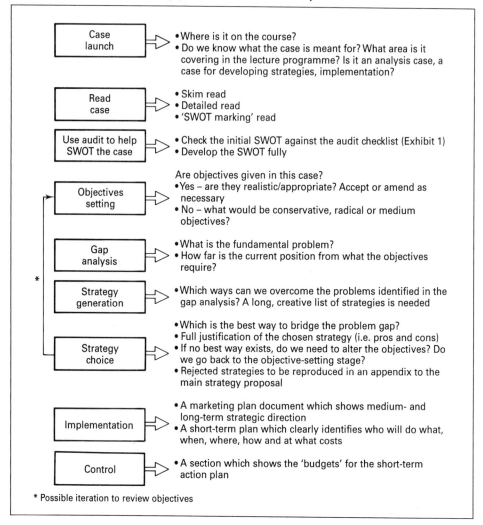

Case launch
•Where is it on the course?
• Do we know what the case is meant for? What area is it covering in the lecture programme? Is it an analysis case, a case for developing strategies, implementation?

Read case
• Skim read
• Detailed read
• 'SWOT marking' read

Use audit to help SWOT the case
• Check the initial SWOT against the audit checklist (Exhibit 1)
• Develop the SWOT fully

Objectives setting
Are objectives given in this case?
•Yes – are they realistic/appropriate? Accept or amend as necessary
• No – what would be conservative, radical or medium objectives?

Gap analysis
•What is the fundamental problem?
• How far is the current position from what the objectives require?

Strategy generation
•Which ways can we overcome the problems identified in the gap analysis? A long, creative list of strategies is needed

Strategy choice
•Which is the best way to bridge the problem gap?
• Full justification of the chosen strategy (i.e. pros and cons)
• If no best way exists, do we need to alter the objectives? Do we go back to the objective-setting stage?
• Rejected strategies to be reproduced in an appendix to the main strategy proposal

Implementation
• A marketing plan document which shows medium- and long-term strategic direction
• A short-term plan which clearly identifies who will do what, when, where, how and at what costs

Control
• A section which shows the 'budgets' for the short-term action plan

* Possible iteration to review objectives

3. They are European by way of focus. This is to redress the balance of American cases which are still the most numerous.

4. They are complex in that they do not focus on a small area but typically cover several intertwined issues which need to be addressed.

5. No questions are supplied with each case. This is a deliberate move to allow your case leader to provide relevant questions if deemed

necessary. It also allows you to determine the issues yourself if you are a more advanced case user.

6. Some general guidance is provided, however. The cases have been chosen because of their coverage of a wide range of marketing themes. The matrix in Exhibit 3 shows the areas covered by each case in terms of the chapter headings from the textbook *Principles of Marketing* by Kotler *et al.* (1995). This should help both student and tutor to ascertain the broad parameters of the case at the outset.

Exhibit 3 *Case and content matrix*

	Polo Mints	Virgin Atlantic	Midelectric	Project G	Victoria	Nivea Sun	Gedas	Marks & Spencer	ABB	Sport-Trax Ltd	GPA	Gatorade	Magnum	IKEA	Carlsberg
Marketing process															
1. Marketing in a changing world	S	S	M									M			
2. Marketing and social responsibility			M											S	S
3. Marketing planning						M	M		M	S	M		S	S	M
Marketing setting															
4. Marketing environment			M	M	M			S	S	S	S	M	S	S	S
5. Global market						M			M			M	M		M
6. Market research and forecasting	M			M								S	M		M
Buyer behaviour															
7. Consumer marketing	M	S	S			M		M				M		S	M
8. Industrial marketing							M		M	M					
Core strategy															
9. Segmentation	M	M			S	M	S		M	S		M	M		M
10. Positioning	M	M			M	M	S		M	M		M	M		M
11. Building customer satisfaction		M			M	M	S			S	M	S			S
12. Competitive advantage	S	M			M	M	M				M				S
Product															
13. NPD	S			M					M	S					M
14. Product design		S		M					M				M		M
15. Services		M	S					S						S	
Price															
16. Pricing concepts						M				S		S	M		S
17. Pricing strategy		S				M				M		S	M		S
Promotion															
18. Communications						M		M			M	M	M	M	M
19. Advertising and sales		S				M	M					S	M		M
20. Personal selling							S			M					
Place															
21. Channels and physical dish						M		S	M			M		M	S
22. Retailing and wholesaling						M			M			S	M	M	S

M = Main area covered; S = Secondary area covered

Some Final Thoughts

Although this chapter aims to give you a greater awareness of what is required from you in your case work, there will still be some uncomfortable moments awaiting you. This should not cause you undue concern. Remember the complexity of what you are doing. It would be worrying if you did not run into some problems as this would signify a shallowness of analysis that needs addressing. Remember that any skill takes time to get right, but when it is mastered you will wonder what all the fuss was about. Treat the uncertainty in case study work as a necessary phase of the learning process which will recede as long as you keep working at it. Remember, it is better to get things wrong now so that you get things right in your later business career.

Bibliography

Kotler, P., Armstrong, G., Saunders, J. and Wong, V. (1995) *Principles of Marketing*, European Edition, Prentice Hall Europe.

Smith, G. (1987), 'The use and effectiveness of case study method in management education: A critical review', *Management Education and Development*, 18 (1), 51–61.

CASES

Polo Mints

Gareth Smith and **John Saunders**
Loughborough University Business School, UK

It had never ceased to amaze Dave Nunn just how unpredictable life could be. A few days ago he was happily learning the brand manager's job on one of Nestlé's smaller brands (they have several hundred around the world) when he had been summoned to the head office in York at short notice. He left the meeting with a new job as UK brand manager for one of the company's flagship and oldest products – Polo Mints.

Within Nestlé, Polo Mints is viewed as one of the thirteen 'strategic brands', so called because they are global rather than national/multinational in their appeal and marketing. Polo Mints is currently the eighth best selling confectionery item for Nestlé in the UK behind the flagship brand, Kit Kat. These two brands have annual turnovers of over £30 million and £200 million, respectively. In the mints market, Polo Mints is the second best selling product behind Trebor Extra Strong Mints. Dave thought back to his induction training with the company when he learned that one hour's production of Polo Mints stacked on top of each other would be two miles high.

The previous incumbent of the job had been promoted to a marketing job in Vevey, on the shore of Lake Geneva in Switzerland where Nestlé's international headquarters is based. Her new job was as part of a business group responsible for coordinating advertising and branding strategy across Nestlé's global business in countlines (chocolate-based confectionery products, typically sold individually on the counters of general stores and petrol stations or near supermarket checkouts). Nestlé countlines include such well known brands as Aero, Rolo, Drifter, Smarties, Lion bars, Munchies and of course Kit Kat. Before leaving her post she had been analysing the results of a novel and wide ranging market segmentation study into the UK confectionery and snacks market. Included in the study was a valuable

This case is based on research carried out for the Nestlé organization. It is intended to be used as a basis for class discussion rather than to illustrate either effective or ineffective handling of an administrative situation. For reasons of commercial sensitivity some names, dates and figures have been altered.

insight into the way mints were perceived by differing segments of the confectionery market. The task of analysing the report was now Nunn's, and he pondered this and other new challenges as his taxi drove him slowly through York to the station.

He made a mental note that after getting to know his new staff and dealing with the urgent correspondence he would set aside two days to read, analyse and consider the implications of the report. As he half expected, the immediate tasks took longer than planned and so it was ten days later that with a clear desk and no diary appointments he gathered the relevant report in front of him and began to read. Three hours later and with his mind spinning from the detail he had just read, he considered how the data helped him in his job.

According to the report's stated objectives, the segmentation study could be used in a number of ways, namely:

1. To provide a framework in which to position all brands.
2. To identify opportunities:
    (a) for new products;
    (b) for the repositioning of existing products.
3. To identify brand strengths and weaknesses which can assist the development of strategies for individual brands.
4. To provide an understanding of threats.
5. To identify product categories which would benefit from promotional links.
6. To help with the development of advertising strategies.
7. To provide recruitment criteria for research purposes.
8. To provide a framework for research.

To illustrate these ideas the report included a worked example using the pet food market as a focus (see Exhibit 1.1). Even at this early stage, and only having read the report once, Nunn realized that the study was not going to help him with all of these things. The study, for example, covered all of the confectionery and snacks market, not just the market for mints. As such it did not concentrate solely on Polo Mints and its market. It did, however, provide a lot of relevant data on the customer segments in the snack market. How to use this insight was still the big question.

Nunn had spent some of the first days in his new job talking to his predecessor in the post, Jane Foster. During this general handover period the issue of the new study had been aired and it soon became obvious that Jane either did not really understand its implications or was honestly critical of the lack of clear direction coming from the findings. She used expressions like 'blinding us with science' and 'not being able to see the woods for the trees'. On a more positive note, he and she had considered how Nestlé compared with its competition as regards the way the company segmented the confectionery market. They agreed with the view within the business that prior to this study the company was trailing the competition in its

Exhibit 1.1   *Example of segmentation in the pet food market*

1. A segmentation study provided a framework for understanding how brands were positioned in the marketplace.

The pet food study established that it was the relationship between the pet and owner which determined which brand of cat food they bought, all the brands could be positioned in the market.

Brand	Market segment
None	Cat lovers who feed *fresh* food, i.e. human or pet quality fresh meat and see the cat as *part* of the family.
'Dine' (premium)	Cat lovers who feed *prepared* food and see the cat as *part* of the family.
'Whiskas' (mid range)	Cat lovers who feed *prepared* food and see cat as *extension* of family.
'Kit-e-Kat' (economy)	Cat tolerators – no relationship with the cat, belongs to the kids but mum has to feed it and wants it to be healthy.

Competitor brands were also positioned, often after rather unexpected results, e.g. own-label fish varieties were positioned alongside Dine; previously they were thought to compete with Kit-e-Kat in the economy end of the market.

Snappy Tom which previously was thought to compete with Whiskas was also positioned alongside Dine.

This example also illustrates how segmentation can provide a framework of reference for a market, against which current thinking can be checked.

2. Segmentation identified opportunities to be exploited by *new products* or the *repositioning* of *existing* brands.

Opportunity for new products
The first consumer segment (i.e. cat lovers feeding fresh food) were obviously not being catered for by the prepared tinned food market. Sheba was developed and introduced specifically to fit this opportunity. Sheba used high quality meats and was packaged in plastic rather than metal. It was also a single serve size to convey freshness.

Repositioning of existing brands
Kit-e-Kat had originally been positioned as an economy brand, but it was repositioned to meet the needs of the cat tolerators. Cat tolerators want to be reassured that the animal will be healthy and not cause any problems.

The economy price is part of the equation but health is also important.

3. Segmentation identified brands' strengths and weaknesses which assisted the development of strategies for individual brands.

Prior to the segmentation study, Whiskas was positioned as a serious quality cat food with owner endorsement (similar to 'top breeders recommend Pedigree Chum'). It used 'Whiskas time' as the key signature tune. After the segmentation study it became 'Whiskas time: the time you love the best', and the relationship between the owner and the cat was stressed. To express the relationship that cat lovers felt for their cats, the product was also changed to make each variety different and, therefore, make the brand more special.

All the brands had assistance in their strategy development because there was an understanding of why people were buying each brand. This also lead to long-term strategy objectives.

Exhibit 1.1 *Continued*

---

4. It helped provide an understanding of the threats from related product categories and competitive brands.

Identifying own-label fish varieties as a competitor to expensive premium range brands helped develop sales strategies to combat this growing threat. The related product category fresh meat was identified and understood which led to the development of Sheba. In states where fresh meat sales were high, the threat was combated with PR campaigns, stressing that feeding fresh meat did not provide a balanced diet and could cause problems such as rickets in puppies and vitamin deficiencies, etc.

5. It helped identify related product categories which would benefit from promotional links.

Whiskas canned food and Whishettes dry food, both had the same target groups and benefited from promotional links.

6. It helped with the development of advertising strategies consistent with desired image changes required in order to secure long-term brand objectives.

All brands' advertising campaigns became more focused. Each campaign followed on from the last: the overall message trying to be communicated was the same for each campaign but it would be tweaked and improved on each time.

> Dine for the cat that's really a person.
> Kit-e-Kat the brand you can really trust.
> Whiskas time the time you love the best.

Once the desired image and strategy had been identified through the segmentation study, that image was developed, developed and developed again, each campaign building on the last.

7. It provided recruitment criteria for research purposes.

Whenever any research was conducted there was a clear target group to recruit. The statements used in the segmentation study which best discriminate between consumers were used in qualitative and quantitative recruitment.

8. It provided a framework for research to operate in.

It identified competitor sets of products for data analysis and the construction of consumer market segments and qualitative group structures.

It also provided commerical research with the opportunity to be more proactive in identifying new product opportunities and developing marketing strategy.

Overall it became a whole way of thinking.

---

application of segmentation. Two approaches to segmentation were currently used within Nestlé:

1. Demographics – where age, sex and family life cycle predominate.

2. Behavioural – such as traditionalists or experimentalists in the boxed chocolate market, and snack, indulgence or hunger-satisfying segments for countlines.

The result of this had been the tendency for most of the company's brands to compete with one another for the same high-volume customers. For instance, all countlines are aimed at 16 to 24 year olds, where the majority of countline volume comes from. Also, 'indulgent countlines' compete for women who tend to eat the majority of indulgent brands. In the mint market, Polo Mints targeted the 16 to 65+ males and females, while Triple X was aimed at 25 to 65+ males; hardly tight, accurate segmenting, and overlapping with the bulk of the competition.

A major stimulus to the segmentation study, therefore, was this perception that the company was competitively disadvantaged in the whole area. For example, Cadbury was known to employ usage occasion segmentation, and in their research used such statements as: 'eat on your own', 'convenient to eat', 'only for children', 'good for sharing', 'suitable for parties', 'for special occasions', 'eaten while watching TV', 'husbands/partners like them' and 'eaten with a hot drink'. The fruits of this research was beginning to be seen in the way their advertising developed the usage occasion theme to communicate more meaningfully to target segments. This type of research was also widely credited with highlighting the potential of the 'bitesize' market which targeted primarily children.

The other major competitor in the UK was the Mars Company. Mars was known to have made a long-term commitment to market segmentation and the use of sophisticated brand image preference models. Jane Foster had a file which contained a mass of data on Mars in the UK, including trade press articles, salesforce observations, the results of 'competition brainstorming' sessions and the like. She photocopied a particularly relevant section on segmentation for Dave (Exhibit 1.2).

The Segmentation Study

The segmentation study was commissioned by an external market research agency between 16 November and 6 December 1995. The research objectives were provided by Nestlé's marketing department. They were:

1. To provide a behavioural frame for snacking (overall and by product category).
2. To identify opportunities for new products or to reposition existing ones.
3. To assist in the development of brand strategies.
4. To identify the links between brand image and consumer preference for market segments.
5. To understand threats from related product categories.

To conduct the survey, 1,500 child and adult respondents were recruited using quota controls (Exhibit 1.3). Using a self completion questionnaire, attitudinal data about snacks and brand images were obtained from this sample.

A second questionnaire was administered to all respondents to provide information of demographics, awareness of brands eaten over the previous four

Exhibit 1.2   *What is known about segmenting by Mars*

Mars use two-way segmentation, i.e. consumer segmentation and usage occasion segmentation. This results in a grid:

Usage occasion segments

Consumer segments

The grid represents all snack food and chocolate eating, including crisps, cakes, biscuits and ice-cream.

The consumer groups that Mars identified in the USA in 1982 were:

1. Carefree
2. Rationalization
3. Controlled

These emerged from seven adult segments and four teenager segments.

Adult
1. Rationalizers
2. Compulsive eaters
3. Hedonists
4. Controlled indulgers
5. Logical independent thinkers
6. Successful restrictors
7. Casual fatalists

Teenager
1. Self-rewarding chocolate lovers
2. Narcissistic restrictors
3. Carefree hedonists
4. Independents

The usage occasions they identified were:

1. When hungry
2. For low energy
3. For a mood/emotion
4. For cravings
5. For children
6. Social eating

I believe they also include in the UK whether you are eating on your own or with people, watching TV, etc.

Evidence of this is the introduction of such products as funsize bars, ice-creams, Twix biscuit variants, snacksize bars. Umbrella promotions for related product categories, i.e. the World Cup sponsorship with Mars, M&Ms, kingsize Mars and Snickers, Mars miniatures and bitesize ice-creams.

Exhibit 1.3   *Survey bases and definition of terms*

(a) Survey bases (unweighted)	Adults	Children	Total	Average
Survey respondents	1,324	163	1,487	
Diary respondents	864	114	978	
Eating occasions	21,153	3,255	24,408	(25)
Snack occasions	12,864	2,118	14,982	(15)
Items recorded	30,958	4,888	35,846	(37)
Snack items recorded	20,235	3,471	23,706	(24)

(b) 'Snack' definitions
Snack occasion
- Any 'snack or nibble'
- Any meal or meal-replacement occasion containing a snack item

Snack item
- Chocolate confectionery
- Sugar confectionery/mints
- Biscuits
- Crisps
- Fruit
- Sandwiches
- Ice-cream

weeks, frequency of snacking by occasion-types, suitability of brands for up to four snacking occasions and overall brand ratings on a five-point scale.

One thousand of the respondents were asked to complete a diary giving detailed consumption of snacks over one week. For the purpose of the study, snack items included chocolate confectionery, sugar confectionery/mints, biscuits, crisps, fruit, sandwiches and ice-cream and a snack occasion was defined as any 'snack or nibble' or 'any meal or meal-replacement occasion containing a snack item'.

General Results of the Segmentation Study

Factor analysis[1] was used on the attitudinal data about snacks to identify eight groups of consumers ranging from the heavy-using 'depressive chocolate lover' to a small group of 'male savoury eaters' who are low consumers of confectionery items. The eight segments identified were:

---

[1] *Factor analysis is an advanced technique for analysing masses of data and identifying common/ linked areas within these data. In this case the views of a sample of consumers are analysed based on their attitudes to snacks and snacking, and factor analysis is used to develop subgroups or segments from within the larger group. These subgroups are made up of people who have similar views to each other about snacking and generally dissimilar views to those in the other groups or segments identified.*

1. Confectionery opportunists
2. Apathetic/inactive
3. Energetic males
4. Depressive chocolate-lovers

5. Ageing easy-going
6. Upmarket female diet-conscious
7. Older opinionated snackers
8. Male savoury eaters

More detailed profiles of the segments and the rationale for the titles given to them by the agency are provided in Exhibits 1.4–1.12.

Ten broad classifications of snacking occasions were derived which accounted for almost 98 per cent of all the snacking occasions identified (described in Exhibit 1.6). They are then tabulated against the attitudinal segments to show the adult snacking market broken down into eighty (ignoring 'unclassified') segments (Exhibit 1.11).

Exhibits 1.8 and 1.9 show how the consumption occasion for mints and chewing gums varies across the eighty segments. In Exhibit 1.8, several of the cells are blank where the small cell size meant too few occasions were found.

Significant variations in attitudes were identified when the suitability of brands for snacking occasions were tabulated against segments (Exhibit 1.11 provides the relevant research findings for mints). Overall, 'other food items' such as fruit, crisps and sandwiches came out as more suitable across all snacking occasions. More relevant to Nestlé's products, CBCL (chocolate biscuit countlines) and countlines were also thought of as being widely appropriate to many snacking occasions. In contrast, the mints were seen as only appropriate for a few snacking occasions.

Dave decided that it was necessary to reduce the mass of information to reasonable proportions and therefore 'dumped' a lot of the information which was focused on other parts of the snack market. In practice this meant stripping out data on the CBCL market (products such as Kit Kat two fingers, Club, Penguin, Twix), the countlines market (snacks such as Kit Kat four fingers, Mars, Flake, Snickers,

Exhibit 1.4   *Adult consumer segments*

	% of adult popn	% of snack occns	% of confec. items
Confectionery opportunists	15	14	20
Apathetic/inactive	20	21	20
Energetic males	15	15	18
Depressive chocolate-lovers	12	14	17
Ageing easy-going	12	10	10
Upmarket female diet-conscious	8	9	7
Older opinionated snackers	12	12	5
Male savoury eaters	6	6	4

Rolo), sugar sweets (Fruit Pastilles, Opal Fruits, Toffo, Chewits, etc.), chocolate blocks (Cadbury Dairy Milk, Galaxy, Yorkie, Aero, etc.), and the boxed chocolate market (Roses, Quality Street, After Eight, Milk Tray, etc.). Not surprisingly this significantly reduced the size of the report. Looking at the remains of the depleted study Dave briefly scribbled a list of what was left:

1. An example of segmentation in the pet food market (Exhibit 1.1)
   Useful to help clarify some of the possible uses of this study.

2. What is known about segmentation by Mars (Exhibit 1.2)
   Useful if only to see what the competition is up to.

3. Survey bases and general definition of terms (Exhibit 1.3).
   General outline of who we talked to and how, plus some basic terms used.

4. The consumer segments (Exhibits 1.4 and 1.5)
   The eight segments which were identified by the research – also some pretty pictures to go with them.

5. Snacking occasions definitions (Exhibit 1.6)
   The ten periods when people snack throughout the day.

6. Study results: demographic profiles of segments (Exhibit 1.7)
   Reasonably self-explanatory.

7. Study results: share of mint and chewing gum market by segment (Exhibit 1.8 and 1.9)
   So to the nitty gritty!

8. Study results: psychographic/attitudinal profiles of segments (Exhibit 1.10)
   Interesting but need to think more about how I can use this.

9. Consumption occasion by segments (Exhibit 1.11)
   Ditto.

10. Brand suitability by segment and consumption occasion (Exhibit 1.12)
    This shows in ranked order where competing brands were placed by the segments. If a brand is mentioned it is seen as appropriate for that snacking occasion and vice versa (I've included the countline data by way of comparison). Again, I'm sure this must be useful, but how?

Dave Nunn's notes told him that there was still a lot of work to be done on the research before he could use it to aid his decision making for Polo Mints' future development. He metaphorically rolled up his sleeves and set to the task.

Exhibit 1.5 *Pictorial representation of the eight consumer segments*

Exhibit 1.6 *Snacking occasions defined (adults)*

Snack or nibble, first thing in the morning, for or with breakfast	9%
With a lunchtime meal (knife and fork)	12%
Normal lunchtime snack or nibble	10%
Mid-morning or mid-afternoon snack or nibble with a hot drink	17%
Mid-morning or mid-afternoon snack or nibble without a hot drink	9%
With an evening meal	13%
Something instead of a usual meal	4%
Evening snack or nibble at home	19%
Evening snack or nibble with a cold drink, away from home	4%
Snack or nibble while travelling in a car or on public transport	<1%
Unclassified	2%

Exhibit 1.7 *Demographic profiles of segments (diary adults)*

Weighted base: 1,349	Popn share %	Sex (%)		Age (%)			Social class (%)				Total %
		Male	Fem.	16–34	35–54	55–65	AB	C1	C2	DE	
Conf. opportunists	15	49	51	49	29	22	9	24	31	36	100
Apathetic/inactive	20	52	48	34	44	22	13	32	22	33	100
Energetic males	15	73	27	63	32	5	14	28	34	23	100
Depressive choc-lovers	12	37	63	53	40	7	16	26	31	27	100
Ageing easy-going	12	39	61	23	50	27	23	27	21	30	100
Upmkt female diet-cons.	8	15	85	46	43	11	30	28	28	14	100
Older opinionated snckrs	12	45	55	23	48	29	18	37	22	23	100
Male savoury eaters	6	75	25	46	40	14	13	29	31	27	100
Average	n.a.	49	51	42	40	18	16	29	27	28	

Exhibit 1.8 *Percentage share of total confectionery market (diary adults)*

Base: confectionery items	Popn share	Confectionery category (%)									Total conf. %
		CBCL	Sugar	Mints	Choc CL	Blks	Ass				
Conf. opportunists	15	13.1	25.9	27.6	19.3	17.6	11.8				19.9
Apathetic/inactive	20	23.5	20.1	15.2	18.5	22.9	20.4				19.9
Energetic males	15	17.5	12.2	14.0	20.3	15.8	15.1				17.5
Depressive choc-lovers	12	16.3	16.8	13.6	18.7	16.8	14.5				16.9
Ageing easy-going	12	9.8	7.9	11.5	9.2	11.1	14.5				10.0
Upmkt female diet-cons.	8	6.7	9.5	2.9	6.7	8.2	12.5				6.8
Older opinionated snckrs	12	5.2	2.1	10.3	3.1	3.6	7.9				4.6
Male savoury eaters	6	3.9	5.5	4.9	3.7	3.9	3.9				4.1
Total %	100	100	100	100	100	100	100				100.0

CBCL = chocolate biscuit countlines; Blks = blocks; Ass = assortments

Exhibit 1.9 *Percentage share of mint/chewing gum market (diary adults)*

Base: mints and gums	Consumption occasions (%)											
	With Brkfst	Lnch meal	Lnch snck	Morn./ Aft.w. drnk	Morn./ Aft.w/o drnk	With Eve. meal	Meal-repl.	Eve. at home	Eve. away home	Whle trav.	Uncl. %	Total %
Conf. opportunists	4.94	1.65	1.23	1.85	6.79	3.09	0.82	2.88	2.06	0.82	1.44	27.57
Apathetic/inactive	0.41	0.82	0.82	0.62	7.41	0.82	–	0.82	2.06	0.21	1.03	15.23
Energetic males	0.21	0.62	0.82	1.23	4.32	1.85	–	2.47	1.03	–	1.23	13.99
Depressive choc-lovers	1.44	0.62	1.85	1.44	3.09	0.62	0.41	0.82	3.29	–	–	13.58
Ageing easy-going	1.03	0.21	0.62	1.03	5.56	0.41	0.21	0.41	2.06	–	0.21	11.52
Upmkt female diet-cons.	–	0.21	0.21	0.41	1.44	0.41	–	–	–	–	–	2.88
Older opinionated snckrs	0.41	1.44	0.41	–	2.26	1.44	–	1.65	0.82	0.21	1.44	10.29
Male savoury eaters	–	0.41	1.03	–	2.06	0.21	0.41	0.41	0.21	–	0.21	4.94
Total %	8.85	5.97	6.70	6.58	33.13	8.64	2.06	9.26	11.73	1.23	5.76	100.0

Exhibit 1.10 *Psychographic/attitudinal profiles (adults)*

(Attribute means) (1–5 score, hi = agree)	All adults	Confec. opportunists	Apathetic/ inactive	Energetic males	Depressive choc-lovers	Ageing easy-going	Upmarket female diet-consc.	Older opinionated snacker	Male savoury eater
Percentage of adults	**100%**	**15%**	**20%**	**15%**	**12%**	**12%**	**8%**	**12%**	**6%**
Average snack occasions/week	**14.9**	**16.2**	**14.8**	**14.8**	**15.8**	**15.1**	**16.1**	**13.1**	**11.0**
Chocolate is healthy	2.4	3.1	2.4	2.4	2.1	2.6	1.9	2.1	2.1
Reckless shopper	2.9	3.5	2.5	3.5	3.5	2.4	2.4	2.0	2.6
Prefer savoury	3.4	2.9	3.3	3.3	2.6	3.7	3.3	4.3	4.5
Health objections	2.2	1.9	1.8	2.0	1.6	2.7	2.2	3.2	3.0
Handy packet of sweets	2.9	4.2	2.5	2.8	3.3	3.6	2.0	1.6	2.5
Choc up large bars	2.7	3.1	2.7	2.7	2.1	3.2	2.7	2.3	1.8
Buy prepared meals	2.2	2.3	1.8	2.5	2.8	2.0	2.2	2.0	2.0
Drink wine at home	2.7	2.3	2.4	3.0	3.0	3.1	2.7	2.7	2.7
Work harder than others	3.0	2.9	2.5	3.3	3.0	3.2	2.7	3.1	3.6
Sweets handy when travel	3.5	4.5	3.3	3.3	2.4	4.0	3.2	2.2	2.7
Job physically tiring	2.9	3.1	2.2	3.5	2.9	3.2	2.6	2.4	3.8
Packed lunch everyday	2.8	2.7	2.6	3.0	2.5	3.3	3.0	2.7	2.8
Like lively places	3.0	3.4	2.5	3.7	3.2	2.7	3.0	2.5	3.5
Eat low calorie sweets	2.2	2.0	1.6	2.1	2.1	3.0	3.2	2.3	1.5
Exercise regularly	3.1	3.5	2.4	3.8	2.3	3.1	3.5	3.3	3.6
Buy chocolate to share	3.0	3.5	2.8	3.2	2.9	3.5	3.4	2.1	2.4
Indulge at weekend	2.1	2.2	1.6	2.1	2.0	2.7	3.1	1.8	1.5
Eat choc. in a hurry	3.0	3.7	2.8	3.4	3.7	3.1	2.7	1.9	2.5
Traditional Sunday roast	3.8	4.2	3.8	3.5	3.7	3.9	3.7	3.5	4.1
Try unusual food	3.4	3.3	3.0	3.6	3.6	3.7	4.0	3.2	3.2
Eat choc. regardless	3.2	4.1	3.0	3.3	4.2	2.9	3.5	1.7	1.8
Watch calories	2.5	2.1	1.9	2.1	2.3	3.6	3.8	3.4	1.7
Mints bad for teeth	2.5	1.8	2.4	2.8	2.2	2.3	3.2	3.3	2.0
Taste important	3.5	3.9	3.6	3.8	4.0	3.0	2.7	2.7	3.7
Do not like chocolate	1.7	1.2	1.5	1.6	1.1	1.9	1.5	2.8	2.5
Exercise lots	2.7	3.4	2.3	3.6	1.9	2.5	2.0	2.2	3.5
Use a lot of energy	2.6	3.3	2.1	3.6	2.3	2.3	1.8	2.0	3.6
Buy fast-food	2.5	2.7	2.1	3.3	3.3	2.1	2.1	1.9	2.9

Exhibit 1.10 *Continued*

(Attributable means) (1–5 score, hi = agree)	All adults	Confec. opportunists	Apathetic/ inactive	Energetic males	Depressive choc-lovers	Ageing easy-going	Upmarket female diet-consc.	Older opinionated snacker	Male savoury eater
Percentage of adults	**100%**	**15%**	**20%**	**15%**	**12%**	**12%**	**8%**	**12%**	**6%**
Average snack occasions/week	**14.9**	**16.2**	**14.8**	**14.8**	**15.8**	**15.1**	**16.1**	**13.1**	**11.0**
Eat what I like	3.9	4.6	4.2	4.0	4.3	3.5	2.9	3.1	4.4
Eat when depressed	3.1	3.6	2.5	2.7	4.2	3.3	3.8	2.3	2.0
Choc. for breakfast	1.7	2.5	1.5	1.8	2.4	1.4	1.5	1.2	1.3
Choc. to unwind	2.5	3.6	2.0	2.2	3.6	2.7	2.5	1.3	1.3
Mints freshen breath	3.7	4.4	3.6	3.4	4.0	4.3	3.0	3.0	3.9
Eat choc. when bored	3.1	4.1	2.7	3.2	4.4	3.1	3.3	1.5	1.7
Buy choc. whenever	3.4	4.0	3.4	3.6	4.1	3.1	3.5	2.1	2.7
No sweet tooth	2.7	2.1	2.8	2.4	1.8	3.1	2.5	4.0	4.0
Do not buy choc. myself	2.8	1.9	2.7	2.5	1.8	3.1	2.6	4.2	4.1
Suck and concentrate	2.5	3.5	2.2	2.2	2.8	3.4	1.6	1.5	2.8

Exhibit 1.11   *Consumption occasions by segment for all confectionery items (adults)*

Base: all confectionery items	With Brkfst	Lnch meal	Lnch snck	Morn./ Aft.w. drnk	Morn./ Aft.w/o drnk	With Eve. meal	Meal-repl.	Eve. at home	Eve. away home	Whle trav.	Uncl. %	Total %
					Consumption occasions (%)							
Conf. opportunists	1.65	1.59	1.83	2.86	2.55	2.70	0.88	3.53	1.06	0.28	0.77	19.8
Apathetic/inactive	0.49	2.14	1.47	3.50	3.24	1.86	0.69	4.63	1.06	0.20	0.67	19.9
Energetic males	0.98	2.23	1.08	2.66	3.40	1.90	0.98	2.99	0.67	0.07	0.62	17.5
Depressive choc-lovers	0.93	1.62	1.16	2.73	2.93	1.88	0.59	3.47	1.21	0.05	0.31	16.9
Ageing easy-going	0.46	1.11	0.90	1.49	1.62	1.39	0.46	1.44	0.82	0.00	0.28	10.0
Upmkt female diet-cons.	0.05	0.54	0.57	1.16	1.54	0.95	0.21	1.54	0.18	0.00	0.08	6.8
Older opinionated snckrs	0.31	0.62	0.23	0.46	0.80	0.80	0.00	0.93	0.33	0.03	0.28	4.6
Male savoury eaters	0.13	0.23	0.46	0.51	1.06	0.41	0.07	0.59	0.21	0.03	0.28	4.1
Total %	5.0	10.1	7.7	15.4	17.5	11.9	3.9	19.0	5.5	0.7	3.3	100.0

Exhibit 1.12 *Brand suitability by consumption occasion: mints and countlines*

Mints	First thing in the morning/ breakfast	Lunchtime meal	Lunchtime snack	Morning/ afternoon with a hot drink	Morning/ afternoon without a hot drink	With evening meal	Meal replacement	Evening snack at home	Evening snack away from home	When travelling
Confectionery opportunists	Polo Mints		Gum		Ex.Str.Mints Polo Mints Trebor Softmints Gum Murraymints XXX			Trebor Softmints Polo Mints	Polo Mints Ex.Str.Mints XXX Trebor Softmints Gum Murraymints	Polo Mints Gum Trebor Mints Ex.Str.Mints XXX Minties Trebor Softmints
Apathetic/ inactive					Ex.Str.Mints Polo Mints Trebor Softmints					Trebor Softmints Polo Mints Ex.Str.Mints Gum
Energetic males										Polo Mints Ex.Str.Mints Glaciermints Trebor Softmints Trebor Mints Gum
Depressive chocolate-lovers					Ex.Str.Mints Polo Mints XXX Glaciermints Trebor Softmints				Gum Polo Mints	Ex.Str.Mints Trebor Softmints Polo Mints XXX Glaciermints

Exhibit 1.12 *Continued*

Mints	First thing in the morning/breakfast	Lunchtime meal	Lunchtime snack	Morning/afternoon with a hot drink	Morning/afternoon without a hot drink	With evening meal	Meal replacement	Evening snack at home	Evening snack away from home	When travelling
Ageing easy-going	Polo Mints				Polo Mints					Gum Polo Mints Trebor Softmints Clorets Glaciermints Ex.Str.Mints
Upmarket female diet-conscious					Trebor Softmints					Polo Mints Ex.Str.Mints XXX
Older opinionated snackers										Gum Polo Mints Trebor Softmints Clorets Glaciermints
Male savoury snackers					Gum Polo Mints Ex.Str.Mints XXX					Polo Mints Ex.Str.Mints XXX Trebor Softmints

Exhibit 1.12 *Continued*

Countlines	First thing in the morning/breakfast	Lunchtime meal	Lunchtime snack	Morning/afternoon with a hot drink	Morning/afternoon without a hot drink	With evening meal	Meal replacement	Evening snack at home	Evening snack away from home	When travelling
Confectionery opportunists	KitKat 4, Mars		D.Decker, Mars, Twirl, Crunchie, Flake, T.Crisp, KitKat 4, Lion, Aero, Wispa	Flake, Caramel, KitKat 4, Crunchie, Wispa, Snickers, Aero, Twix 2, Twirl, T.Crisp	D.Decker, Flake, Rolo, T.Crisp, Aero, Wispa, Crunchie, KitKat 4, Twix 2, Lion	Walnut Whip, Flake, Mars	Snickers, Picnic, D.Decker, KitKat 4, Crunchie, T.Crisp, Mars, Twix 2	Caramel, Walnut Whip, Crunchie, Picnic, D.Decker, T.Crisp, Rolo, Aero, Flake		Snickers, Maltesers, D.Decker, Revels, KitKat 4, Lion, Aero
Apathetic/ inactives			KitKat 4, Crunchie	KitKat 4, Twix 2	Flake, KitKat 4, Wispa, Crunchie, Mars			KitKat 4, Mars		Wispa, Crunchie, Rolo, Mars
Energetic males	Flake, Mars		KitKat 4, Twix 2, Snickers	KitKat 4, Twix 2, Snickers, T.Crisp, Lion, Mars, Aero, Wispa, Crunchie	Caramel, Boost, Twix 2, D.Decker, Aero, Crunchie, Flake, T.Crisp, Mars		KitKat 4, Topic, Twix 2, Snickers, Mars	Flake, KitKat 4, Aero, Topic, Snickers, Mars	Mars	Aero, Caramel, Minstrels, Picnic, Mars, Lion, KitKat 4, Snickers, Twirl

Exhibit 1.12 *Continued*

Countlines	First thing in the morning/breakfast	Lunchtime meal	Lunchtime snack	Morning/afternoon with a hot drink	Morning/afternoon without a hot drink	With evening meal	Meal replacement	Evening snack at home	Evening snack away from home	When travelling
Depressive chocolate-lovers		Twix 2	D.Decker Twix 2 Flake Mars KitKat 4 Twirl	Flake Snickers KitKat 4 Lion Mars Twirl	Caramel T.Crisp Walnut Whip Topic Spira Flake		KitKat 4 Twix 2 Mars	Crunchie Boost D.Decker Minstrels Maltesers Picnic	Mars	Boost Maltesers Walnut Whip Picnic Mars Buttons
Ageing easy-going				KitKat 4 Twix 2	Mars			Flake Mars		Twirl Mars
Upmarket female diet-conscious		KitKat 4			KitKat 4 Twirl Crunchie Mars			Wispa Crunchie Mars KitKat 4		Mars
Older opinionated snackers										
Male savoury snackers	KitKat 4	KitKat 4			Topic					Mars

Virgin Atlantic Airways
Ten Years After

Pantéa Denoyelle
INSEAD, France

ĭ

June 1994. Virgin Atlantic Airways celebrated the tenth anniversary of its inaugural flight to New York. Richard Branson, the airline's chairman and founder, reminisced about its tremendous growth. In ten short years, he had established Virgin Atlantic as Britain's second largest long-haul airline, with a reputation for quality and innovative product development. Richard Branson turned his thoughts to the challenges that lay ahead.

Origins of the Virgin Group

'Branson, I predict you will either go to prison, or become a millionaire.' These were the last words that the 17-year-old Richard Branson heard from his headmaster as he left school. Twenty-five years later, Richard Branson ruled over a business empire whose 1993 sales exceeded £1.5 billion.[1] He had started his first entrepreneurial business at the age of 12, selling Christmas trees. Soon after leaving school, he set up *Student*, a national magazine, as 'a platform for all shades of opinion, all beliefs and ideas . . . a vehicle for intelligent comment and protest'. The magazine, whose editorial staff had an average age of 16, featured interviews by Richard Branson with celebrities and articles on controversial issues.

In 1970, Richard Branson founded a mail-order record business – called Virgin to emphasize his own commerical innocence. The first Virgin record shop was opened in London's Oxford Street in 1971, soon followed by a recording studio and a label which produced records for performers such as Phil Collins, Genesis and Boy George. The Venue nightclub opened in 1978. In 1980, Virgin Records began expanding overseas, initially on a licensing basis; it later set up its own subsidiaries.

This case was prepared by Pantéa Denoyelle, research associate, under the supervision of Jean-Claude Larréche, Alfred H. Heineken Professor of Marketing at INSEAD. It is intended to be used as a basis for classroom discussion rather than to illustrate either effective or ineffective handling of an administrative situation. Copyright 1995 INSEAD, Fontainebleau, France.

Virgin Vision was created in 1983, followed by Virgin Atlantic Airways and Virgin Cargo in 1984, and Virgin Holidays in 1985.

In November 1986, the Virgin Group, which included the music, communication and retail divisions, was floated on the London Stock Exchange. The airline, clubs and holidays activities remained part of the privately owned Voyager Group Ltd. In its first public year, Virgin Group Plc had profit of £13 million on £250 million turnover – far beyond expectations. Its public status, however, was short-lived: Richard Branson believed he could not be an entrepreneur while chairing a public company. In October 1988, he regained full control by buying back all outstanding shares. The constraints that he had struggled with during the company's public life were replaced by an overwhelming sense of relief and freedom. A partnership with Seibu Saison International, one of Japan's largest retail and travel groups, was equally brief. In 1990, Richard Branson sold 10 per cent of the equity of Voyager Travel Holdings, the holding company for Virgin Atlantic, to the Japanese group in return for an injection of £36 million of equity and convertible loan capital – only to buy out his Japanese partner for £45 million in 1991.

In 1992, Richard Branson sold Virgin Music (by then the world's sixth largest record company) to Thorn EMI for £560 million. By 1994, the Virgin Group consisted of three holding companies: Virgin Retail Group, Virgin Communication and Virgin Investments which controlled over one hundred entities in twelve countries. Exhibit 2.1 summarizes the group's actitivies.

Creation of Virgin Atlantic Airways

In 1984, Richard Branson was approached by Randolph Fields, a 31-year-old lawyer who wanted to start a transatlantic airline. Fields' plan was to operate a business-class-only B747 service to New York. Richard Branson quickly made up his mind. He announced that the new airline, to be named Virgin Atlantic Airways, would be operational within three months. Needless to say, his decision struck Virgin's senior management as completely insane.

Richard Branson, who knew nothing about the airline business, set out to learn from the downfall of Laker Air, an airline launched in 1970 by Freddie Laker with six planes and 120 employees. Laker Air was originally designed as a low-risk business, flying under contract for package-holiday firms; in 1971, however, it introduced a low-budget, no-frills service between London and New York. Laker's overconfidence led to several mistakes, including purchasing three DC-10s before the US government had approved his London–New York line, and generally ordering more aircraft than he could afford. He accumulated a £350 million debt while the big transatlantic carriers slashed prices. This eventually led to Laker Airways' demise in 1981.

Richard Branson hired two former Laker executives, Roy Gardner (who later became Virgin Atlantic's co-managing director) and David Tait. Branson decided that his new airline should not be all business class, but combine an economy section

Exhibit 2.1 *The Virgin Group of Companies*

Virgin consists of three wholly-owned separate holding companies involved in distinct business areas from media and publishing to retail, travel and leisure. There are over one hundred operating companies across the three holding companies in twelve countries worldwide.

Virgin Retail Group	Virgin Communications	Voyager Investments		
		Virgin Group	*Voyager Group*	*Virgin Travel Group*
• Operates a chain of megastores in the UK, Continental Europe, Australia and Pacific selling music, video and other entertainment products	• Publishing of computer entertainment software	• Investments: joint ventures	• Clubs and hotels	• UK's second largest long-haul international airline: Virgin Atlantic Airways
• Operates games stores in the UK	• Management of investments in broadcasting including Music Box. Investments in related publishing and entertainment activities, television post production services	• Property developments	• Airship and balloon operations	• Freight handling and packaging
• Wholesale record exports and imports	• Book publishing	• Magnetic media distribution	• Storm model agency	• Inclusive tour operations: Virgin Holidays
	• Virgin Radio, Britain's first national commercial contemporary music station	• Management and corporate finance services to the Virgin organization		

Notes:
1. Marui of Japan owns 50 per cent of Virgin Megastores Japan.
2. W.H. Smith owns 50 per cent of Virgin Retail UK

Source: Virgin Atlantic.

with a first class section at business class prices. His goal was clear: 'To provide all classes of travellers with the highest quality travel at the lowest cost.' Richard Branson also leased a secondhand 747. The contract he negotiated with Boeing had a sell-back option at the end of the first, second or third year; a clause protected Virgin against currency fluctuations. Another priority was to recruit air crews. Fortunately, British Airways had recently lowered the optional retirement age for its crew, creating a pool of experienced pilots from which Virgin could draw; this gave it the most experienced crew of any British airline.

Obtaining permission to fly to New York from American regulatory bodies was not easy; authorization to land at Newark was granted only three days before Virgin's first flight was scheduled. Forbidden to advertise in the US until the approval, Virgin decided to launch a teaser campaign. Skywriters festooned the Manhattan sky with the words 'WAIT FOR THE ENGLISH VIRGI . . .'

Virgin Atlantic's inaugural flight took off from London on 22 June 1984, packed with friends, celebrities, reporters and Richard Branson wearing a First World War leather flight helmet. Once the plane had taken off, passengers were surprised to see on the video screen the cockpit, where the crew – Richard Branson and two famous cricketers – greeted them. Although this was obviously a recording, it was a memorable moment for passengers.

Early Years (1984–89)

Virgin Atlantic's early years were slightly chaotic. 'I love the challenge,' Richard Branson said. 'I suspect that before I went into the airline business, a lot of people thought I would never be able to make a go of it. It made it even more challenging to prove them wrong.' Richard Branson's determination and enthusiasm, as well as the experienced management team that he assembled, made up for the initial amateurism.

Virgin Atlantic extended its operations progressively. Its early routes, all from London, were to New York (Newark since 1984 and John F. Kennedy airport since 1988), Miami (1986), Boston (1987), and Orlando (1988). Flights to Tokyo and Los Angeles were added in 1989 and 1990. In 1987, Virgin celebrated its one millionth transatlantic passenger. Until 1991, all Virgin flights left from London's Gatwick airport, which is much smaller than Heathrow. Virgin countered this commerical disadvantage with a free limousine service for Upper Class passengers and a Gatwick Upper Class lounge, inaugurated in 1990.

While Richard Branson had always befriended rock stars, he had otherwise kept a low profile. This changed when he launched the airline: 'I knew that the only way of competing with British Airways and the others was to get out there and use myself to promote it,' he explained. Richard made a point of being accessible to reporters and never missed an opportunity to cause a sensation, wearing a stewardess's uniform or a bikini on board, or letting himself be photographed in his bath. What really caught the public's attention were his Atlantic crossings. In 1986 his Virgin Atlantic Challenger II speedboat recorded the fastest time ever across the Atlantic with Richard Branson on board. Even more spectacular was the 1987 crossing of the Virgin Atlantic Flyer – the largest hot-air balloon ever flown and the first to cross the Atlantic. Three years later Richard Branson crossed the Pacific in another balloon from Japan to Arctic Canada, a distance of 6,700 miles, breaking all existing records with speeds of up to 245 miles per hour.

The Years of Professionalization (1989–94)

The professionalization of Virgin Atlantic's management began in 1989. Until then Virgin Atlantic had had a flat structure, with 27 people reporting to Richard Branson directly. As the airline expanded, it had outgrown its entrepreneurial ways, and needed to become customer-driven.

Richard Branson asked Syd Pennington, a veteran Marks & Spencer retailer, to look into the airline's duty-free business in addition to his other responsibilities at Virgin Megastores. Some time later, Pennington, coming back from a trip, learned that he had been promoted to co-managing director of the airline. When Pennington expressed his surprise, Richard explained: 'It's easier to find good retail people than good airline people.' Syd Pennington saw that Virgin Atlantic lacked controls and procedures, and he devoted himself to professionalizing its management. His objective was to infuse the business with Richard Branson's charisma and energy while also making it effective enough to succeed. Exhibit 2.2 has a five-year summary of Virgin Atlantic's financial performance and labour force. Exhibit 2.3 shows the three-year evolution of passengers carried and market shares.

Exhibit 2.2 *Financial results and labour force of Virgin Atlantic Airways*

Financial year[a]	Turnover (£m)	Profit (loss) before tax (£m)
1988–89	106.7	8.4
1989–90	208.8	8.5
1990–91	382.9	6.1
1991–92	356.9	(14.5)
1992–93	404.7	0.4

[a] The reporting year ends on 31 July until 1990, and on 31 October as of 1991. The 1990–91 period covers 15 months.

Year	Number of employees[a]
1988	440
1989	678
1990	1,104
1991	1,591
1992	1,638
1993	1,627
1994	2,602

[a] As of 31 December (31 May for 1994).
Source: Virgin Atlantic.

Exhibit 2.3   *Market shares of Virgin Atlantic Airways (revenue passengers)*

Route[a]	1993	1992	1991
New York (JFK and Newark)	19.6%	17.2%	18.0%
Florida (Miami and Orlando)	33.2%	30.6%	25.2%
Los Angeles	23.6%	21.8%	25.8%
Tokyo	18.4%	15.5%	16.0%
Boston	22.2%	20.0%	15.3%
Total passengers carried	1,459,044	1,244,990	1,063,677

[a]: Flights from Gatwick and London Heathrow.
Source: Virgin Atlantic.

After years of campaigning, Virgin Atlantic was granted the right to fly out of Heathrow in 1991. Heathrow, Britain's busiest airport, handled 100,000 passengers a day – a total of 40 million in 1990, compared with 1.7 million at Gatwick. Virgin Atlantic was assigned to Heathrow's Terminal 3, where it competed with thirty other airlines serving over seventy-five destinations on five continents. In Richard Branson's eyes, gaining access to Heathrow was a 'historic moment and the culmination of years of struggle'. His dream to compete with other long-haul carriers on an equal footing had come true. A new era began for Virgin. Flying from Heathrow enabled it to have high load factors all year and to attract more business and full-fare economy passengers. It could also carry more interline flyers and more cargo, since Heathrow is the UK's main air freight centre. On the morning of the airline's first flight from Heathrow, a Virgin 'hit squad' encircled the model British Airways Concorde at the airport's entrance and pasted it over with Virgin's logo. Richard Branson, dressed as a pirate, was photographed in front of the Concorde before security forces could reach the site. A huge party marked the end of the day.

In April 1993, Virgin ordered four A340s from Airbus Industries, the European consortium in which British Aerospace had a 20 per cent share. The order, worth over £300 million, reflected the airline's commitment to new destinations. 'We are proud to buy an aircraft which is in large part British-built, and on which so many jobs in the UK depend,' said Richard Branson. The A340, the longest-range aircraft in the world, accommodated 292 passengers in three cabins, and had key advantages such as low fuel consumption and maintenance costs. When the first A340 was delivered in December, Virgin became the first UK carrier to fly A340s. Virgin also ordered two Boeing 747-400s and took options on two others. It also placed a $19 million order for the most advanced in-flight entertainment system available, featuring sixteen channels of video, which it planned to install in all three sections. In keeping with the airline's customization efforts, the new aircraft's cabin was redesigned. Upper Class passengers would find electronically operated 54-inch wide seats with a 55 degree recline and an on-board bar. There was a rest area for flight and cabin crew.

In June 1993, Virgin scheduled a second daily flight from Heathrow to JFK. 'We've given travellers a wider choice on their time of travel,' said Richard Branson. 'The early evening departure is timed to minimize disruption to the working day, a welcome bonus to both busy executives and leisure travellers.' In March 1994, Virgin put an end to British Airways' and Cathay Pacific's long-standing duopoly on the London–Hong Kong route, launching its own A340 service.

Virgin's first Boeing 747-400 was delivered in May 1994. Only days later, Virgin opened its San Francisco line (until then a British Airways/United duopoly). In a press release shown in Exhibit 2.4, Virgin emphasized the continuation of its expansion plans, the renewal of its fleet, and the 'better alternative' that it offered

Exhibit 2.4 *Press release for the opening of the San Francisco route*

17th May 1994

NEW SAN FRANCISCO ROUTE MARKS CONTINUED EXPANSION
FOR VIRGIN ATLANTIC

A new service to San Francisco, its sixth gateway to the US, was launched today (17th May 1994), by Virgin Atlantic Airways, marking another stage in the airline's development as it approaches its tenth anniversary.

The daily Boeing 747 service from London's Heathrow airport follows further route expansion in February 1994 when the airline introduced a daily service to Hong Kong, using two of four recently acquired Airbus A340 aircraft.

Virgin Atlantic Chairmand Richard Branson said: 'San Francisco was always on our list of the 15 or so great cities of the world that we wanted to fly to, so it's a very proud moment for us finally to be launching this new service today.

'We regularly receive awards for our transatlantic flights so I hope that this new service will be able to provide consumers on both sides of the Atlantic with a better alternative to the current duopoly which exists on the San Francisco/London route.

'Today's launch is also the culmination of a number of significant developments at Virgin Atlantic, not least of which is our recent acquisition of two new Boeing 747-400s and four Airbus A340s. This comes on the back of our $19 million investment in new 14 channel in-flight entertainment, which, unlike other airlines, we have made available to all of our passengers.'

Mr Branson added that it was the airline's intention to have one of the most modern and passenger-friendly fleets in the world. Virgin's current fleet comprises: eight B747s, three A340s, and an A320 and two BAe 146 Whisper Jets which are jointly operated with franchise partners in Dublin and Athens.

A daily service will depart Heathrow at 11.15, arriving in San Francisco at 14.05 local time. Flights leave San Francisco at 16.45, arriving in the UK the following day at 10.45. For reservations call 0293 747747.

For further information:

James Murray
Virgin Atlantic Airways
Tel: 0293 747373.

customers on both sides of the Atlantic. During the inaugural flight 150 guests – and some fare-paying flyers who had been warned that it would not be a quiet flight – were entertained with a fashion show and a jazz band. In San Francisco the aircraft stopped near a giant taximeter. The door opened, Richard Branson appeared, and inserted a huge coin in the taximeter, out of which popped the Virgin flag. Airport authorities offered Richard Branson a giant cake decorated with a miniature Golden Gate Bridge. Guests were entertained for a whirlwind five days which included a tour of the Napa Valley and a visit to Alcatraz prison where Richard Branson was jailed in a stunt prepared by his team. Virgin also took advantage of the launch to unveil a recycling and environmental programme. A stewardess dressed in green – rather than the usual red Virgin uniform – gave passengers information on the programme, which had delivered savings of £500,000 since it was launched in late 1993.

At the time of Virgin's tenth anniversary, its fleet comprised eight B747-200s, a B747-400 and three A340s. The airline awaited delivery of its second B747-400 and fourth A340 and also planned to retire two older B747-200s by the end of 1994. By then, half of its fleet would be brand new. By comparison, the average age of British Airways' fleet was eight years.[2] Richard Branson planned to expand his fleet to eighteen planes which would serve twelve or fifteen destinations by 1995. Proposed new routes included Washington DC, Chicago, Auckland, Singapore, Sydney, and Johannesburg. The London–Johannesburg license, granted in 1992, had been a moral victory for Virgin: when exploited, it will end a fifty-year duopoly enjoyed by British Airways and South African Airways.

All Virgin Atlantic planes were decorated with a Vargas painting of a red-headed, scantily dressed woman holding a scarf. The names of most Virgin aircraft evoked the Vargas Lady theme, starting with its first aircraft Maiden Voyager (Plate 3 lists the aircrafts' names). The first A340, inaugurated by the Princess of Wales, was christened The Lady in Red.

Virgin Classes

Richard Branson originally proposed to call Virgin's business and economy classes Upper Class and Riff Raff respectively; in the latter case, however, he bowed to the judgement of his managers, who urged him to desist. Virgin Atlantic strove to offer the highest quality travel to all classes of passengers at the lowest cost, and to be flexible enought to respond rapidly to their changing needs. For instance, Virgin catered to the needs of children and infants with special meals, a children's channel, pioneering safety seats, changing facilities and baby food.

'Offering a first class service at less than first class fares' had become a slogan for Virgin Atlantic. Marketed as a first class service at business class prices, Upper Class competed both with other carriers' first class and with their business class. Since its 1984 launch, this product has won every major travel industry award.

Plate 1

VIRGIN • ATLANTIC
TO AND FROM FLORIDA

VIRGIN • ATLANTIC
TO AND FROM NEW YORK CITY

VIRGIN • ATLANTIC
TO AND FROM LONDON

VIRGIN • ATLANTIC
TO AND FROM ATHENS

VIRGIN • ATLANTIC
TO AND FROM HONG KONG

Source: Virgin Atlantic. Copyright © 1995 INSEAD, Fontainebleau, France

Plate 2

Virgin Atlantic Fleet

Aircraft	Type	Name	Into Service
G-VIRG	B747-287B	Maiden Voyager	1984
G-VGIN	B747-243B	Scarlet Lady	1986
G-TKYO	B747-212B	Maiden Japan	1989
G-VRGN	B747-212B	Maid of Honour	28/08/89
G-VMIA	B747-123	Spirit of Sir Freddy	09/05/90
G-VOYG	B747-283B	Shady Lady	10/03/90
G-VJFK	B747-238B	Boston Belle	06/03/91
G-VLAX	B747-238B	California Girl	28/05/91
G-VBUS	A340-311	Lady in Red	16/12/93
G-VAEL	A340-311	Maiden Toulouse	01/01/94
G-VSKY	A340-311	China Girl	21/03/94
G-VFAB	B747-4Q8	Lady Penelope	19/05/94
G-VHOT	B747-4Q8		delivery 10/94
G-VFLY	A340-311		delivery 10/94

Plate 3

Virgin Atlantic's Three Classes

UPPER CLASS

- Reclining sleeper seat with 15" more legroom than other airlines

- Latest seat arm video/audio entertainment

- Unique Clubhouse lounge at Heathrow featuring health spa (includes hair salon, library, music room, games room, study and brasserie)

- Virgin Arrival Clubhouse with shower, sauna, swimming pool and gym

- Inflight beauty therapist on most flights

- Onboard lounges and stand up bars

- "Snoozzone" dedicated sleeping section with sleeper seat, duvet and sleep suit

- Complimentary airport transfers including chauffeur-driven limousine or motorcycle to and from airport

- Free confirmable Economy ticket for round trip to US/Tokyo

Plate 4

Virgin Atlantic's Three Classes

MID CLASS

● Separate check-in and cabin

● Most comfortable economy seat in the world with 38″ seat pitch (equivalent to many airlines' business class seat)

● Complimentary pre-take off drinks and amenity kits

● Frequent Flyer programme

● Priority meal service

● Priority baggage reclaim

● Armrest/seatback TVs and latest audio/video entertainment

ECONOMY CLASS

● Contoured, space-saving seats, maximizing legroom, seat pitch up to 34″

● Three meal option service (including vegetarian) and wide selection of free alcoholic and soft drinks

● Seatback TVs and 16 channels of the latest inflight entertainment

● Pillow and blankets

● Advance seat selection

● Complimentary amenity kit and ice cream (during movies on flight from London)

Source: Virgin Atlantic.
Copyright © 1995 INSEAD,
Fontainebleau, France

Plate 4 (continued)

Virgin Atlantic Clubhouse

Plate 5

Load Factors of Virgin Atlantic Airways

Year	Newark %	Miami %	Tokyo %	JFK %	Los Angeles %	Boston %
1990-1991	82.0	89.5	65.9	76.9	84.5	83.3
1989-1990	83.3	92.1	68.3	74.2	79.8	
1988-1989	82.8	86.7	52.4			
1987-1988	77.1	85.0				
1986-1987	74.4	76.4				
1985-1986	72.9					
1984-1985	72.0					

Source: Virgin Atlantic promotional materials.
(Copyright © 1995 INSEAD, Fontainebleau, France)

Plate 6

They must be on a different planet.

It's a brave airline that claims to be the world's favourite.

Now it seems the world has a different idea.

For at the 1989 Executive Travel Airline of the Year Awards, Virgin Atlantic have emerged victorious.

Those most demanding and, dare one say, discerning of people, the readers of Executive Travel Magazine voted Virgin Atlantic, Best Transatlantic Carrier.

It's not just over the Atlantic that they hold sway. For Virgin were also named Best Business Class in the World, above airlines they admire such as Singapore and Thai.

A choice that was quickly seconded by Business Traveller Magazine.

It's not hard to see why Virgin's Upper Class commands such respect.

AIRLINE OF THE YEAR AWARDS 1989

VIRGIN ATLANTIC AIRWAYS
EXECUTIVE TRAVEL MAGAZINE

Best Transatlantic Carrier
Best Business Class in the World
World's Best In-flight Entertainment

BUSINESS TRAVELLER MAGAZINE

World's Best Business Class

Passengers enjoy a free chauffeur driven car* to and from the airport plus a free economy standby ticket.†

On the plane there are first class sleeper seats that, miraculously, you can actually sleep in and on-board bars and lounges.

And your own personal Sony Video Walkman with a choice of 100 films.

As you might expect from Virgin, this entertainment is truly award winning. It helped scoop a third major award. Best In-Flight Entertainment.

So the next time you want to travel across the world in style, you know who to favour.

For details call *0800 800 400* or for reservations *0293 551616*, or see your travel agent.

*First 40 miles with our compliments †Not available on Tokyo route

LONDON   •   NEW YORK JFK AND NEWARK   •   MIAMI   •   MOSCOW   •   TOKYO

Plate 7

Virgin Atlantic Aircraft After New Corporate Identity Program (1994)

Plate 8

Plate 9

Plate 10

Plate 11

The Economy Class promised the best value for money, targeting price-sensitive leisure travellers who nevertheless sought comfort. It included three meal options, free drinks, seat-back video screens, and ice-cream during movies on flights from London.

After years of operating only two classes, business and economy, Virgin had introduced its Mid Class in 1992 after realizing that 23 per cent of Economy passengers travelled for business. Mid Class was aimed at cost-conscious business travellers who required enough space to work and relax. This full-fare economy class offered flyers a level of service usually found only in business class, with separate check-in and cabin, priority meal service, armrest or seat-back TVs, and the latest in audio and video entertainment. Plate 4 shows Virgin's three sections: Upper Class, Mid Class and Economy.

Virgin's B747 configuration on the Heathrow–JFK route consisted of 50 seats in Upper Class, 38 in Mid Class, and 271 in Economy. The typical British Airways B747 configuration on the same route was 18 First Class seats, 70 seats in Club World, and 282 in World Traveller Class.[3]

Service the Virgin Way

Virgin Atlantic wants to provide the best possible service while remaining original, spontaneous and informal. Its goal is to turn flying into a unique experience, not to move passengers from one point to another. It sees itself not only in the airline business but also in entertainment and leisure. According to a staff brochure:

> We must be memorable, we are not a bus service. The journeys made by our customers are romantic and exciting, and we should do everything we can to make them feel just that. That way they will talk about the most memorable moments long after they leave the airport.

Virgin Atlantic saw that, as it became increasingly successful, it risked also becoming complacent. The challenge was to keep up customers' interest by keeping service at the forefront of activities. Virgin is often distinguished for the quality and consistency of its service (as shown in Exhibit 2.5); it won the Executive Travel Airline of the Year award for an unprecedented three consecutive years. Service delivery, in other words 'getting it right the first time' was of key importance. The airline is also perceived to excel in the art of service recovery, where it aims to be proactive, not defensive. It handles complaints from Upper Class passengers within twenty-four hours, those from Economy Class flyers within a week. If a flight is delayed, passengers receive a personalized fax of apology from Richard Branson or a bottle of champagne. Passengers who complain are occasionally upgraded to Upper Class.

Exhibit 2.5 *Awards won by Virgin Atlantic Airways*

1994

Executive Travel
Best transatlantic airline
Best business class
Best in-flight magazine

Travel Weekly
Best transatlantic airline

1993

Executive Travel
Airline of the year
Best transatlantic carrier
Best business class
Best cabin staff
Best food and wine
Best in-flight entertainment
Best airport lounges
Best in-flight magazine
Best ground/check-in staff

Travel Weekly
Best transatlantic airline

Travel Trade Gazette
Best transatlantic airline

TTG Travel Advertising Awards
Best direct mail piece

1992

*Executive Travel (Awards given
   for 1991/92)*
Airline of the year
Best transatlantic carrier
Best long-haul carrier
Best business class
Best in-flight food
Best in-flight entertainment
Best ground/check-in staff

Business Traveller
Best airline for business class –
   long haul

Travel Weekly
Best transatlantic airline

Travel Trade Gazette
Best transatlantic airline

Courvoisier Book of the Best
Best business airline

ITV Marketing Awards
Brand of the year – service

Frontier Magazine
Best airline/marine duty free

BPS Teleperformance UK Winner
Overall European winner

Meetings and Incentive Travel
Best UK-based airline

Ab-Road Magazine
Airline 'Would most like to fly'
Best in-flight catering

1991

Executive Travel
(Awards given in 1992)

Business Traveller
Best business class – long haul

Travel Weekly
Best transatlantic airline

Travel Trade Gazette
Best transatlantic airline
Most attentive airline staff

*Avion World Airline
   Entertainment Awards*
Best in-flight videos – magazine
   style
Best in-flight audio –
   programming
Best in-flight audio of an original
   nature

Which Airline?
Voted by the readers as one of
   the top four airlines in the
   world (the only British airline
   amongst these four)

The Travel Organization
Best long-haul airline

Conde Nast Traveller
In the top ten world airlines

Air Cargo News
Cargo airline of the year

1990

Executive Travel
Airline of the year
Best transatlantic carrier
Best in-flight entertainment

Business Traveller
Best business class – long haul

*Travel News (now Travel
   Weekly)*
Best transatlantic airline
Special merit award to Richard
   Branson

Travel Trade Gazette
Best transatlantic airline
Travel personality – Richard
   Branson

*Avion World Airline
   Entertainment Awards*
Best overall in-flight
   entertainment
Best video programme
Best in-flight entertainment
   guide

Onboard Services magazine
Outstanding in-flight
   entertainment programme
Outstanding entertainment (for
   Sony Video Walkmans)

The Travel Organization
Best long-haul airline

1989

Executive Travel
Best transatlantic airline
Best business class in the world
Best in-flight entertainment

Business Traveller
Best business class – long haul

*World Airline Entertainment
   Awards*
Best overall in-flight
   entertainment
Best in-flight audio
   entertainment
Best in-flight entertainment
   guide (Outside magazine)

Onboard Services Magazine
Overall on-board service award
   (Upper Class)

Which Holiday?
Best transatlantic airline

Nihon Keizai Shimbun (Japan)
Best product in Japan – for Upper
   Class

1988

Executive Travel
Best business class – North
   Atlantic

Business Traveller
Best business class – long haul

Travel Trade Gazette
Best transatlantic airline

1986

The Marketing Society
Consumer services awards

What to Buy for Business
Business airline of the year

Source: Virgin Atlantic.

Innovation

Virgin's management, who want passengers never to feel bored, introduced video entertainment in 1989. They chose the quickest solution: handing out Sony Watchmans on board. Virgin later pioneered individual video screens for every seat, an idea that competitors quickly imitated. In 1994, Virgin's on-board entertainment offered up to twenty audio and sixteen video channels, including a shopping and a game channel. A gambling channel would be introduced at year-end. In the summer, a 'stop smoking program' video was shown on all flights – Virgin's contribution to a controversy over whether smoking should be permitted on aircraft.

The presence of a beauty therapist or a tailor is an occasional treat to passengers. The beautician offers massages and manicures. On some flights to Hong Kong, the tailor faxes passengers' measurements so that suits can be ready on arrival. In 1990, Virgin became the only airline to offer automatic defibrillators on board and to train staff to assist cardiac arrest victims. A three-person Special Facilities Unit was set up in 1991 to deal with medical requests. Its brief was extended to handle arrangements for unaccompanied minors or unusual requests such as birthday cakes, champagne for newly weds, public announcements or mid-flight marriage proposals. The unit also informed passengers of flight delays or cancellations, and telephoned clients whose options on tickets had expired without their having confirmed their intention to travel. Another service innovation was motorcycle rides to Heathrow for Upper Class passengers. The chauffeur service used Honda PC800s with heated leather seats. Passengers wore waterproof coveralls and a helmet with a built-in headset for a cellular phone.

In February 1993, Britain's Secretary of State for Transport inaugurated a new Upper Class lounge at Heathrow: the Virgin Clubhouse. The £1 million lounge, shown in Plate 5, had an unusual range of facilities: Victorian style wood-panelled washrooms with showers and a grooming salon offering massages, aromatherapy and haircuts; a 5,000-volume library with antique leather armchairs; a games room with the latest computer technolgy; a music room with a CD library; a study with the most recent office equipment. Many of the furnishings came from Richard Branson's own home: a giant model railway, the Challenger II Trophy, a three-metre galleon model. A two-ton, five-metre table made in Vienna from an old vessel had to be installed with a crane. Upon the opening of the Hong Kong route, a blackjack table was added at which visitors received Virgin bills that the dealer exchanged for tokens. There was also a shoeshine service. Passengers seemed to enjoy the lounge. One remarked in the visitors' book: 'If you have to be delayed more than two hours, it could not happen in a more pleasant environment.'

Customer Orientation, Virgin Style

Virgin tried to understand passengers' needs and go beyond their expectations. While it described itself as a 'niche airline for those seeking value-for-money travel', its standards and reputation could appeal to a broad spectrum of customers. It managed to serve both sophisticated, demanding executives and easy-going, price-sensitive leisure travellers in the same aircraft. According to marketing director Steve Ridgeway, Virgin attracted a broader range of customers than its competitors because it managed this coexistence between passenger groups better. This had enabled the airline to reach high load factors soon after opening new lines, as shown in Plate 6.

Virgin Atlantic had initially marketed itself as an economical airline for young people who bought Virgin records and shopped at Virgin stores, but gradually its target shifted. The danger, which Richard Branson saw clearly, was that people would perceive it as a 'cheap and cheerful' airline, a copy of the defunct Laker Airways. Richard Branson knew that his airline's survival depended on high yield business travellers. After establishing a strong base in leisure traffic, Virgin turned to the corporate segment and strove to establish itself as a sophisticated business class airline that concentrated on long-haul routes. The idea of fun and entertainment, however, was not abandoned. Upper Class was upgraded and incentives were added to attract the business traveller. By 1991, 10 per cent of the airline's passengers and 35–40 per cent of its income came from the business segment. Virgin's competitive advantage was reinforced through the combination of corporate travel buyers' price-consciousness and the rising service expectations of travellers. Richard Branson actively wooed business customers by regularly inviting corporate buyers to have lunch at his house and seeking their comments.

As part of Virgin's drive to meet customers' standards, thirty passengers on each flight are asked to fill out a questionnaire. Their answers form the basis of widely distributed quarterly reports. Virgin's senior managers fly regularly, interviewing passengers informally, making critical comments on the delivery of service and circulating their reports among top management. Richard Branson himself, who welcomes every opportunity to obtain feedback from customers, takes time to shake hands and chat with passengers. The preoccupation with service is so strong that staff are often more exacting in their evaluation of each other than the customers are.

Business exceecutives, unlike younger leisure travellers, do not readily relate to other aspects of the Virgin world: the records, the Megastores, the daredevil chairman. Their good feelings about Virgin stem mainly from their positive experiences with the airline. These tough and demanding customers appreciate Virgin's style, service, innovations and prices. Some are enthusiastic enought to rearrange their schedules in order to fly Virgin despite punctuality problems. Aside from complaints about flight delays, their only serious criticism is that Virgin does not serve enough destinations.

Virgin's People

Virgin Atlantic attract quality staff despite the relatively low salaries it pays. In management's eyes, the ideal employee is 'informal but caring': young, vibrant, interested, courteous and willing to go out of his or her way to help customers. Richard Branson explained:

> We aren't interested in having just happy employees. We want employees who feel involved and prepared to express dissatisfaction when necessary. In fact, we think that the constructively dissatisfied employee is an asset we should encourage and we need an organization that allows us to do this – and that encourages employees to take responsibility, since I don't believe it is enough for us simply to give it.

Richard Branson believes that involving management and staff is the key to superior results: 'I want employees in the airline to feel that it is *they* who can make the difference, and influence what passengers get,' he said. He writes to employees regularly to seek their ideas and to ensure that relevant news is communicated to them. His home telephone number is given to all staff, who can call him at any time with suggestions or complaints.

Virgin Atlantic's philosophy is to stimulate the individual. Its dynamic business culture encourages staff to take initiatives and gives them the means to implement them. Staff often provide insights into what customers want or need – sometimes anticipating their expectations better than the customers themselves. Virgin Atlantic has a formal staff suggestion scheme and encourages innovation from employees, both in project teams and in their daily work. Employees' suggestions are given serious consideration; many were implemented, such as the idea of serving ice-cream as a snack, although formal marketing research had never shown the need for such a service.

Richard Branson himself is open to suggestions and innovations. He talks to everyone and is a good listener, inquisitive and curious about all aspects of the business. He spends time with passengers, and visits the lounge without any advance notice. While he personifies a hands-on approach to management, he never appears controlling or threatening. His contant presence is a sign of involvement and a source of motivation for staff, who feel a lot of affection for him. It is not unusual to hear crew discuss his recent decisions or activities, mentioning 'Mr Branson' or 'Richard' with admiration and respect.

In the difficult environment of the late 1980s and early 1990s, most airline employees were anxious to keep their jobs. With most operating costs – fuel prices, aircraft prices, insurance, landing and air traffic control fees – beyond management's control, labour costs were the main target of cutbacks. In 1993, the world's top twenty airlines cut 31,600 jobs, or 3.6 per cent of their workforce, while the next eighty airlines added nearly 14,000, or 2.4 per cent. That same year, Virgin Atlantic maintained its labour force, and was in the process of recruiting at the end of the year. In June 1994, Virgin Atlantic had 2,602 employees and recruited 880 cabin crew members. Opening a single long-haul line required hiring about 400 people.

The Airline Industry

Deregulation of the US air transport industry in 1978 had reduced the government's role and removed protective rules, thereby increasing competition among American airlines. A decade later, deregulation hit Europe. The liberalization movement began in an effort to end monopolies and bring down prices. In fact, European carriers had been engaged in moderate competition in transatlantic travel while the domestic scheduled market remained heavily protected through bilateral agreements. Most European airlines were state-owned, in a regulated market where access was denied to new entrants. In April 1986, the European Court of Justice ruled that the Treaty of Rome's competition rules also applied to air transportation. Deregulation took place in three phases between 1987 – when price controls were relaxed and market access was opened – and 1992, when airlines were allowed to set their own prices, subject to some controls.

In this atmosphere of deregulation and falling prices, traffic revenue grew briskly until 1990, when a global recession and the Gulf War plunged airlines into their worst crisis since the Second World War. The twenty-two members of the association of European airlines saw the number of passengers plummet by 7 million in 1991. Traffic recovered in 1992, when the world's one hundred largest airlines saw their total revenue, measured in terms of tonnage or passengers, increase by just over 10 per cent. However, the airlines recorded a net loss of $8 billion in 1992, after losses of $1.84 billion in 1991 and $2.66 billion in 1990. Some experts believed that the industry would ultimately be dominated by a handful of players with a larger number of mid-size carriers struggling to close the gap. Exhibit 2.6 and Exhibit 2.7 show financial and passenger load data for some international airlines, while Exhibit 2.8 ranks Europe's top twenty airlines.

Virgin's Competitors

Virgin's direct competitor was British Airways (BA). Both carriers were fighting each other intensely on the most attractive routes out of London. BA, the number one British airline, was fifteen times the size of second-placed Virgin. Exhibit 2.9 and Exhibit 2.10 compare Virgin's and British Airways' flights and fares.

British Airways became the state-owned British airline in 1972 as the result of a merger between British European Airways (BEA) and British Overseas Airways Corporation (BOAC). In the early 1980s, BA was the clear leader in the highly lucrative and regulated transatlantic route, where operating margins were approximately 15 per cent of sales. However, its overall profitability was shaky when Lord King became chairman in 1981. He transformed BA into a healthy organization and prepared it for its successful privatization in 1987. Since this time, BA has remarkably outperformed its European rivals.

British Airways traditionally benefited from a strong position at Heathrow, but competition toughened in 1991 when TWA and Pan Am sold their slots to American and United Airlines for $290 million and $445 million, respectively. In the same year, Virgin also received slots at Heathrow. These slot attributions so infuriated Lord King that he scrapped BA's annual £40,000 donation to Britain's

Exhibit 2.6 *Financial results of selected international airlines*

Airline company	Ranking 1992	Ranking 1991	Sales (US$ million) 1992	% change	Operating results US$ million	Net results US$ million 1992	Net results US$ million 1991	Net margin % 1992	Jet and turbo fleet	Total employees	Productivity sales/employee $000
American	1	1	14,396	11.7	(25.0)	(935.0)	(239.9)	−6.5	672	102,400	140
United	2	2	12,889	10.5	(537.8)	(956.8)	(331.9)	−7.4	536	84,000	153
Delta	3	4	11,639	15.7	(825.5)	(564.8)	(239.6)	−4.9	554	79,157	147
Lufthansa	4	5	11,036	7.1	(198.5)	(250.4)	(257.7)	−2.3	302	63,645	173
Air France	5	3	10,769	−1.1	(285.0)	(617.0)	(12.1)	−5.7	220	63,933	168
British Airways	6	6	9,307	6.5	518.4	297.7	687.3	3.2	241	48,960	190
Swissair	16	16	4,438	7.0	152.8	80.7	57.9	1.8	60	19,025	233
TWA Inc.	18	18	3,634	−0.7	(404.6)	(317.7)	34.6	−8.7	178	29,958	121
Singapore	19	19	3,443	5.4	548.0	518.5	558.4	15.1	57	22,857	150
Qantas	20	20	3,099	2.9	79.1	105.7	34.6	3.4	46	14,936	207
Cathay Pacific	21	21	2,988	11.3	464.0	385.0	378.0	12.9	49	13,240	225
Southwest	34	41	1,685	28.3	182.6	103.5	26.9	6.1	141	11,397	148
Virgin Atlantic	62	62	626	7.3	(22.0)	Not reported	3.8	Not reported	8	2,394	261

Source: 'Much pain, no gain', *Airline Business*, September 1993. Productivity computed for this exhibit.

Exhibit 2.7 *Passenger load factors of selected international airlines*

Airline company	1992 revenue Tonne km million			% change	1992 revenue passenger km Million	% change	1992 passengers Million	% change	Passenger load factor 1992 %	1991 %	Year end	1992 rank
	Passenger	Freight	Total									
American	14,223	2,176	16,399	19.7	156,786	18.3	86.01	13.3	63.7	61.7	Dec. 92	1
United	13,489	2,522	16,010	12.0	149,166	12.6	67.00	8.1	67.4	66.3	Dec. 92	2
Delta	11,761	1,765	13,525	20.2	129,632	19.6	82.97	11.8	61.3	60.3	Dec. 92	3
Lufthansa	5,882	4,676	10,725	14.4	61,274	17.1	33.70	14.2	65.0	64.0	Dec. 92	4
Air France	5,238	3,970	9,208	5.3	55,504	4.0	32.71	3.4	67.4	66.8	Dec. 92	5
British Airways	7,622	2,691	10,313	13.2	80,473	15.6	28.10	10.5	70.8	70.2	Mar. 93	6
Swissair	1,573	1,063	2,684	9.1	16,221	7.0	8.01	0.4	60.3	61.6	Dec. 92	16
TWA Inc.	4,258	734	4,992	1.4	46,935	1.8	22.54	8.5	64.7	64.7	Dec. 92	18
Singapore	3,675	2,412	6,086	14.2	37,861	8.5	8.64	6.3	71.3	73.5	Mar. 93	19
Qantas	2,684	1,220	3,904	4.9	28,836	7.2	4.53	9.4	66.2	66.0	Jun. 92	20
Cathay Pacific	2,695	1,671	4,366	13.3	27,527	12.7	8.36	13.1	73.5	73.6	Dec. 92	21
Southwest	2,032	49	2,082	23.4	22,187	22.0	27.84	22.6	64.5	61.1	Dec. 92	34
Virgin Atlantic	984	285	1,269	27.4	9,001	8.7	1.23	5.6	76.1	81.6	Oct. 92	62

Source: 'Much pain, no gain', *Airline Business*, September 1993.

Exhibit 2.8 *Europe's top twenty airlines, 1993*

Rank	Airline company	Sales (US$ m)	Global rank
1	Lufthansa	11,036.5	4
2	Air France Group	10,769.4	5
3	British Airways	9,307.7	6
4	SAS Group	5,908.2	12
5	Alitalia	5,510.7	14
6	KLM Royal Dutch	4,666.3	15
7	Swissair	4,438.5	16
8	Iberia	4,136.7	17
9	LTU/LTU Sud	1,836.1	31
10	Sabena	1,708.3	33
11	Aer Lingus	1,381.0	38
12	Aeroflot	1,172.1	43
13	Finnair	1,132.2	45
14	TAP Air Portugal	1,110.1	47
15	Austrian Airlines	1,003.8	49
16	Britannia Airways	924.0	53
17	Olympic Airways	922.5	54
18	Turkish Airlines	736.5	59
19	Airlines of Britain Holdings	687.7	61
20	Virgin Atlantic	626.5	62

Source: 'Much pain, no gain', *Airline Business,* September 1993.

governing Conservative Party. At the time of the Heathrow transfer, BA scheduled 278 flights a week across the Atlantic from London, with 83,000 seats, while American had 168 flights with 35,000 seats and United 122 with 30,000. Virgin had 84 flights with 30,000 seats.

Despite these competitive pressures and the recent airline recession, BA remained one of the world's most profitable airlines. The largest carrier of international passengers, serving 150 destinations in 69 countries, it was making continuous progress in terms of cost efficiency, service quality and marketing. BA recruited marketing experts from consumer goods companies who implemented a brand approach to the airline's classes. Some of the actions undertaken by BA in the early 1990s include the £17.5 million relaunch of its European business class Club Europe and spending £10 million on new lounges (with a traditional British feel), check-in facilities and ground staff at Heathrow. It was also rumoured that BA was preparing to spend nearly £70 million on an advanced in-flight entertainment and information system for its long-haul fleet before the end of 1994.

British Airways and Virgin had fiercely competed against one another from the onset. One major incident that marked their rivalry was what became known as the Dirty Tricks Campaign. In 1992, Virgin Atlantic filed a lawsuit against BA, accusing it of entering Virgin's computer system and spreading false rumours. In January 1993, Virgin won its libel suit against BA in London. The wide press

Exhibit 2.9   *Virgin Atlantic and British Airways: comparison of routes, 1994*

Destination from London to:	Airline	Frequency	Departure–Arrival (local times)	Aircraft
New York (JFK)	Virgin Atlantic	Daily (LHR)	14.00–16.40	747
			18.35–20.55	
	British Airways	Daily (LHR)	10.30–09.20	Concorde
			11.00–13.40	747
			14.00–16.40	747
			18.30–21.10	747
			19.00–17.50	Concorde
		Daily (Gat)	10.40–13.20	D10
New York (Newark)	Virgin Atlantic	Daily (LHR)	16.00–18.40	747
	British Airways	Daily (LHR)	14.45–17.40	747
Boston	Virgin Atlantic	Daily (Gat.)	15.00–17.10	A340
	British Airways	Daily (LHR)	15.45–18.00	747
			09.55–12.30	767
Los Angeles	Virgin Atlantic	Daily (LHR)	12.00–15.10	747
	British Airways	Daily (LHR)	12.15–15.15	747–400
			15.30–18.30	747–400
Miami	Virgin Atlantic	W,F,S,Su (Gat.)	11.15–15.45	747
		Th (Gat.)	11.15–15.45	747
	British Airways	Daily (LHR)	11.15–15.40	747
			14.30–18.55	747
Orlando	Virgin Atlantic	Daily (Gat.)	12.30–16.40	747
	British Airways	Tu,W,Su (LHR)	11.15–19.15	747
		M,Th,F,S (Gat.)	11.00–15.10	747
San Francisco	Virgin Atlantic	Daily (LHR)	11.15–14.05	747
	British Airways	Daily (LHR)	13.15–16.05	747–400
			10.50–13.40	747
Tokyo	Virgin Atlantic	M,T,Th,F,S,Su (LHR)	13.00–08.55 (next day)	747/A340
	British Airways	Daily (LHR)	12.55–08.45 (next day)	747–400
		M,T,Th,F,S,Su (LHR)	16.30–12.15 (next day)	747–400
Hong Kong	Virgin Atlantic	Daily (LHR)	20.30–16.35 (next day)	A340
	British Airways	F (LHR)	13.55–09.55 (next day)	747–400
		M,T,W,Th,S,Su (LHR)	14.30–10.30 (next day)	747–400
		Daily (LHR)	21.30–17.30 (next day)	747–400

LHR = London Heathrow; Gat. = Gatwick

Sources: The Guide to Virgin Atlantic Airways, May/June 1994, and *British Airways Worldwide Timetable*, 27 March–29 October 1994.

Exhibit 2.10 *Virgin Atlantic and British Airways' fares, 1994*

Route	Virgin Atlantic			British Airways			
	Upper Class[a] £	Mid Class[a] £	Economy 21 Day Apex[b] £	First Class[a] £	Club[a] £	Economy £	21 Day Apex[c] £
New York	1,195	473	489	1,935	1,061	620	538
San Francisco	1,627	595	538[d]	2,179	1,627	920	638
Los Angeles	1,627	604	538	2,179	1,627	920	638
Tokyo	1,806	783	993	2,751	1,806	1,580	993
Hong Kong	979	600	741	3,280	2,075	1,808	741
Boston	1,082	473	439	1,935	1,061	620	538
Miami	1,144	529	498	2,085	1,144	780	598
Orlando	1,144	529	498	2,085	1,144	780	598

[a] One-way weekend peak-time fares.
[b] Economy fare for Virgin is Economy 21 day Apex (reservation no later than 21 days prior to departure).
[c] 21 day Apex round-trip ticket.
[d] Between 17 May and 30 June 1994 a special launch fare round trip ticket was sold at £299.

coverage caused much embarrassment to British Airways. Later that year, Virgin
filed a $325 million lawsuit in the Federal Court of New York, accusing BA of using
its monopoly power to distort competition on North American routes.

In addition to British Airways, Virgin competed with at least one major carrier
on each of its destinations. For instance, it was up against United Airlines to Los
Angeles, American Airlines to New York and Cathay Pacific to Hong Kong. Most
of its competitors surpassed Virgin many times in terms of turnover, staff and
number of aircraft. Yet, Virgin was not intimidated by the size of its competitors; it
saw its modest size as an advantage that enabled it to react quickly and remain
innovative.

Virgin Atlantic's Management Structure

Virgin Atlantic's headquarters are in Crawley, a suburb near Gatwick. The airline
has a loose organization combined with a high level of dialogue and involvement,
as well as strong controls. A senior manager explained: 'Our business is about
independence, entrepreneurial flair, and people having autonomy to make
decisions; yet we pay a great deal of attention to overhead and cost levels.' Members
of the management team, whose structure is shown in Exhibit 2.11, came from other
airlines, other industries, or other divisions of the Virgin Group. The three top
executives – co-managing directors Roy Gardner and Syd Pennington and finance
director Nigel Primrose – report directly to Richard Branson.

Exhibit 2.11   *Virgin Atlantic Airways Ltd organizational structure, 1994*

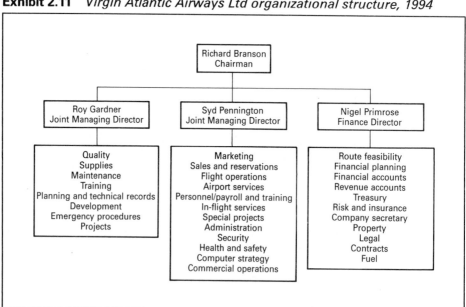

Gardner had joined Virgin Airways as technical director in 1984 after working at Laker Airways and British Caledonian Airways. He is responsible for the technical aspects of operations: quality, supplies, maintenance, emergency procedures. Pennington oversees commercial operations, marketing, sales and flight operations. Primrose, a chartered accountant with twenty years of international experience, was part of the senior team that set up Air Europe in 1978 and Air UK in 1983 before joining Virgin Atlantic in 1986. He was Virgin Atlantic's company secretary with responsibility for route feasibility, financial planning, financial accounts, treasury and legal affairs.

Steve Ridgeway heads the marketing department (Exhibit 2.12). After assisting Richard Branson in several projects, including the Transatlantic Boat Challenge, he had joined the airline in 1989 to develop its frequent traveller programme, becoming head of marketing in 1992. Paul Griffiths, who had fourteen years of commercial aviation experience, became Virgin Atlantic's director of commerical operations after spending two years designing and implementing its information management system. Personnel director Nick Potts, a business studies graduate, was recruited in 1991 from Warner Music UK where he had been the head of the personnel department.

Marketing Activities

Steve Ridgeway's marketing department covered a variety of activities, as shown in Exhibit 2.12. Some traditional marketing disciplines, such as advertising, promotions, planning and the Freeway frequent flyer programme, reported to Ruth Blakemore, head of marketing. Catering retail operations (for example, duty-free sales), product development and public relations reported directly to Steve Ridgeway.

Exhibit 2.12 *Virgin Atlantic Airways' marketing department*

Source: Virgin Atlantic.

Virgin Atlantic spent an average 2 per cent of turnover on advertising, well below the 5–7 per cent industry norm. Virgin's advertising had featured a series of short campaigns handled by various agencies. The winning of a quality award was often a campaign opportunity as in Plate 7, as was the opening of a new line. On one April Fool's Day, Virgin announced that it had developed a new bubble-free champagne. It also launched *ad hoc* campaigns in response to competitiors' activities, as in Exhibit 2.13. The survey in Exhibit 2.14 shows that Virgin Atlantic enjoyed a strong brand equity, as well as a high level of spontaneous awareness and a good image in the UK. In order to increase the trial rate, its advertising had evolved from a conceptual approch to more emphasis on specific product features.

In 1990, the airline launched its Virgin Freeway frequent travellers programme in Britain (it started in the USA in 1992). While Virgin Freeway was an independent division of the Virgin Travel Group, it operated with the airline's marketing department. Freeway miles were offered to members who flew Mid Class or Upper Class or who used the services of international companies such as American Express, Inter-Continental Hotels, British Midland, SAS and others. Miles could be exchanged for free flights to Europe, North America and Japan, as well as a wide range of activities: hot-air ballooning, polo lessons, rally driving, luxury country getaways for two, five days skiing in the USA. As part of the Freeway programme, Virgin offered a free standby ticket for every Upper Class ticket purchased.

The Virgin Freeway was run in partnership with SAS and other international groups which, according to Ruth Blakemore, enabled it to compete with British Airways. Virgin also had ties with SAS through another Freeway partner, British Midland, wholly-owned by Airlines of Britain in which SAS had a 35 per cent stake. Virgin delivered significant interline traffic to British Midland, and Blakemore believed that there was a useful common ground for all three to join forces against British Airways.

In May 1993, Virgin Atlantic unveiled a promotional campaign targeting BA passengers who had never tried Virgin. Members of BA's Executive Club USA programme who had accumulated 50,000 miles or more qualified for a free Upper Class Companion ticket on Virgin; those with 10,000 to 49,999 miles qualified for a free Mid Class ticket. The campaign was launched with a radio commerical in which Richard Branson said: 'In recent years, Virgin has done about everything we can think of to get those remaining British Airways' passengers to try Virgin Atlantic.'

The marketing department handled the franchising of the Virgin Atlantic brand, which included two routes. London–Athens, launched from Gatwick in March 1992 in partnership with South East European Airlines of Greece, was transferred to Heathrow seven months later. London City Airport–Dublin, with City Jet, was launched in January 1994. In both cases, the aircraft and crew bore Virgin's name and colours, but Virgin's partner was the operator and paid royalties to Virgin for the use of its brand, marketing and sales support, and for assistance in the recruitment and training of flight staff.

In April 1994, Virgin announced a partnership with Delta Air Lines – its first alliance with a major international airline. Delta would purchase a set percentage

Exhibit 2.13 *Virgin Atlantic Airways advertising response to a British Airways campaign, spring 1994*

The world's favourite airline?
Not in our book.

BEATS THE PANTS OFF BA!
VERY GOOD SERVICE.
JAMES ARMSTRONG
B. S. LIMITED

Excellent.
Keep BA on the run!
JEREMY HATTON
NORWICH CRUISE CENTRE

The best service from the best airline in the World!
Absolutely Fabulous - !!
VINCE CRAWLEY
COUNTRY CASUALS LTD

With a deal like this,
who the hell wants to
fly BA anyway!!
BOB BROWN
FILMCO EUROFORM

A previously dedicated and loyal
British Airways customer, now
a dedicated and loyal Virgin
customer!
ROBERT CASSON
PFIZER INC

Best Business Class price
service in the air.
GEOFF TOVEY
SMITHKLINE BEECHAM

Such a refreshing change from BA! Great
entertainment & service! - Looking forward
to another flight!
ANDREW TURNER
REED TRAVEL GROUP

I am your biggest fan -
I promise never to fly
another airline if I can
help it. It is always
a pleasure on Virgin!
KATHY BRADY
BANKERS TRUST

As ever, Virgin
leads the field.
PAUL JACKSON
CARLTON TV

My first time too on Virgin Atlantic and it's
unquestionably better than the equivalent BA.
The service, for example, was first class.
SHERBAN CANTACUZINO
ROYAL FINE ART COMMISSION

Virgin Atlantic's Upper Class costs the same as BA Club Class. And it's not just
the comments in our visitors' book that are better. Hope to see you soon.

Exhibit 2.14   *Brand equity survey*

	Perceived strongest brand name in transatlantic travel % of respondents	Spontaneous awareness %	Usage %	Rating of brand names 0–100 scale
BA	70	96	93	85
Virgin	24	74	48	80
American	2	49	44	61
United	1	22	23	58

Source: Business Marketing Services Limited (BMSL). Based on 141 interviews of executives from the UK's top five hundred organizations.

of seats on Virgin flights between London and Los Angeles, New York (Newark and JFK), Miami, San Francisco, Orlando and Boston which it would price and sell independently. The alliance, which increased Virgin's annual revenue by $150 million and gave Delta access to Heathrow, has received the blessing of the British government and is awaiting US approval.

Virgin Atlantic's public relations department, known as 'the press office' and led by James Murray, plays an important role. 'We are not here just to react to press inquiries,' explained Murray. 'We also try to gain publicity for the airline's products and services and to show how much better we are than the competition.' Virgin Atlantic enjoys excellent relations with the media – not the rule in the airline industry – because of a combination of factors: Richard Branson's persona, the airline's openness in dealing with the press, its 'David versus Goliath' quality, the news value of its innovations and a good management of media relationships.

For instance, Virgin had readily accepted an invitation to participate in BBC television's prime-time *Secret Service* series, in which investigators posing as customers test service at well-known firms. Failures in service delivery were exposed and discussed. British Airways, which the BBC had approached first, had declined. While the programme did identify some shortcomings in Virgin's operations, including delays in meal service (due to oven problems) and in answering passenger calls, it gave a lively demonstration of the quality of service in Upper Class and of Virgin's willingness to take corrective action.

The public relations department comprised three people in Crawley and two in the group press office, where James Murray spends two days a week. Originally set up in Richard Branson's own house, the group press office had to move next door as the amount of work increased. Staff were on call round-the-clock, sometimes taking calls from journalists in the middle of the night. During a one-hour car ride with James Murray, the authors watched him handle a constant flow of requests ranging from invitations to the inaugural San Francisco flight to questions on Virgin's position on privatizing the Civil Aviation Agency or the possible banning of peanuts on flights after reports of allergy risks – all on the car phone.

A five-member product development department evaluates and develops innovations. It handles a broad range of new product activities – a new identity programme for the aircraft, selection of seat design and internal decoration, the catering system or new lounges – and coordinates the input from other departments. Typically, the marketing, engineering, commercial and sales departments also participate in developing new products. For example, the airport services department played a crucial role in setting up the Clubhouse lounge.

By June 1994, Virgin had taken steps to correct its main weaknesses: the age of its fleet and its punctuality problems. More than half the fleet would be renewed by the end of the year, and Virgin was undertaking an On-time Initiative in which cabin crew were to shut doors exactly ten minutes before departure time, even if late passengers had not boarded – even Richard Branson, who was notorious for being late. Virgin was also implementing a new corporate identity programme. In addition to the Virgin logo and the Vargas Lady, all aircraft would bear the words 'virgin atlantic' in large grey letters, as shown in Plate 8.

Challenges for the Future

During its first decade, Virgin Atlantic has confronted great challenges and survived the worst recession in the history of air transportation. Amidst rumours over the airline's financial health, Richard Branson has always stressed his personal commitment. 'I would put everything I had into making sure that Virgin Atlantic was here in twenty years time,' he said.

Virgin Atlantic has demonstrated its capacity to innovate, to satisfy customers and to be financially viable in difficult times. As the world economy began to recover, the airline was poised for a quantum leap in the scale of its operations. When Richard Branson founded it in 1984, his ambition had been to build an airline unlike any other. Ten years later, what set Virgin apart was its reputation for giving customers what they wanted at prices they could afford, pioneering new concepts in service and entertainment, and restoring a sense of pleasure and excitement to long-distance travel.

The main challenge the airline faced as it celebrated its tenth anniversary was to foster this difference throughout the 1990s. What sort of airline should it be? How could it achieve that goal? How could it remain profitable? How could it retain its competitive edge in innovations? Was it possible to grow while retaining the organizational advantages of a small entrepreneurial company? How could it keep employees motivated and enthusiastic? How would it keep the momentum of its success? These were some of the questions that went through Richard Branson's mind as he and his four hundred guests watched a Virgin 747 Jumbo fly over the Thames and Westminster to mark Virgin's first decade.

Notes

1.   In June 1994, £1 = US$1.51.
2.   BA's fleet had 240 aircraft, including some 180 Boeings, 7 Concordes, 10 A320s, 15 BAe ATPs and 7 DC10s.
3.   As of April 1994, the Club World and World Traveller (Euro Traveller for flights within Europe) were the names given to British Airways' former Business and Economy Classes respectively.

Midelectric Ltd
A Market Electrified

Timo Ranta

Helsinki School of Economics and Business Administration, Finland

> Decisions made in the capital-intensive electricity industry
> tend to have extensive effects. If hasty decisions are made
> as the market is opened to competition, short-term decisions
> may have undesirable long-term effects.
> Antero Pohjola, Midelectric Annual Report 1992

In 1994, pressure was felt thoroughout the Finnish electricity market. A draft version of the new electricity market act had been distributed for evaluation and the electricity utilities knew that they would have to prepare for free competition in the production and sale of electricity – for the first time in their existence.

This posed no threat to Mr Pohjola, managing director of Midelectric Ltd, a large Finnish electrcity utility company operating in central Finland, as he was sitting in his office on a hot July morning in 1994. He knew what was going to happen:

> Now, as the electricity market is being opened to competition, major electricity consumers such as industrial firms will start to evaluate electricity suppliers not only according to price and quality but also according to all the expertise they can get from their suppliers. They have no money for and no interest in employing energy experts themselves, which is why they will be looking for electricity suppliers that are able to save their money and design environmentally acceptable systems together with them. This has nothing to do with fashion.

Midelectric was no novice in customer orientation. Throughout its existence it had focused on enhancing welfare, economic development and home comfort in its distribution district. For Midelectric, it had always been obvious that energy is a means to an end and that this end should not be forgotten. Midelectric also knew what the requirements of sustainable development meant in the field of energy.

Once the new law took effect, however, things would change for Midelectric too. The company would be in a novel environment and conditions would probably never be the same again. Mr Pohjola considered what the future might look like for Midelectric and for the whole market. There was noise outside. He closed the window of his office and listened to the low hum of the air-conditioning system.

Company Profile

The history of Midelectric goes back to the first quarter of the century. The company was founded by a group of local electricity distributing companies in order to secure a supply of electricity. In 1960 the distribution companies were merged into Midelectric. In the 1990s the company was in the business of providing electricity to households and companies in its distribution district as well as carrying out installation and cable construction operations. It also took part in the distribution of district heating and gas, which was conducted mainly through its shareholding companies.

By 1994 Midelectric had become one of the largest electricity utilities in Finland. In 1994 it was expanding rapidly, aiming at strengthening its foothold in the concentrating electricity market of Finland (Exhibit 3.1).

The turnover of Midelectric had increased from FIM 500 million[1] to FIM 600 million between 1993 and 1994, owing partly to acquisitions. For a company like Midelectric, purchasing electricity is a major cost factor. In 1994 it owned only two power plants; this is because the area where it operates is not very conducive to electricity generation. Other major cost factors were personnel, grid maintenance and net financial expenses, all of which had increased owing to recent acquisitions.

Exhibit 3.1   *Midelectric in brief*

		1993	1992
People in the distribution district		236,500	176,500
Distribution district	km²	13,800	11,830
Purchase of electricity	GWh	1,637	1,578
Customers		139,066	108,402
Distribution network			
Substations (110/20 kV)		38	30
Distribution substations (20/0.4 kV)		7,661	6,350
Medium voltage lines (20 kV)	km	8,180	6,650
Low voltage lines (0.4 kV)	km	14,157	11,400
Business activities			
Investments in the distribution network	FIM million[a]	48	48
Turnover	FIM million	499	456
Balance sheet total	FIM million	929	875
Wages and salaries	FIM million	58	61
Personnel		458	450

[a] In 1993, FIM 1 ≃ £0.12.
Source: Midelectric Annual Report 1993.

The remainder was capital costs. Electricity distribution, in general, is a very capital-intensive industry. In Finland, the total turnover of the industry was in the neighbourhood of FIM 14 billion, over 3 billion of which had been invested each year before the recession.

The customer profile of Midelectric was distinctive as compared with some of the other large electricity utilities; a large number of its customers were households and private dwellings (see Exhibit 3.2). This was because the area served by Midelectric was composed mainly of small towns and countryside, which was also popular among holidaymakers. However, 1 per cent of Midelectric's customers consumed 32 per cent of the electricity distributed by it, which was not an atypical ratio in Finland.

A comparison of the customer profile of Midelectric with the national profile of Finland creates an interesting picture and illustrates the distinctive customer profile of Midelectric in more detail (Exhibit 3.3). In fact, the percentages of

Exhibit 3.2 *Electricity consumption by consumer group in the Midelectric distribution district, 1993*

Customer group	No. of customers	Consumption million kWh	kWh/customer
Households	64,718	494	7,626
Other dwellings	27,014	67	2,468
Farms	9,564	153	16,014
Industry and construction	1,453	251	175,231
Transportation and business	4,040	113	27,963
Public	2,806	128	45,606
Retailers	8	333	
Nokia district[a]	29,481	40	
Total	139,066	1,580	

[a] A distribution district purchased by Midelectric in 1993; the figure includes all customers.
Source: Midelectric information leaflet, 1993.

Exhibit 3.3 *Use of electricity by sector*

Sector	Share of all electricity used in Finland %	Share of all electricity supplied by Midelectric %	Share in the Midelectric customer portfolio %
Industry and construction	52	21	1
Households and farms	26	59	93
Public, transportation and business	17	20	6
Losses	5		

Source: Statistical appendix, Midelectric Annual Report 1994.

household and industry electricity consumption in the Midelectric sales portfolio represent a virtual mirror image of the national ratio.

Operating Environment

Finland has many features that make it peculiar in terms of energy. Apart from Iceland, Finland is the only country lying above 60 degrees north latitude. It has long, cold and dark winters. Finland is also part of the Eurasian taiga, one of world's largest forested areas, and over half of Finnish export income stems directly or indirectly from forest-related industries. These factors – the northern climate and dependence on forests – make Finland one of the most energy-intensive nations in the world.

The Finnish framework, thus, requires much more energy than developed economies such as Germany, Belgium and Japan. These latter benefit from warmer climate and the fact that an overwhelming part of their GNP is produced by manufacturing industries. The biggest source of export incomes of Germany, for example, is the automobile industry, and the production of one car requires a very small amount of energy compared with a tone of pulp or paper. Hence, the German price of energy may be two and a half times that of Finland without causing much of a burden to its industries. More detailed statistics about the Finnish energy situation can be found in Exhibit 3.4.

Exhibit 3.4   *Energy consumption in Finland*

Sector	Share of all energy used in Finland %	Breakdown (%)
Households (incl. direct and indirect use of energy)	43	
Indirect		56
• groceries		21
• maintenance of dwellings		12
• goods and services		11
• traffic		8
• clothing		4
Direct		44
• heating of dwellings		20
• gasoline		10
• household electricity		8
• hot water		5
• lighting		1
Export	41	
Investments	10	
Public services	6	

Source: Midelectric information leaflet, 1993.

Furthermore, Finland is sparsely populated. In Finland, there are 130 metres of electric cables per inhabitant, whereas the equivalent figure in the developed industrial countries of the Central Europe is 20–30 metres. The establishment of an electricity system had required more resources per capita in Finland than elsewhere in the industrialized world. The low price of Finnish energy, therefore, has to be related to the efficiency of the entire system. Also, the energy-related environmental pressures may become quite acute in an energy-intensive country like Finland. However, Mr Pohjola, the managing director of Midelectric, thinks that many of the demands presented to the energy industry are ill-informed.

> One often sees people from outside the industry import ideas written 'under a palm tree' to Finland.

In 1994 Finland was characterized by a large number of electricity utility companies, as were Norway and Sweden, but a clear tendency towards concentration was evident. In comparison, immediately after the Second World War countries like the UK and France opted for state-owned electricity utilities. By the 1990s, however, the UK had a half dozen private and regional electricity utilities. In general, electricity utilities had tended to become larger, but they were not allowed to become nationwide monopolies. Japan has had it every way. It has had many small utilities, then a state system and then nine private electricity utilities, which are giants in their own right but still constitute a competitive market. In 1994, Finland had about 120 electricity utilities, a figure which had dropped from 270 during the preceding twenty-five years. This trend was likely to continue. In 1994, however, Finnish electricity utilities were still small and numerous.

It was also common knowledge within the industry that in 1994 Finnish electricity utilities fell into three distinct clusters. The first was formed by the three large utilities operating in the Helsinki area, and these geographically close companies were known to have stuck together at various instances. The second cluster was commonly known as the Group of Ten and it was the backbone of the Finnish Electricity Utilities' Association. These ten utilities were quite large and, geographically, they covered an overwhelming part of the market. Midelectric was one of the strongest companies in this group. The rest of the utilities could be categorized as small. The smaller companies did not cooperate publicly in any way.

New Legislation

The new law regulating the Finnish electricity market was likely to take effect as of the beginning of July 1995. In brief, this would mean that the generation and exchange of electricity would be opened to competition. The new law was supposed to increase the efficiency of the Finnish electricity market and hence safeguard the future competitiveness of the Finnish electricity system. The industry was also prepared for integration of the Nordic and European markets. The new legislation was designed to remove barriers to competition and to deregulate that part of the market where competition was possible, i.e. generation and sales. Competition and deregulation would encourage efficient use of resources in the electricity industry and create cost savings for the consumer and for the economy as a whole.

A set of clear rules would be established for the monopoly activities, i.e. the distribution network. Electricity networks were usually owned by producers and sellers who could prevent outsiders from penetrating their market area. When the new law became effective, all network-owners would have to open their networks to new entrants for a reasonable price. Electricity networks would constitute a marketplace that would have to serve the parties in the electricity trade, both buyers and sellers, on reasonable and equal terms. The price system for the network activity would have to encourage trade.

The network activity would have to be transparent, which would mean public prices as well as readily available information about economic and technical efficiency. In accounting systems, network activities would have to be separated from the other activities of electricity companies. The same applies to other corporate electricity distribution activities where the company has a dominant market position. All network owners would need an operating licence. This would define the geographical region where the network owner has to connect all electricity users to its network. Major network owners would also bear responsibility for the security of the national high-voltage network and they would have the primary responsibility and right to maintain and extend that network.

The selling of electricity, on the other hand, would no longer require an operating licence. Electricity distributors would lose their regional monopolies. To safeguard the interests of small consumers, however, the regional distributors would be required to supply electricity to those customers who are not in the competitive market. The prices and delivery terms for these customers would have to be uniform and public.

The freedom of the buyer to choose an electricity supplier would increase under the new legislation. In particular, this would apply to large industrial firms, wholesalers and small and medium-sized enterprises. The possibilities for households to select a new supplier would, in the beginning, be limited by transaction costs, which were, however, expected to decline with technological progress. Small customers would first benefit indirectly from the increased competition in the wholesale market. Electricity prices for consumers would not depend on their location within the distribution area.

This revolution in the electricity market would encourage the use of renewable energy. Open networks reduce barriers to market entry, which might be a significant change for local small power plants, for example. In addition, the change would give local electricity utilities more scope to encourage energy conservation by their customers. There would be new opportunities to include the costs of energy conservation services in electricity tariffs.

The licensing procedure required for building large power plants (more than 250MW) would be removed as was done for the small power plants in 1989. Even imports and exports of electricity would be freed from much of the existing bureaucracy, although imports would still be subject to licensing because of environmental and security aspects. Also, licences would still be needed for power plant construction owing to legislation on the environment, nuclear energy, water and construction, for example.

The new law for the electricity market would implement the changes concerning electricity distribution, pricing and accounting within a one-year transition period. The new electricity safety law would take effect simultaneously. Thus, the current electricity market legislation would be replaced in its entirety.

Orientation of Midelectric

Midelectric perceived itself as a service company in the field of energy aiming at enhancing economic welfare and living comfort in its distribution district. The operation of the company was guided by the interests and needs of its customers and other interest groups. It sought to maintain and strengthen its position in the energy sector in order to support development in its district efficiently and competitively. The company had set internal efficiency, economic profitability, professionalism, environmental protection, flexibility and quality as its strategic guidelines. In line with these guidelines, the company also had strong strategic capabilities in efficient electricity production, demand-side management, and the efficient use of energy. These latter are discussed in turn.

Efficient Electricity Production

As the purchasing of electricity constituted a major part of the costs of Midelectric, efficient electricity production and consumption structures were essential. Midelectric, therefore, attempted to influence developments in the electricity market and the economy as a whole. It had, for example, been trying to monitor and direct public opinion so that wise energy decisions would be made at the national level. As Mr Pohjola put it:

> We try to influence public opinion so that Finnish electricity will not have to be produced by 'burning small pine cones'.

Midelectric had been trying to explain to the general public that it was in their own interests that electricity should be produced as efficiently as possible in a country like Finland where there is no more water power to be employed. Parliament had also decided that no more nuclear power plants would be built in Finland, which meant that the proportion of expensive thermal electricity would increase steadily. It was difficult for Mr Pohjola to hide his disappointment about this national course taken in the autumn of 1993.

It was also important for Midelectric to acquaint the general public with the nature and effects of electricity. One distinction is especially relevant but not very well understood: the distinction between energy and electricity. Energy, in general, is power used in order to accomplish various goals but not all energy is in the form of electricity. If all energy consumed in Finland, for example, is transformed into equivalent oil-tons, 300 billion tons were consumed each year in the 1990s, about one-third of which was electricity. Considering the reasons behind energy conservation aims – avoidance of emissions and concern for global energy reserves – one has to bear in mind this distinction because, for example, the emission problem is far more acute in direct consumption of gasoline than in electricity consumption. This is one of the reasons why the electric car is seen as one solution to the pressing environmental problems of today.

An illustrative example of this distinction was the question of electrical heating. Normal household heating per cubic metre of housing required 70–80 kWh in Finland in the 1950s. In the 1960s, the possibility of electrical heating was introduced, which had a number of positive effects. Owing to the higher unit price of electricity as compared with oil, increasing attention was paid to proper construction and reasonable heating levels, and soon the relative consumption of heating energy began to drop. By 1994 there were houses where heating required 30–35 kWh per cubic metre. Increased use of electricity had therefore decreased the use of energy.

Midelectric had also been experimenting with renewable energy sources, solar power in particular. It did not, however, see them as a relevant solution to the Finnish environment on a large scale. The solar power plant of Midelectric, for example, was worth FIM 70,000 but it produced only 600 kWh of electricity a year, which was worth about FIM 250. The return on investment was not high.

Demand-side Management

Electricity consumption in Finland is characterized by strong seasonal fluctuations. Of particular importance is the increased electricity consumption in the winter, for example in February 1994, the national average was 11,000 MW (11 GW) per hour. Weekly fluctuations are also important owing to the predominance of industry in electricity consumption.

Explicit efforts to cut the peaks of energy consumption are often referred to as demand-side management (DSM). Demand-side management is sometimes considered to be the sole responsibility of national and international energy policy officials and institutions. The energy conservation programme introduced by the Finnish government in September 1992, for example, had set as a target that 15 per cent of household-related, 10 per cent of industry-related, 15 per cent of service-related and 10 per cent of transport-related energy consumption be conserved in the near future. Midelectric, however, had made a conscious effort to institute explicit and effective demand-side management as one of its strategic goals.

As an example, Midelectric received the Eta Award in 1993 for its success in restructuring the production process of an industrial company. That company shifted from butane to electricity and its energy consumption dropped by 50 per cent, production and productivity increased, and working conditions improved. In many factories it was also possible to 'recycle' process energy as heating energy, which amounted to enormous energy savings in the long run. This example also illustrated how economic and ethical considerations combine in the marketing orientation of Midelectric. By installing energy-conserving systems, which was the right thing to do ethically, Midelectric, at the same time, was attracting new customers.

Demand-side management, however, has to be effectively targeted in order to work. Attention also has to be focused on the return from energy investments. Mr Pohjola illustrates:

> If somebody invented a lamp that consumes no energy at all, replacing every lamp in Finland with that new invention would reduce household energy consumption by 1 per cent.

Specific attention should, therefore, be paid to heating, hot water and transport. Moreover, as Midelectric attempted primarily to enhance development and housing comfort, it was careful not to make its customers compromise their safety, health or happiness in the name of energy conservation.

As a consequence, Midelectric had principally relied on tariff measures in its demand-side management. The idea was to reduce peak consumption on winter weekdays by trying to shift it to nights, weekends and summer with the aid of the tariff structure, which is presented in Exhibit 3.5. In 1994, only one-third of the electricity sold by Midelectric was invoiced with the more expensive general tariff. General tariff 2, the so-called efficiency tariff, was particularly popular among larger customers, whereas the night tariff was widely accepted in the household sector as well.

The tariff measure had basically met with good results, especially the cheaper night tariff. Sometimes, however, customers were unwilling to switch to a new tariff because it was hard for them to understand the logic behind the request. Mr Pohjola gives an example:

Exhibit 3.5 *Tariff structure of Midelectric at 1 April 1994*

	General tariff	General tariff 2	Night tariff	Seasonal tariff
Fixed tariff (FIM/month)	49	110	110	110
Energy tariff (FIM/kWh)				
Daytime	0.36	0.33	0.36	
Night-time	0.36	0.33	0.17	
Winter weekdays				0.56
Other times				0.16

Source: Midelectric customer magazine 2, 1994, p. 3.

We sent a letter to a small company telling them that they did not have the best possible tariff arrangement and called them afterwards asking whether they wanted to change the tariff. They said they had sent the letter to their headquarters because they thought something must be wrong when a seller wants to get less money from the buyer.

Also, Mr Lampinen, the tariff expert, thinks that savings have to be substantial before they make people actually do something about their tariffs. FIM 300 a year, for example, is not enough.

Sometimes, however, the peak problem had become so acute that Midelectric had resorted to more drastic measures. Since 1992, it had published an advertisement in all major newspapers in its distribution district whenever a peak was approaching, asking people to burn more wood for heating and not to heat their saunas at the same time as everybody else. It had also made a survey about the effects of these campaigns and found that 75 per cent of its customers thought the campaign had had a significant effect on their electricity consumption at that time.

The motivation behind these peak-cutting measures was twofold. First, the tariff system enabled alert customers to make large savings in their electricity bill. This in turn kept existing customers happy and attracted new ones. Secondly, it was in everybody's interest that no new capital investments should be made because of a temporary peak since this would raise electricity prices and perhaps create dormant overcapacity for the rest of the year, which is obvious waste. Again, economic and ethical considerations went hand in hand.

Providing feedback information to customers had also been used as a demand-side management measure. It had entailed, however, many problems, including the difficulty of finding meaningful points of comparison and problems of presentation – a kilowatt means little to the average household. Feedback had consequently been employed with the larger customers in particular.

Efficient Use of Energy

The concepts of energy and energy conservation are abstract, alien and sometimes even frightening to the average consumer. This is why Midelectric attempted to be as practical and as positive as possible in its provision of consumer advice. As Mrs Asikainen, the household advisor put it: 'We prefer to talk about the wise use of energy and invite people to see what it means in practice.' Mrs Asikainen stands in the kitchen established at the company premises and starts heating water with a kettle and with an electric boiler at the same time. In about two minutes, water boils in the electric boiler and it is switched off. The kettle is nowhere near boiling. A meter on the wall counts the energy used by both appliances in watts and pennies and the kettle is clearly losing. Mrs Asikainen explains:

This is what we do. We get people to come here and show them the difference it makes to your electricity bill if you operate your kitchen efficiently. First, they say it's peanuts but when we start counting, it turns out to be a lot of money.

Mrs Asikainen admits that much impact hinges on the gadgetry. Midelectric does not, however, promote any particular brand. It is more important for them to see that existing equipment is employed wisely. Much energy is wasted: for example, not enough attention is paid to freezers. The approach, though, to giving advice has to be gentle:

> We are not saying to people: 'look how much energy you waste all the time.' We try instead to make them think about these things. They come here and do what they would normally do and just keep an eye on the energy meter for a while. That usually does it.

Enter 1995

This is where Midelectric stood in 1994. Mr Pohjola had been with the company since 1963 and he obviously knows the ropes. What about everybody else in the company? Mrs Seppälä, the communications manager explains:

> We have invested a great deal in internal marketing. We think that everybody in the company should be knowledgable of our basic aims, such as energy conservation. Every electrician who goes into the field has to be able to advise the customer about energy conservation.

What about everybody else in the industry? As news about the new electricity market act spread, it became obvious that the whole market would eventually be restructured. This would not, however, happen very soon. The law itself was very much open to interpretation and a lot of case law would be needed in order to make it operative.

In any case, it would be difficult to go back to regional selling monopolies, which is probably why a new phenomenon was in the offing. Electricity utilities would form a competitive market, which was bound to lead to the establishment of marketing principles as business practice in this field as well, However, the question was whether it would be good or bad marketing. Would companies overdo it and create a mess resembling the deregulated financial and telecommunications markets of Finland? Mr Pohjola pondered how his company could, in the new environment, continue to enhance sustainable growth and competitiveness. It was getting late. He opened his window and felt the cool breeze coming in.

Note

1.   In 1993, the FIM/£ average exchange rate calculated by the Bank of Finland was 8.582.

CASE 4

Project Gemini

Margaret Bruce and **Barny Morris**
Manchester School of Management, UMIST, UK

Introduction

'We have an opportunity here to dominate the construction powertool market, but time is not on our side,' said John Schofield, the international product marketing manager based at the UK headquarters of Ingersoll–Rand (IR). The product he wanted was to be best in its class for power, vibration and ergonomics. These were important criteria considering the imminent introduction of rigorous work, health and safety regulations that were to put European working practice legislation two to three years ahead of its American counterpart.

Graham Dewhurst, the project engineer, agreed with the objectives of the project, but after all the team's effort, did not want to enter the market with an inferior product. He believed that by exploiting the Vibra-Smooth, a vibration-reducing device he had worked on for many months, their market leadership would be assured for a number of years. He believed passionately that the company was poised to produce an innovative power tool specifically for the European market that was far ahead of the competition. He envisioned a tool that would position Ingersoll–Rand as a leader and innovator in the European construction tool market and wanted his colleagues to share his enthusiasm. The company had developed a vibration-reducing device, Vibra-Smooth, that gave them a product advantage, but to exploit the device fully meant radical design changes for which they did not have the in-house expertise. They would therefore have to rely on an external design consultant's competence for the first time, which added to the project risks.

Aware of the critical timing of product introduction, John turned to Graham and said, 'We've got to get this resolved now, Graham, as we need to present a unified front at the briefing meeting tomorrow and decide a realistic date for our market launch.' The people involved with the production and marketing of the Vibra-Smooth and who would be present at ther next day's briefing were:

- John H. L. Schofield (project leader), international product marketing manager. Started his career in the computer industry and joined IR in 1983.

80

- Graham Dewhurst, design engineer. Started as a mechanical apprentice in 1976, and joined IR in 1989 as a design engineer.
- Dave Hill, production/shopfloor.
- Bob Buxton, industrial design consultant. Senior founding partner of Buxton Wall McPeake Design Consultancy.

Ingersoll–Rand: History and Culture

In the mid- to late nineteenth century, the American nation was expanding rapidly. Cities were growing, new roads, railways, canals and buildings were being excavated and engineered. Coal was needed to supply vital energy, and gold fever was running high. All of this meant that huge quantities of rock had to be removed. Before this could be done, the rock had to be drilled and then blasted. Opportunities for innovation in drilling technologies were vast and new companies were formed to develop products for the construction industry. Ingersoll–Rand was one company to emerge and the milestones in its history are as follows:

1849   First powered rock drill invented by J. J. Couch, Phildelphia.
1871   Simon Ingersoll, New York, received a patent for his steam-driven rock drill.
1871   Formation of the Ingersoll Rock Drill Company.
1875   First Ingersoll product, the Eclipse Rock Drill. Recognition of the benefits of compressed air over steam-driven drills, particularly in underground conditions.
1882   The Eclipse Rock Drill is sold in England, France and Spain.
1902   Merger of the Ingersoll Rock Drill Company. Company produces the world's first truly portable compressor.

In this same period, Laffin & Rand was a New York firm specializing in the manufacture and sale of explosives used in blast holes. Albert Rand, a senior partner, recognized that powered rock drills would permit the drilling of larger holes than could be achieved by hand – and that could only be good for business. The Rand Drill Company was formed and produced powered hand-drills under the name Little Giant and, like the Ingersoll company, moved into the design and production of compressors.

1905   Ingersoll Sergeant Holdings merge with the Rand Drill Company to form Ingersoll–Rand. The merger allowed economies in administration, manufacturing and selling.
1913   Ingersoll–Rand produces the first Jack Hammer Drill using a mechanism that allowed the product to be light enough to be used by one person.

The Ingersoll–Rand story is one of expansion throughout the years to the point reached today where the company has manufacturing establishments in seventeen countries and worldwide sales and distribution. The company continues to

Exhibit 4.1   *Financial data of Ingersoll–Rand*

In the early 1980s, the over-valued US dollar cost Ingersoll–Rand a good piece of its important export business. At the same time, oil prices collapsed, and Ingersoll–Rand counted on energy for 50% of its revenues. To lessen dependence on oil, President James Perella and Chairman Theodore Black diversified in an way calculated to broaden their customer base. The company also increased its manufacturing outside the US. Today, 70% of Ingersoll–Rand's foreign sales are generated by products manufactured abroad, up from 30% a decade ago.
P. Klebnikov, in *Forbes*, 151 (2), 1993, pp. 83–84

Demand is surging for Ingersoll–Rand's industrial equipment. In 1993's first quarter, profits jumped 20% on a revenue increase of 10%. Further earnings gains are expected in the quarters ahead. Ingersoll's fortunes have traditionally tracked the world's leading economies. Ingersoll is likely to earn between $1.50 and $1.60 a share this year, up from last year's $1.11. Ingersoll's stock price has been strong, climbing to a record high of 36 3/8 in February.
J. Palmer, in *Barron's* 73 (25), 1993, p. 12

Capital equipment industry is voted fourth in the top six industries by the stock market which show the most market promise in 1994. This is good news for Ingersoll Rand.
R. S. Teitelbaum, *Fortune*, 128 (10), 1993, pp. 102–113

manufacture rock drills, but the Ingersoll–Rand range has now been significantly expanded to all types of process plant and portable air compressors, mining equipment, pumps, oilfield equipment, automated assembly systems and a comprehensive range of air powered construction tools. Ingersoll–Rand is a multinational company with a turnover of $4.2 billion in 1993 and employs 35,000 people worldwide. (See Exhibit 4.1 for more financial information).

Ingersoll-Rand operates in the following main capital equipment markets: automotive industry, energy industry, construction industry and general industry. In 1993, the total world market for construction hand tools was estimated at 250,000 units. This was reduced from a peak in 1990 of an estimated 328,000 units, reflecting ther worldwide recession in the interval. However, the construction industry was predicted to grow in 1994 by between 1 and 4 per cent. Mr Schofield believed that the demand for power tools would begin to show once pre-recession sales levels had been reached.

Power Tools Group, UK

The UK company was established in 1921 in London, and later that year a warehouse was acquired in Trafford Park, Manchester. Manufacturing commenced in Trafford Park in 1933 and the range of products produced was extensive. Post-war growth in production meant expansion was vital, and the company now has their manufacturing establishments in the north of England. One of the UK plants is part of the

International Power Tools Group of Ingersoll–Rand and forms an integral part within that group, alongside US sister plants in Athens, Pennsylvania and Roanoke, Virginia. The three-hundred-strong workforce is concerned with the manufacture, sales and marketing of hand-held air-powered tools such as scalers, chippers, drills, impact tools and sand-rammers for use in all industries where air power is used. Design and development of all products has traditionally been the sole responsibility of the sister plant in Athens, Pennsylvania, until the Irgo-Pic project (named originally Project Gemini) began at the UK plant.

Strategy

Ingersoll–Rand's strategy has been to broaden its customer base and to manufacture more of its products abroad. Europe was identified as a major emerging market, and in accordance with the company's long-term strategy, an application was made by the general manager for Europe, supported by the plant manager in the UK, and authorized by the divisional general manager in the USA to set up a European design centre in the UK. Authorization to access appropriate resources for the project took almost two years to process. Whilst this was happening, John Schofield took the initiative and started to lay the groundwork for Project Gemini. It was imperative for Schofield to get an early start with the project in order to meet the market gap created by changes in health and safety legislation, especially in the German market.

European Design Centre

The aim was to set up, as a long-term commitment, a European design centre for Ingersoll–Rand that was responsible for new products for Europe. Part of the initiative involved the employment of Graham Dewhurst as a design engineer. However, John Schofield needed a starting point for the project, as he explains:

> We had nothing. We had no in-house experience of developing products from scratch. We had no supplier base. This has positive and negative benefits. Starting from fresh meant that we could do what we wanted. However, the rest of management saw it as 'opening a can of worms' as they weren't sure how it was going to work.

John was highly motivated to become involved with setting up the design centre because he saw very clearly the potential for changing market conditions and market opportunities, and wanted to sell a product that had European equity rather than Amercian. It was decided to base the organization of the project along similiar lines to that of Project Lightning (an air-powered grinder) which ran in the USA and in which product design teams, concurrent engineering, user groups and rapid prototyping were used to develop products quickly and effectively. As John Schofield commented: 'It was not so much a decision as an acceptance that if we were to collapse the time-frame with a market-orientated product, there was no other way to be organised.'

The Design Team

The stated aim was to bring to market within twelve months and within budget a product in the ten kilogram weight range that would be best in class for power, vibration and ergonomics. The product had to also contribute $X million of revenue within three years.

John Schofield was responsible for setting up a design team. He decided that the team approach would be best used as a way of cutting down the development time from four years, as was typically the case for new product development in Ingersoll–Rand, to one year. However, a number of questions were raised by senior management. Could the company organize an efficient and effective design team? Who would be the members of the team? Would this team be able to manage the process having little experience of new product development? Would the team be able to source external design expertise successfully? Would the project be to schedule, meet all customer requirements and still be within budget?

After much discussion, John Schofield managed to gain support for his idea and a small, full-time team was put together consisting of representatives from marketing, design engineering and manufacturing from within the company (i.e. John Schofield, Graham Dewhurst, Dave Hill); product design was sourced externally. Dave had been with Ingersoll–Rand on the 'shopfloor' for almost thirty years, and so knew the capability of the UK manufacturing plant and what it could and could not make. The characteristics of a good product design team are expounded in Exhibit 4.2.

This core team was given sole responsibility for all decisions concerning the project, and reported to a steering committee made up of directors of different functions. John Schofield persuaded his peers that this was the only way to get real commitment:

> Unless you give the team the authority to do the job, they won't take any of the responsibility for it. It helps get the motivation. By getting everyone in the room together it meant that everyone knew what was going on. We all believe that everyone can contribute to the design of the product, not just the engineers, and not just the core team members either.

Exhibit 4.2   *Product design teams*

> If firms are to tap the full potential of their employees, they must bring them together in teams. Unlike the rigid, topdown teams of the past, the new team is an organic, living system characterized by partnership: it's a smart team. Like other organisms, smart teams are self-managing, self-renewing and self-transcending. Ingersoll–Rand used teams like this to improve its power tool division's product development cycle.
> C. Garfield, *Executive Excellence*, 10 (7), 1993, pp. 3–4

Each team member contributed on an equal footing. This meant that they bounced ideas between each other, giving different views on subjects that were not ordinarily within their traditional area of expertise. Normal traditional hierarchical forms of authority were also forgotten. Instead, the project leader's duties were rotated amongst the group so that different people took command at different times.

Control was exercised through goal orientation so that the team collectively focused on achieving tasks and the satisfaction accruing from solving problems together, rather than individual conformity to meeting a series of established milestones, or from subservience to an authority figure. The members of the team viewed their relationships with each other as being akin to a marriage; whilst there was bound to be conflict (since the free flow of opinions and ideas were encouraged) the members always made up afterwards. Dave's personality, particularly his sense of humour 'kept the banter going' whenever there were heated discussions.

The Steering Committee

The steering committee oversaw the team but took no part in the team's decision-making process. The committee could advise and guide the team, but not make the final decisions. Its responsibilities were:

1. To set and concur with the team vision for the project.
2. To review change in the scope of the project.
3. To review changes in time, budgets and key product features.
4. To project status and milestones.
5. To remove strategic barriers.

The committee consisted of top management from finance, quality, purchasing, manufacturing and the general manager. The committee knew at any given point in time what the team had done, where the team were, and the team's direction for the next few weeks. This could only be achieved by the core team and steering committee interacting closely together throughout the project. Conflict occasionally arose when the traditional bosses of the team members found it difficult to accept that Project Gemini took priority over other projects.

Market Analysis

Market research and analysis was carried out throughout the project's duration. The type of information and the means of generating and collecting market information were carefully planned in order that an appropriate marketing strategy could be put together.

The main areas that the team had to consider were:

1. Market research that would generate product specifications, e.g. user needs/customer needs, industry regulation and legislation.

2. Product positioning.

3. Sales: past, present and predicted (and estimations of market size and value).

4. Competitor information.

Market Research

Remaining close to the customer was an overriding concern of the product development team. Accordingly, the team worked closely with a core user-group which consisted of the following:

1. Ingersoll–Rand distributors.

2. Competitors' distributors.

3. Salespeople (Ingersoll–Rand staff).

4. End-users.

The user-group members (UGM) were mainly from Europe, although regular input was also solicited from America, Canada, South America, Asia and the Pacific Rim. The fifty to sixty members of the group were used to evaluate concepts and to verify that the product was on the right track in terms of the product specification's ability to satisfy market requirements. Most of the user information and specifications were compiled via close interaction with the UGM. Three approaches were used to talk to the UGM:

1. The UGM were asked for product feature preferences.

2. The UGM were then asked for direct requirements in order to create a wish-list of product features.

3. Finally, the UGM was asked what product features they disliked.

The team had difficulty in getting customers to generalize their own exact and precise needs. So throughout the product development processs the UGM were shown a number of competitor tools (and, in the final stages of the process, prototype tools) to elicit a better response. By having tools in front of them to criticize, the UGM were better able to focus on key issues.

John Schofield already knew that health and safety features of power tools were becoming important purchase criteria of Ingersoll–Rand's customers. This demand was driven primarily by regulations that were laid down to protect the end-user (Exhibit 4.3). Whilst at the time there was no regulation in force that limited the use of tools with a high level of vibration, the pace of regulation in the industry, particularly in Europe, suggested that this would soon become an issue. John

Exhibit 4.3 *Ergonomics*

The new Irgo-Pic demolition tool from Ingersoll–Rand brings together two objectives of construction tools which have previously seemed totally incompatible – power and comfort. Until now, powerful tools have meant heavy tools, tools which are uncomfortable to hold and impossible to use for any length of time, and operators have had to stop frequently to rest. The Irgo-Pic is the most powerful hammer in its class. A combination of advanced materials and focused design effort have resulted in a tool which weighs in at just 10 kg (22 lb) yet delivers the performance of 13 kg (29 lb) competitive tools.

It has also been ergonomically designed for maxium operator comfort. The uniquely styled housing is a natural fit to the hand, making it easier to grip and operate, and the advanced composite material of the exterior reduces vibration, temperature effects and noise to give the smoothest performance with no penalty to the operator. Special grip areas moulded into the housing are correctly angled for the most efficient operation, top handle and front breakthrough guards have been included to protect the operator's hands and a special three-finger grip has been designed to spread force and reduce stress. The Irgo-Pic has been designed with the following existing specifications in mind, and certain recent research:

1. Grip inclination and D-handle profile conforming to US military specification MIL-STD-1472C.
2. Machinery Safety Directive (89/392/EEC) under which manufacturers have to state vibration levels if above 2.5 ms^2.
3. Cumulative trauma disorders (CTDS) resulting from vibration to the hand and arm have increased significantly in recent years, leading to reduced productivity and increased costs. However, employers have been faced with a dilemma: how to reduce the exposure of their workers to vibration without allowing excessive stops for rest which affect productivity.
4. Vibration-related disorders are now eligible for compensation payments in the UK and form a large proportion of all claims.
5. Extensive research linking serious skeletal and circulatory disorders with exposure to hand/arm vibration.

Buxton Wall McPeake had used an ergonomics consultancy on past projects to look at the human factors of the product. The consultant helped BWMc in the initial concept stage and early development stage with anthropometrics such as size of handgrip (the clearance for fingers, etc.), and the T-handle (the angle of handgrips to each other, whether they should be parallel, angled down, etc). John Schofield saw the ergonomic input as a seal of approval on the project, and features this in the product literature.

> The Irgo-Pic demolition tool embodies key ergonomic principles, and Ingersoll–Rand is to be commended upon the application of these principles in engineering design.
> Joe Langford BSc (Hons), MErgS, Consultant Ergonomist, Human Factors Solutions

identified that the European market was ahead of the American in terms of concern for health and safety legislation at work, and a concern for the ergonomics of the product. He explained that:

> We have legislation two or three years in advance of the US market. We have an opportunity for designing products specifically for the European market, which will not only benefit us in Europe, but give us a product advantage in the US market.

Product positioning

The intention was for the product to be the best on the market. There was no premium sector of the market, and John Schofield wanted to break away and create a new market with a radically designed product. This was reflected in his approach to his pricing strategy, where his starting point was to see how 'high' he could go rather than, in the more traditional sense, how 'low' he could go.

Competitor Analysis

Ingersoll–Rand and Atlas Copco (including Chicago Pneumatic – Consolidated Pneumatic in Europe) were the only two worldwide suppliers in the construction tool market. However, each major geographical market has its own indigenous manufacturer who challenged strongly in that area. Using competitive benchmarking, Schofield categorized the competitor products into a particular power/weight/vibration/cost ratio – low weight (in the 10 kg range), low vibration and low cost coupled with high power being the optimum for hand-held tools (Exhibit 4.4).

Exhibit 4.4   *Rating of competitor products*

Product	Weight kg	Blow energy Nm	Power p.h.	Vibration ms^{-2}
Irgo-Pic (IR)	11.2	29	1.37	6.7
Atlas Copco Tex11	12.4	12	0.59	11.1
C.P. FL22	10.4	12	0.57	7.9
Thor 16D	8.2	8	0.49	16.2
Maco P43	13.0	29	1.32	17.3
Bohler A140	11.5	20	0.64	20.5
Compair U9	11.75	14	0.59	18.8
Maco P105	8.4	18		17.6

Project Gemini

John Schofield realized early on that lack of in-house skills meant that suitable expertise would have to be bought into three areas: business, engineering and design.

1. Business

The idea was to enlist the help of a local university's business services centre, so that as the project progressed the team could learn the necessary skills for design and development of a product with a view to being able to manage future projects autonomously.

2. Engineering

The team was looking for a particular power cycle for the product, and successfully used computing facilities at a local university to simulate this power cycle.

3. Design

A local design consultancy was used to model the power tool. Whilst this partnership was productive, it was not the long-term relationship that the team were looking for. As Graham Dewhurst laments: 'When it came down to actually solving our problems they didn't have the expertise to do it.' The consultancy was in essence a specialist in model-making rather than in offering a full design service such as detailing the design from concept models. Therefore it was unable to provide the expertise the company was looking for. Whilst this was a setback to the team, they learnt the importance of sourcing the appropriate skills from design consultancy. John Schofield explains his approach to using the design consultancy as follows:

> We wanted someone who wanted to come to the party. He had to take on some of the responsibility, and put his own stake in as well. If we fell, then we all fell together. We said to the consultants that we didn't want the standard consultancy relationship. In other words, we didn't want someone to come and listen to our problems, go away and solve them and come back with a solution. We had the objective of starting a product design facility in Europe that went beyond this initial project. We wanted someone who was part of the team.

This failure to choose the right consultancy caused a rift between the team members. Should they stay with this consultant or start fresh with another? This dilemma also coincided with the development of Vibra-Smooth – a vibration-reducing device that would give the product massive advantage over current competitor products. The inclusion of Vibra-Smooth would radically change the shape of the product, although the detailed design of this device had still to be undertaken. Whilst in theory the idea was proven, it was unknown whether the device could work in practice or even be engineered into the product, along with a new body shell, within the allotted time.

This caused a second major dilemma within the team. The Vibra-Smooth device would meet the customer requirement of less vibration. Should they try to incorporate this device into the product at the risk of missing the deadline, losing their market opportunity and potentially their market leadership position? Alternatively, perhaps it would be less risky to go into production and try to sell the product without the vibration requirement but to schedule? After much discussion, the team took the decision to use an alternative design supplier to detail design. John Schofield used Buxton Wall McPeake, a multi-disciplinary design consultancy in

Manchester. Buxton Wall McPeake had expertise in rapid prototyping and had in-house computer-aided design (CAD) facilities.

Background to Buxton Wall McPeake, Product Design Consultants

Buxton Wall McPeake (BWMc) is one of the north west's leading multi-disciplinary design consultancies. When the company was formed in 1979, the directors recognized the potential to bring together the disciplines of product and graphic design to provide a comprehensive range of design services.

The consultancy aims to achieve the optimum design solution for the market, by working closely with clients' marketing and production teams during a design project. The consultancy has the capability to manage projects from initial concepts through to production, dealing with many other design-related activities throughout the process.

Bob Buxton, one of the company's founders, believes that design and development are the key to strategic market positioning of all successful products. For a specific target sector, it is vital to have the appropriate blend of appearance, function, economic manufacture and presentation.

BWMc is listed as a consultancy with the Design Council, the Chartered Society of Designers and the Department of Trade and Industry. Directors are fellows and members of the Chartered Society of Designers and as such are bound by the society's code of professional conduct. The importance of designers to the success of the product development process is emphasized in Exhibit 4.5.

BWMc's Approach to Client Management

At the beginning of a project the senior partners of BWMc try to establish with each client a framework which defines the degree of freedom the consultancy can work within. However, this framework has to be flexible to allow for change in a product's development: for this reason, communication with the client at all times is seen to

Exhibit 4.5 *Designers*

A few smart companies are making industrial design one of their core competencies and are using it to drive their entire product development process, sharply increasing their chances of generating successful products. One problem that design can help solve is how to transfer new technology out of the labs and into the market. Because they can identify customer needs, designers can do a better job than engineers of selecting technologies that can solve real-world problems.
B. Nussbaum, *Business Week,* 7 June 1993, pp. 54–57.

be crucial to a project's success. Awareness of the market requirements and what the client desires is also critical. Bob Buxton describes the process:

> The first meeting covers the definition of the brief and agreeing the brief. In other words, agreeing what the product's all about. After this, it's a question of good communication. If we're thinking of doing something slightly different, or some detail needs to be changed, we ask the client's opinion first. You have to tell the client everything, otherwise at the end of the project, the product is not acceptable. This takes a lot of time, and typically we have put more time in than we wanted to. However, one can go on designing for ever; a line has to be drawn at some point. As long as everyone's aware of, and has agreed to, what's happening and why it's happening, then there's no problem.

The philosophy at BWMc is to get all of their designers contributing to every client project in the inital stages. Ideas generated are pooled and laid out on a table for evaluation from which perhaps a couple of ideas are taken further for presentation to the client. Designers are involved with the client from the start of the project, with one of the partners as project leader.

In December 1991 the partners of the consultancy were cold-calling local businesses to drum up some business. Fortunately, Ingersoll–Rand was on their list. In mid-December of 1991, Alan Wall and Bob Buxton were on their way to Ingersoll–Rand for an initial interview with the core team. Bob Buxton explains how he felt:

> I always feel a little apprehensive at these initial meetings. We have never met them before, so we are going in cold and it's so important that we make the right impression to the client to begin with. His initial reaction to us will tell us whether he will give us the work. It's a very fragile situation that requires careful handling. There's no way round it really.

At this initial meeting John Schofield explained that they had already used a design consultancy firm and a prototype had been built. However, the vibration requirement had not been incorporated into the design and, to date, no decision had been taken to incorporate the device. The team welcomed the design consultants' views in this matter. With time pressing, the Ingersoll team needed a design consultancy that was flexible, highly committed and could work quickly to design the product to schedule. BWMc agreed to meet again in early January for a project briefing session.

Design and Development Process

The project between BWMc and Ingersoll–Rand was divided into four design and development stages:

1. Briefing
2. Feasibility study and detail design

3. CAD development

4. Rapid prototyping and tooling up

Other suppliers were used for particular jobs:

1. CTR Plastics Co. were used to injection mould the outer casing.

2. T. Wright and Co. Ltd made the tools for the moulders, used by CTR Plastics.

3. Formation Engineering turned the two-dimensional drawings created by BWMc into three-dimensional computer models, which in turn, created the three-dimensional pattern required by the toolmakers.

Exhibit 4.6 outlines the project history which is now described in some detail.

Exhibit 4.6 *Project history in brief*

December 1991	Initial meeting with Ingersoll–Rand. Briefing to design a new power tool.
January 1992	Initial concept work carried out for a nominal fee. Accepted well by IR staff. BWMc asked to set out a design programme.
January 1992	Initial development work: liaison with IR team and Thomas Wright Ltd, toolmaker, and CTR Plastics, moulder, both of Liverpool; prepare layout drawings, make full-size foam model.
February 1992	Design T-handle, liaison with Joe Langford, Human Factors Services, for advice and evaluation of handle sizes and ergonomics in general. Advice on materials and design details DuPont. Visit Formation Engineering with drawings; Formation produces 3D CAD model, then SL model.
April 1992	CAD model to toolmaker. SL model used as pattern for polyurethane castings for prototypes. Design work continues on nose ring, exhaust insert, etc. IR tests prototypes.
May 1992	Detail engineering drawing of T-handle. Liaison with toolmaker and moulder.
June 1992	Prepare definitive visual for final version of product with T-handle.
October 1992	Finish T-handle foam model for photography.
November 1992	Product launch for D-handle version.
May 1993	Product launch for T-handle version.

1. Briefing

- Mid-December 1991   Initial discussion between IR and BWMc.
- 6 January 1992   BWMc project briefing at IR, and initial feasibility study by BWMc signifying the start of stage 1.
- 12 January   Presentation to IR team. End of stage 1.
- 13 January   Debrief at BWMc.
- 4 February   Fax sent of breakdown of consultancy cost and of the product costings (not including the design of the T-handle). IR were more focused on completing the job rather than the cost of the job.

The two companies met again in early January to discuss the details of the project. Having already had a false start with the first design consultancy, John Schofield was cautious in making sure that the working relationship and the envisaged design quality were right. The briefing at this stage was very informal, as John's introduction indicates:

> What I'm looking for, gentlemen, is a new image for the product. I don't just want the product to be a market-beater functionally, I want our customers to be able to look at a product and know it instinctively to be made by Ingersoll–Rand.

The team was still undecided as to whether to incorporate the Vibra-Smooth Isolater. Whilst some members of the core team wanted to do some minor modification to the existing prototype, others wanted to make use of the Vibra-Smooth device. Time was running out and the possibility of starting a new design was not viewed with particular relish given the pressure they were all under. Before making a final decision, they decided to welcome some fresh input from Buxton Wall McPeake. Whilst the team described their requirements, Bob Buxton made small thumbnail sketches. Graham Dewhurst, the design engineer, commented later to the rest of the team that he was particularly impressed with the way the consultant 'put pencil to paper' and started sketching in this initial discussion. This briefing was critical for a number of reasons as the consultancy needed to know the following:

1. How the product was to be made.
2. The effect that the additional Vibra-Smooth device would have on the internal geometry.
3. The type of material and process to be used for the moulding, and how it was to fit to the inner mechanisms.
4. Other existing Ingersoll–Rand products, and how this new product was to fit into, or be a departure from, the existing range.
5. The critical elements in the design as perceived by the end-user and customer.
6. Project management.

7. The number of units (as batches) to be produced in the first and second years.

8. The handle configurations (T- or D-shaped).

As Bob Buxton walked around the Ingersoll–Rand factory and was shown the existing product range by Graham and John, he soon realized that the product was going to be used in a tough environment. Bob thought back to his student days. He had worked on a building site and on motorways during summer vacations and remembered the way the workmen had treated the tools, leaving them exposed to all weather conditions, never cleaning them, and treating them roughly, Bob believed that, as a designer, these briefing situations were invaluable as a way to absorb the approach, or the culture of the company.

Design Considerations
During the briefing process, Bob Buxton realized that the Vibra-Smooth device would give the product immense added value. If the Vibra-Smooth device was to be included in the product, it meant a new product image and a change in dimensions so that from an industrial design standpoint, they would have to start again. Bob Buxton's view was that the Vibra-Smooth device should be included and he saw this as an opportunity to do something very different. Bob's view was strongly supported by Graham Dewhurst, and eventually they managed to persuade John Schofield that a radical redesign had greater benefits than the modified project.

With the team united, the steering committee were convinced that this was the way forward since their worry was that a 'me-too' product would be developed. It was decided that an inital feasibility study conducted by the design consultancy would allow other possibilities to be explored. John Schofield appreciated the idea of an initial trial period as this allowed him to evaluate the work of BWMc and the potential of the working relationship that was to ensue. Bob Buxton was enthusiastic not only at the prospect of redesigning the product from scratch, but also because he was entrusted with some freedom in this process by Ingersoll–Rand. Aware that time was short, John gave BWMc less than two weeks to come up with a conceptual design for the product. Lack of time also meant that Ingersoll–Rand was unable to give BWMc any payment for services rendered up-front, thus BWMc had to take John Schofield on trust at this initial trial stage.

Graham Dewhurst explained that the product had to be used in a variety of situations. It needed to have interchangeable D- and T-handle components. Both tools were to be used with two hands and have triggers which could be inside or outside the handle. Bob soon realized that the barrel, which tapered towards the pneumatic chisel, was the common component in each variation of the product. Thus, the key was to arrange a suitable universal fixing system between the different types of handle and the main barrel, which was durable enough to withstand the product's usage.

Regarding product styling, the original prototype model was short and stumpy. The new product was going to be longer, and the main problem would be hiding the fixings used to attach the handle to the barrel. This last problem ended up dictating the final styling of the product.

The Presentation

Following a two-week period, Buxton Wall McPeake returned to Ingersoll-Rand with some conceptual sketches. Bob Buxton had been told of the project time constraints, and whilst normally at stage 1 of a project he would show a range of proposals to his client, he homed in on just one proposal to save time. To illustrate his proposal, full-size, two-dimensional representations were produced, along with a cardboard cutout of the product for the core team to evaluate. Back-up sketches were also brought.

When the colour illustrations were unveiled, the reaction to the concept from the core team was positive. Bob Buxton's instincts were right about the proposal, and the concept was considered for further development. What surprised the consultants was the reaction to the cardboard cutout model. Graham Dewhurst remarked on how this gave a clear indication of scale and the ergonomic problems involved.

The two companies discussed how to progress from concept stage to product development. Bob Buxton was asked to cost the components that made up the barrel housing and handles, and was given the name of the moulder and toolmaker, which had been previously sourced by IR.

John Schofield reiterated the time pressure on the project. He felt that this could not be stressed too much. They had already spent over nine months of their allotted time, and had another nine months to go. This meant that the exterior of the product had to be designed, developed and manufactured well within that timescale. Bob Buxton voiced his worry about proceeding from development to manufacture without a prototyping stage.

> How are we going to have time to produce an appearance model? It's important to realize that once we reach the tooling-up stage, it's very difficult to change the design at that point and so it's far better to model the product now whilst the design is still on paper. Are you confident that the design will be exactly what you want?

Bob Buxton had known other clients miss out this important stage in the development process and regret it later. However, John Schofield had already paid for a prototype from the previous consultancy and felt that, with time running out, it was best to proceed to full manufacture as quickly as possible. He also knew that the earlier the product was produced, the more advantage it had over its competitors, and the higher price premium the market would be prepared to pay for it. He believed that Bob Buxton was able to visualize the product well enough without the need for an appearance model, and so took the risk that Bob's expertise would avoid the need for another prototype.

2. Feasibility

When Buxton Wall McPeake started work on the external casing of the product, Graham Dewhurst was still completing details for the Vibra-Smooth device and testing the product, right up until the end of March. Graham's work affected the overall internal geometry, and in turn the external geometry of the product. Bob Buxton needed to stay in constant contact with Graham in case any significant development occurred. He noted that:

> We received sketch drawings with general sizes of components, and where they fitted internally. Elements were still changing, such as the diameter of the isolator and the barrel, because these were still being developed, and this affected the appearance, obviously. That's the frustrating stage where things keep changing. Everything's fluid, but again, you have to expect that. It's a normal part of development.

Bob Buxton now knew enough about the moulding to produce some preliminary detailed development drawings that would enable the toolmaker and moulder to put some more exact costs together. These general arrangement (GA) drawings were done manually, but more detailed views had to be worked out using BWMc's CAD software. Whilst two-dimensional CAD is a mechanization of traditional manual drawing, it is not necessarily quicker. As Bob Buxton explained, the advantage of CAD was that it was quicker to perform many iterations of drawings.

By the beginning of April, the team knew that all of the components would fit together without any problem. They knew how they were going to mount the internal components, and the exhaust baffle had also been finalized. Bob Buxton commented:

> We spent quite a lot of time detailing the bosses [where the bolts attaching the handle to the casing located] and the rib sections that connected the bosses to the case, so a lot of the later development was to do with those sorts of detail. There was more work inside this moulding than there was outside.

3. CAD Development

- 12 February 1992   Bob Buxton visits IR to discuss engineering details with Graham Dewhurst.

- 13 February   Bob Buxton gains John Schofield's approval to enlist the help of an ergonomics consultant. Ergonomist is sent the original model made by the first design consultancy.

- 19 February   Received relevant ergonomic data on the product.
  Visit to Gloucester to see Formation Engineering and to explain detailed general arrangement drawings.

- 27 March   BWMc receive fax from Formation that the CAD model had been completed.
- 30 March   BWMc change the outside of the foam model to incorporate the fixing bolts for the handles and the ergonomic specifications.
- 16 April   IR invoiced by BWMc for work completed in stage 2. Stage 2 involved BWMc working very closely with IR, such that over thirty-five hours were spent in meetings between the two companies between early February and late March.

One of the reasons that BWMc was chosen by Ingersoll–Rand was for their expertise with CAD/CAM (computer-aided design/computer-aided manufacture) and particularly rapid prototyping using a process known as stereo-lithography (see Exhibit 4.7). The process of using such technology was divided into stages:

Exhibit 4.7 *Rapid prototyping*

British Companies are cutting up to 70 per cent of product development costs by adopting the technology of rapid prototyping which allows designers to turn two-dimensional computer drawings swiftly into solid models. Lee Styger, manager of the Rapid Prototyping and Tooling Consortium at Warwick University says:

> Complex designs often require many iterations, a major factor affecting product lead times. This is overcome by rapid prototyping, which converts computer-aided design data into real models, typically in a matter of hours.
> 'Designs you can grasp', *Independent on Sunday*, 1993

Almost all rapid prototyping systems work on a layering technique. Special software cuts a computer-aided design of the component into slices, feeding the data for each layer to the rapid prototyping machine, most commonly via a technique called stereo-lithography. The data describing each slice controls a laser which 'draws' the slice on a layer of photosensitive resin that is instantly soldified by the laser. The slice is then lowered into the bath of resin and the next layer constructed on top, and so on until the model is complete. Models are typically accurate to ±1 micron (the thickness of a human hair).

Rapid prototyping is used to make models to assist in the visualisation of a new product. Philip Dickens of the Centre of Rapid Prototyping in Manufacturing at the University of Nottingham believes:

> The main use of these machines will be for visualization. Most models will have a life of just a few minutes before they are thrown in the bin because the designer realizes there is a mistake.

BWMc believes that:

> There will always be a place for traditional modelmakers because there are some things that you cannot do on screen, such as doing the characterization of figures. Solid modelling is appropriate where lead times need to be kept as little as possible. The real advantage of CAD/CAM is in an engineering team situation, where all the members work on the model at once – simultaneous engineering. For instance, the designer produces the solid model to begin with, then quite rapidly, people who are going to do testing and analysis can take that into another workstation for other purposes (such as impact testing/stress analysis). That way, problems can be avoided at a much earlier stage in the process.

1. The design was developed to a detailed design stage in a way similar to the traditional design process (see stage 2).

2. The detailed development work was translated from two dimensions to a three-dimensional solid model using sophisticated CAD software. (This development stage could have been reduced or missed out entirely if the product had been detail designed with CAD to begin with.)

3. The CAD model was then loaded into a stereo-lithographic machine which, through a chemical process, can reproduce physically the shape designed on computer.

4. The resultant shape was finished off quickly by traditional modelmakers and used by the toolmaker as a pattern. Using a spark erosion process, this pattern was used to form the metal injection moulding tool.

5. The moulder then used the tool to make the plastic moulds in the traditional manner.

Whilst BWMc could produce all the information necessary for stage 1 of the process depicted above, and another supplier, Formation Engineering, was used to produce the three-dimensional model on computer (stages 1–3), stage 4 would be undertaken by T. Wright & Co. (the toolmakers), and stage 5 by CTR Plastics. The advantage of this concurrent engineering approach in which designers and engineers work closely are set out in Exhibit 4.8.

4. Rapid Prototyping and Tooling up

- 13 April 1992   Meeting with Formation Engineering to approve pattern for tooling-up.
- 15 April   Meeting with toolmaker to progress the casting of the injection moulding tool.
  After mid-April much of the liaison with the toolmakers and moulders was carried out by Graham Dewhurst, the design engineer, as IR had financial constraints concerning the commissioning of BWMc to do this.
- 28 April   Preparation of final detailed General Arrangement (GA). Remodelling of certain details required with the toolmaker.

Rapid prototyping was an expensive but fast and effective way of progressing from drawings on paper to prototypes that could be used to form the core mouldings for manufacture. For instance, the normal price for a model made by a modelmaker in the traditional manner could cost between £2,000 and £5,000. Rapid prototyping (RP) cost a minimum of £10,000 but produced a pattern far more quickly (see Exhibit 4.7). The IR team had not used rapid prototyping before because of the cost, but the project had to be to schedule, and the fortuitous sourcing of a competitively

Exhibit 4.8 *Concurrent engineering*

> Concurrent engineering is an approach to product development in which engineers work
> on design and manufacturability at the same time. The ultimate goal of concurrent
> engineering is to reduce time to market while improving quality. For concurrent
> engineering to be effective, designers and manufacturing engineers must be able to share
> information. Concurrent engineering also needs long-term career development planning.
> R. E. Anderson, *Training and Development Journal* 47, (6), 1993, pp. 49–54.

priced RP supplier, Formation, meant that rapid protopying was a realistic option.
Normally BWMc would have been given the task of finding a supplier, but because
of the cost issue, this task was given to IR. Their experienced purchasing staff, and
their company size, gave them more bargaining power than BWMc, and in John
Schofield's view, BWMc were being paid to design, not to source suppliers.

Before the product design could be finalized and put onto CAD, the
toolmakers, moulders and designers had to agree on the way that the product was
to be manufactured. Bob Buxton, Graham Dewhurst and John Schofield arranged
to meet the CAD engineers from Formation and the traditional toolmakers from
T. Wright together. The mix of manufacturing tradition (toolmakers) and manufacturing innovation (IR, BWMc and Formation) gave rise to a lively discussion. Bob
Buxton commented:

> If everyone sat around the table agreeing then you're not going to get progress. If there
> is this sort of argument, push and determination to look along a certain route, then new
> things can happen. John's team were great because they wanted to be progressive.

The main argument was about how the product casing was to be moulded, as
this affected the shape of the CAD model and ultimately the SL prototype. Whilst
the toolmaker was sure that a one-piece moulding was feasible, he took a little
convincing that it was a practical route to follow. There was also a cost involved, as
a one-piece moulding compared with a clam shell arrangement (e.g. a mould that
came in two halves, similar to the construction of DIY hand-drills) meant more
expense. John Schofield was adamant:

> Our customers want to see a continuous surface on the products they buy, any lines or
> cracks may indicate a weakness to them. I don't want to be able to see any split lines
> on the outside surface, so the casing must be moulded in one piece.

Whilst John knew little about injection moulding, he knew that the outside of
the product had to look strong. He was especially aware that any 'seams' apparent
on the surface of the product would be perceived as a point of weakness by his
customers. Whilst both the moulder, toolmaker and Bob Buxton all suggested that
a clam shell design would be easier and cheaper to mould, John wanted a one-piece
moulding. This was a brave route to follow as it presented quite considerable
moulding and tooling problems.

Bob Buxton wanted to make sure that the translation of his drawings into a three-dimensional shape was performed correctly. Despite IR not being able to pay him for his time, Bob decided it was good investment to take the effort to ensure that his design turned out right:

> I think at that point John had hit some cost limitations so Graham took over at this point. However, we were still needed as we had to closely liaise with Formation Engineering because we were getting queries back from them. The product may look a fairly simple thing, but it's actually fairly tricky to model on computer because of some quite subtle blends and changes. For instance, if you look at the shape of the handle grip, you can draw it in two dimensions, but what's really happening? How do you define that?

Formation Engineering quoted to do the work in four days, but it eventually took ten days to complete the moulding. Bob Buxton lamented:

> I could have done, really, with several visits down to Formation just to sit in. It's like in traditional modelmakers, where you don't just give them the drawings and then go away, you would actually, if there were any problems, call in. You are having to rely on someone else's interpretation otherwise. I did my best using the fax to check the drawings. The whole point is, of course, that you can change a model on CAD quickly and easily because it's a virtual model.

The major part of BWMc's consultancy work finished once their drawings had been translated into the three-dimensional CAD model. BWMc's input from this point was to finish off some small details (such as the exhaust baffle plate) and generally to be available to advise the IR core team should the need arise.

From Design to Manufacture

- 19 May 1992   BWMc still working on the T-handle.
- 30 May   Preparation of component drawings. Sorting out the nose ring detail, exhaust baffle and moulding the D-handle. Stereo-lithography. Project was a mad scramble towards the end.
- 3 June   Logo Label added to the moulding/casting.
- 6 June   IR polyurethane castings.
- 21 July   Ridge for nose ring completed.
                  Toolmaker makes wooden pattern for carbon electrode to spark erode. Also polypropylene exhaust baffle snap fit finished.
- 3 November   Product launch for D-handle expected.

It was not until July 1992 that most of the details of the product were completed. With Graham Dewhurst now overseeing the process from three-dimensional CAD model to manufacture, Bob Buxton did not see the 'real' design until the moulders were starting trial production runs (or first-off sampling).

It was at this point that Bob Buxton noticed a small, almost unnoticeable flaw with the exterior of the product. Where the barrel body meets and blends with the end nozzle section there was a slight ridge, caused purely by the CAD solid modelling process. When Formation had translated Bob Buxton's drawings, the model had been divided into two separate sections and then 'joined' on screen. Because of the limitations of computer screen definition, the join looked perfect. However, once transformed into a solid model, the ridge became evident.

Bob Buxton was tempted to change the model to rectify the flaw. However, as he explained:

> At the end of the day there was so much time pressure the ridge remained although it was feasible to take it out. When I went down to the toolmaker and saw the carbon electrode used to spark erode the tool, I really should have got some wet-and-dry [sand paper] there and then, and removed the detail. I think I would have been thrown out of the workshop if I had done that because it was a fairly traditional workplace. I think this is a good illustration of the process and its pitfalls. It's essential to have the designer right the way through the process.

Product Launch

The product had to be launched by early November and John Schofield was becoming concerned that they would not meet this deadline. He was frustrated at the extra time taken to incorporate the Vibra-Smooth device and to source a new design consultancy. John had already had to change the launch date of the product on two occasions and was under pressure from the steering committee to finalize the date on this third occasion. He had heard rumours that one of their major competitors was also responding to the health and safety legislation and was due to launch a new product. Given all the effort that the team had put into the product, he did not want to miss the market opportunity and become a market follower. He decided to call a meeting of the team to assess the situation and to make a decision before reporting to the steering committee the following morning.

Epilogue

Despite the worst worldwide recession in recent years, the Irgo-Pic has proved a success. The power was immediately recognized as the main selling point, but with the coming of the final stages of the European Union's machinery directive and the increasing awareness of the damage caused by exposure to hand and arm vibration, the ergonomics of the tool have become an important feature too. In terms of the power-to-vibration ratio Irgo-Pic is way ahead of the competition, such that in 1993 Ingersoll–Rand sold twice as many units of Irgo-Pic in Europe as it had sold of the previous model in the previous year. John Schofield commented:

There are many things learned during the project and which, besides being bought into the next project, will also be applied to Irgo-Pic – continuous improvement is the name of the game. There is no doubt this facility will remain the Ingersoll–Rand Power Tool Design Centre for Europe, and for tools for worldwide sales. The Irgo-Pic is the start of the 'right' product image for Ingersoll–Rand. The image of the future will be one of modern styling and super efficiency which are instantly recognisable as Ingersoll–Rand's.

Design Awards

Following the successful launch of the product in November 1993, the product was entered into two award schemes and was successful in attaining best in class for both.

The PRW (Plastic and Rubber Weekly) Awards for Excellence
These awards were first presented in 1990. It was felt that at a time when manufacturing industries were under enormous pressure to compete in worldwide markets, one of the few areas which has consistently expanded its technological boundaries was the polymer industry. This sector had consistently produced components and finished products which were better designed, more cost-efficient, economical on materials and had better strength-to-weight ratios than their non-polymer rivals.

With these characteristics in mind, the Irgo-Pic was the winner of the industrial products category. The heart of the product is the Vibra-Smooth isolator that incorporates three resilient natural rubber balls rolling between two inclined faces which acts as a low axial rate spring while retaining high radial stiffness to maintain tool control. The judges commented:

> Several components exhibit novel designs and uses of materials, some believed to be industry firsts. This is a particularly innovative product which has made good use of polymers in a range of components.

Horners Award
This award was introduced in 1945 and is administered by the British Plastics Federation (BPF) as a joint enterpise with the Worshipful Company of Horners. The 1993 Horners award for plastics was won by Ingersoll–Rand's Irgo-Pic pneumatic hammer. The hammer has the highest power-to-weight ratio recorded for a tool in its class. Weighing only 10 kg, it delivers a blow-energy of 39 Nm, while the vibration transmitted is one-third that of a traditional tool of equivalent power. Designed and engineered in the UK, it is the first such development outside the USA for the US-owned company.

On the advice of the designers, Buxton Wall McPeake, Irgo-Pic uses a variety of thermoplastic mouldings in its construction. Polyamide is used for the case/muffler and nosering, polyurethane for the handles, acetal for the air distribution valve and glassfilled nylon for various small components.

An innovative feature which greatly influenced the adjudication panel was the unique Vibra-Smooth tri-ball isolator. Created by Anthony Best Dynamics, it is largely responsible for the reduction of vibration transmitted to the operator.

CASE 5

Victoria Fruit
Going Bananas?

Ilya Girson
University of Westminster, London

Vitaly Cherenkov
St Petersburg University of Economics and Finance, Russia

One sunny morning in October 1994, Victor Chegirsov, the managing director of Victoria Fruit, drove a BMW from his *dacha* in Zelenogorsk to St Petersburg to attend the company's strategy meeting. After a number of turbulent years and economic upheavals in Russia as it slowly moves towards a more decentralized and mixed economy, Chegirsov concluded that there was an increasing demand for perishable food. There was good reason to be satisfied with his achievements, as much of the credit for founding a well-known perishable goods distribution company in 1992 was owed to Chegirsov.

Chegirsov wanted to capitalize further on the business relationships formed and tested during years of semi-legal activity in the shadow economy of the former USSR which enabled the new entrepreneurs to achieve spectacular results within a short period of time. He was influenced by John van Geest, who started out exporting bulbs from his native Holland to the UK but ended up as a leading importer of bananas from the Caribbean to Europe. Van Geest's business style included ownership or managment of all aspects of the operation, and, in fruit importing, the whole network from the deliveries by sea through ports to supermarkets was under his control.

Wholesale of quickly perishable fresh vegetables and fruit is a capital-intensive enterprise requiring specially equipped warehouses, refrigeration facilities and skilled personnel. Although long-term trends in the demand for fresh vegetables and fruit were anything but clear, the trend was generally accepted to be stable for the foreseeable future, and the transformation of Victoria Fruit from a wholesaler servicing just a few of the adjacent rural regions, to a fully integrated national distributor was considered to be a cornerstone of a successful long-term strategy.

The existence of the company's own distribution network equipped with computerized communication facilities will also enable Victoria Fruit not only to extend its product line to other, possibly non-perishable foods, but also to undertake market research for other companies and thus capture a share of a profitable but almost non-existent business intelligence market. Chegirsov was convinced that Victoria had to change the perceptions of the marketplace as to what a modern distribution network can do. 'We should provide our customers with the details of where the goods are physically in the system, and, crucially, we have to ensure user-friendly access to the information about these goods,' he thought.

In the short term, the main aim of the company was to become the largest supplier of bananas to the Russian market, while preserving and extending the existing assortment of fresh fruit and vegetables. Victoria's turnover is expected to reach US$25 million in 1995 and, according to an optimistic scenario, its revenue may exceed $30 million – a spectacular rise from the anticipated $7.1 million and $2.2 million sales revenue achieved in 1994 and 1993, respectively.

Background

Transition of Russia towards an open market economy created new conditions for entrepreneurial activity, and a novel class of businesspeople was emerging all over the Federation responding to the inadequacies fo the former centrally controlled economy. The new economic framework of the country legitimized the illegal and semi-legal practices of the Soviet black economy.

The offer of fruit and vegetables in the former USSR to the consumer market was limited to a short seasonal period owing to the severe climatic conditions and inadequate transport facilities in the country. In addition, Russia has practically lost its traditional bases of supply in the former Soviet republics, Armenia, Azerbaijan, Georgia, Moldavia, the republics of Central Asia and even Ukraine, where an unstable political and military situation became an impediment to trade.

Although the process of transition from a centralized to a market economy has resulted in a considerable distintegration of the exisiting distribution networks, it has also provided relatively favourable conditions for establishing new, privately owned distribution companies.

Considering that the forecasted demand for fresh fruit and vegetables is stable and only partially satisfied, Victoria's long-term aim of becoming a leading Russian wholesaler in the perishable goods market was successfully under way. The imported products, rarely heard of in the Soviet times, were to provide the bulk of the merchandise, especially in the short term.

Geographical Segments

As the information regarding consumer behaviour in Russia is either lacking or unreliable the market evaluation is based on the population data in the cities where Victoria has had or will establish its subsidiaries in the near future (Exhibits 5.1–5.3).

Exhibit 5.1 *Population of cities where Victoria had established subsidiaries by June 1994*

Cities	Population millions
Nizhny Novgorod	1.8
Novgorod	0.3
Cheliabinsk	1.2
Ivanovo	0.5
Pskov	0.3
Kostroma	0.4
Total	4.5

Exhibit 5.2 *Population of cities where Victoria will establish subsidiaries by January 1995*

Cities	Subsidiaries to be set up by	Population millions
Astrachan	June 1994	0.5
Kirov	June 1994	0.6
Petrozavodsk	July 1994	0.3
Samara	July 1994	0.4
Moscow	July 1994	11.0
Archangelsk	August 1995	0.3
Murmansk	August 1995	0.5
Krasnodar	August 1995	0.5
Kursk	August 1995	0.4
Ekaterinburg	September 1995	2.0
Total		16.5

Overall population including suburbs may total 28 million.

The market demand for the key product lines was established in Russia at Soviet times when the state centralized system imported a limited assortment of fruit, mainly bananas, to a designated number of cities including Moscow and St Petersburg. It is not surprising, therefore, that bananas are the most known fruit in the major Russian markets, especially popular in the winter and spring seasons.

Exhibit 5.3 *Victoria's markets, 1994*

Cities	Market share %
Nizhni Novgorod	53
Ivanovo	5
Pskov	5
Kostroma	2
Cheliabinsk	11
Tver	1
Petrozavodsk	9
St Petersburg	5
Other	9
	100

Competitive Environment

Chegirsov was particularly concerned about the strategies of three companies. Generally, these were well established firms that tended to imitate the marketing strategy of Victoria.

MKM group was set up in 1991 and has acquired strong financial and technological bases for banana treatment. MKM's warehouses and storage facilities belong to the state sector, and its main deliveries are made by sea containers. Yearly turnover of MKM is approximately US$30 million (in Russia the law does not yet require companies to disclose their financial information), and the wholesale price levels are on average 30 per cent lower than Victoria's.

Equator was formed in 1990 and its turnover is $15 million with the average wholesale price levels 10 per cent lower than Victoria's. Lenagro does not operate in St Petersburg, and it is involved mainly in the transportation of goods to the other regions of Russia. Equator's turnover is of the same order as Victoria's and its pricing policies are similar to Victoria's.

By investing $400,000 during summer 1994 into modern imported equipment for ripening bananas, Victoria is now in a position to increase the shelf-life of bananas, adding to the flexibility of its operations. The wholesale price of green bananas delivered by sea and shipped, for example, to Nizhni Novgorod is $12 per box compared with $22.5 per box which is the price of ripe bananas. This differential makes a strong case for a further evaluation of banana-ripening equipment. The product quality, which the company believes to be one of its major advantages, is also maintained by the use of specialized equipment for temperature, humidity and light control in the warehouses and delivery trucks.

Although not as price-competitive as its nearest rivals, Victoria's investment in the distribution network enables it to expand into the new geographical areas and capitalize on a strong corporate image. The company's integrated network also permits it to respond more quickly to the changing conditions of the regional and local markets.

Bulk shipments of produce by sea are still rarely used, and Victoria's price-competitiveness is limited compared with those distributors who acquired interests in shipping lines and use bulk seas shipments frequently. Victoria possesses, however, a sufficient technical base to ensure its product quality, especially the freshness of the produce, and, by investing heavily in the development of distribution network, Victoria aims to achieve a competitive advantage in the quality of its products and services to its regional and local customers.

Recent successes – the company's turnover grew threefold during the past six months to $643,000 per month – are encouraging, but by changing to bulk purchases and shipments by sea, Victoria will be able to provide volume discounts and increase its market share through competitive pricing in addition to its qualitative edge.

Product Line

Fresh fruit and vegetables belong to the group of products that satisfy everyday needs of consumers. Although the proportion of these products in the consumer goods basket in Russia is lower than in the developed Western world, a stable demand for these products exists throughout the year in most of Victoria's markets.

Currently, the company purchases its assortment of vegetables and fruit from suppliers which are divided into two major categories, local producers and importers. Local suppliers, including the republics of the former Soviet Union, provide tomatoes, onions, apples, lemons, aubergines, garlic, carrots, cabbages, pears, peaches, strawberries, water melons, apricots and cucumbers, with the importers delivering predominantly bananas, oranges, kiwi, pineapples, nectarines, coconuts and avocados.

Selection of the produce is based on the analysis of demand in the regional and local markets. Bananas, which can be imported throughout the year, are the key element in this assortment contributing 33 per cent to the total turnover. The Russian market displays a stable demand for this product with little seasonal variation.

Pricing

The projected wholesale price for the goods from importers is based on the purchase price with taxes and custom duties added by the state for imported goods. In addition, all other costs of Victoria, including the storage and treatment of products, are included and an acceptable profit margin is added to reach the lower price limit.

In reality, the prices quoted by Victoria also depend on the economic conditions in the regional and local markets, and the information on these is continuously supplied to headquarters. Control over pricing, especially in the regions where Victoria's major rivals are weak, provides Victoria with an additional competitive advantage.

Victoria's discounting depends on the volume of orders. Experience shows, however, that the overall order levels were not always related to the discount policy. This can partially be explained by imperfections of the regional markets, and the board decided to provide discounting only in special circumstances.

To attract and retain major customers in a highly price-sensitive market, Victoria provides extended credit facilities and payment adjustments in roubles based on the difference between the dollar/rouble exchange rates on the dates of delivery and payment. In times of high inflation and excessive borrowing costs, this approach provides significant benefits to its customers.

The architecture of Victoria's distribution network and its decentralized decision making allows for frequent use of introductory pricing for produce that is unknown or only little known in the local market, e.g. for avocados, papayas, mangos, yuccas, leucoses. Losses from such pricing practices are normally covered by generating extra profit from other commodity items.

Distribution Channels

The company's distribution strategy reflects its major aim to set up an integrated distribution network with St Petersburg as the major point through which the goods enter the whole system.

Only one subsidiary, in Nizhni Novgorod (Exhibit 5.3) reached a satisfactory market share. Growth projections for 1995 assume setting up banana-ripening chambers in St Petersburg, Moscow, Astrachan, Nizhni Novgorod and Cheliabinsk. These cities are also designated by the company to become the regional centres for the global distribution network.

Victoria's distribution strategy is based on establishing centres on three strategic levels:

1. *Main wholesale centres* (MWC). At present, St Petersburg is Victoria's major point of entry for imports by road, and will become an entry port for the deliveries by sea in the first quarter 1995. By the end of 1995, Novorossijsk is planned to become a second entry port for sea deliveries, and in the long term, Murmansk is being considered as a third port of entry.

2. *Regional wholesale branches* (RWB) are set up in the cities where banana ripening chambers either exist or are going to be installed (St Petersburg, Moscow, Nizhni Novgorod, Cheliabinsk, Astrachan). The capacity of these branches can be expanded in the case of unplanned increase in demand. The goods for RWB will be supplied by WSC.

3. *Local wholesale branches* (LWB) do not have banana-ripening chambers at present, so they will receive their produce from RWB. The projected number of LWB centres in the short term is twenty-four, and further

research is being conducted into other geographical territories most suitable to operate as LWB.

A significant feature of the company's distribution network is its ownership of a number of retail outlets providing Victoria with further control over its regional markets in addition to securing data for market testing, assortment and quality of merchandise. At present, retail centres (RC) are in St Petersburg and Nizhni Novgorod.

The current storage capacity in St Petersburg is limited to four rented warehouses with the total space of 1,750 m². Only three warehouses, 450 m² each, specialize in fresh vegetable and fruit storage.

Although all distribution centres have railway service connections, and special refrigeration carriages of 120 ton capacity are available, tariffs for the railroad freight, which is state-owned, are uncompetitive. Victoria Fruit is forced, therefore, to transport its cargo by road with an average speed of only 50 km/h owing to the unsatisfactory condition of the roads.

The company applies a predominantly 'push' stategy to speed up movements of goods within the distribution channels which is combined with aggressive promotional activities at regional and local levels to recruit new customers. The quality of services to the customers is being measured by evaluating the results of meetings with the major customers and mail surveys using questionnaires. Although the majority of customers were satisfied with the level of customer support, some complained that Victoria lacked flexibility in supply; more importantly, though, information from the head office on order status and deliveries was hard to obtain and customers were not forewarned of potential problems with deliveries.

The technological needs of Victoria are determined by the major activities of the company to ensure efficient loading, transportation and the storage of goods. Banana-ripening equipment and the data processing technology are an integral part of the company operations. All the marketing and accounting data to support the information flows from and to the regional and local offices are provided by the network. Every trade transaction is treated as a source of valuable information about the customers, enabling Victoria to start building long-term relationships with them. This information is the prerequisite for opening new marketing channels and helps the company to understand better their customers thereby providing Victoria with further competitive advantages and power within the supply chain.

Organization

In 1994 a board of directors was given responsibility for the company's strategic directions and the operational control up to a regional level. The board included a managing director supported by a financial director, marketing director and a director of personnel.

In May 1994, Victoria Fruit Ltd had headquarters staff of fifty people including security personnel. General managers in the main, regional and local centres are responsible for the flow and storage of goods, and for personnel management. These positions of responsibility are subject to the approval of the board. Personnel selection is carried out on a competitive basis with the assistance of a staff psychologist, and preliminary interviews with subsequent testing are widely applied.

In Victoria Fruit the system of remuneration is based on a fixed salary element in addition to performance-related incentives. One of the important criteria for appraising an employee's contribution to the company is his or her level of customer care, which is novel for companies in Russia.

Victoria Fruit is a family-owned company, and 20 per cent of stock belongs to Victor Chergisov; the rest of the stock is in the hands of his wife and other close relatives. It is planned, however, to allocate company shares to top managers in the parent company including the directors of RWB and LWB. Moreover, Victoria's directors are currently evaluating the possibility of issuing non-transferable shares to all company employees.

The main objective of this scheme is not only to increase the working capital of the company, vital to the company's expansion plans, but to respond to the aspirations and needs of employees from all levels of the company and involve them more closely in the decision-making and daily activities of the business.

'The true spirit of our company', Victor Chegirsov remarked, 'is based on the belief in ourselves, our constant desire to innovate and our willingness to take responsibilities for our actions.' The company's informal atmosphere is reflected in the dress of the employees, casual but neat. Management of human resources is based on strong elements of paternalism. 'People like it,' Victor Chegirsov mentioned, 'and the well-being of personnel is of special importance in this business. We aim to achieve a clear and transparent structure within our organization clearly understood by our employees, customers and suppliers alike.'

Training of the management and other operational personnel is designed by occupational and industrial psychologists and consultants.

Financial Data

The turnover in May 1994 reached $643,000, a threefold growth compared with February turnover, although May figures do not include contributions from Victoria's new subsidiaries in a number of regions.

Payments to suppliers are made within seven days of delivery, and the debt collection has never exceeded seven days from the date of delivery to the customer.

In April 1993, at the start-up stage, the company used three months' loans to finance its expansion, as the banks were unwilling to provide long-term credit. A successful start to its operations made it possible for the company to function without seeking additional capital. Expanding the company's network on the basis of self-financing did not contribute to high profitability (Exhibit 5.4), and the liquidity ratios were also falling. By the end of the year the company should be in a financial position to increase the number of branches to twenty-four.

Exhibit 5.4   *Victoria's financial ratios*

	1993	1994
Current ratio	1.04	0.94
Quick ratio	0.94	0.77
Return on assets	16.00%	5.00%
Net profit margin	1.16%	0.43%

Victoria's Dilemma

Chegirsov knew that a number of options were open to the board; however, he was faced with a dilemma. The investment into the company was hefty, and a good return and payback were required. Victoria needed to build on its expertise in distribution to convince reluctant bankers of the soundness of its approach. 'Did we overlook market reactions or competitor's responses?' Chegirsov thought as he was turning his car into a quiet side-street off the Nevsky Prospect, close to Victoria's headquarters. Chegirsov's genuine belief was that the company's image and professionalism were high and that the main issues facing the company were the speed of growth and its ability to sustain a high level of customer service. Victoria had to convince its various suppliers, customers and bankers that the company could develop a successful presence nationwide.

CASE 6

Nivea Sun

Sabine Kuester
Groupe ESSEC

Bruce Hardie and **Patrick Barwise**
London Business School

Introduction

On 5 September 1994, Lucy Gilbert joined Beiersdorf UK as product manager for Nivea Sun, having previously worked as a product manager for cold and flu remedies in a different company. She was asked to develop her proposed 1995 marketing budget within four weeks. Her main task was to specify the level and nature of the main marketing expenditures: advertising, consumer promotions, trade promotions and public relations. Gilbert started by gathering information on previous years' budget allocations and market data.

Company Background: Beiersdorf and Smith & Nephew

Nivea – for decades one of the world's biggest-selling cosmetics and toiletry brands – was the first major product sold by Beiersdorf, AG. Beiersdorf, based in Hamburg, Germany, manufactured branded products in the fields of toiletries, pharmaceuticals, medical products and technical tapes. During the Second World War, the Nivea brand rights were confiscated in a number of countries and subsequently sold to local companies. The rights for the UK, South Africa and most of the Commonwealth were acquired by the Hull-based company Smith & Nephew in 1954. Smith & Nephew's principal activities were the manufacture and sale of sticking plasters, eye care products, and consumer health care products. Smith & Nephew manufactured the Nivea range and concentrated on making it widely available at the point-of-sale while keeping the brand and its packaging broadly consistent with the rest of Europe.

In December 1992, Smith & Nephew sold the Nivea brand to Beiersdorf for £46.5 million. The contract included an agreement whereby Smith & Nephew continued to be the exclusive distributor for Nivea in the UK.

113

Nivea

Nivea, which means snow white in ancient Greek, was invented by a chemist at the beginning of this century. The product was Nivea Creme, the first-ever water-in-oil emulsion. In many countries, especially in Continental Europe, Nivea Creme was an everyday product bought by women to moisturize and protect their own and their family's skin. Although the brand's formulation and packaging were not identical in every market, the famous Nivea blue and white packaging was based on the design standardized in 1925.

Nivea Sun

The Nivea brand had been extended in multiple ways. At the beginning of the 1990s it covered six product groupings: Nivea Body (Nivea Creme and lotions), Nivea Visage (premium skin care), Nivea Sun, Nivea for Men (not distributed in the UK), Nivea Shower and Bath, Nivea Hair Care and Nivea Deo (deodorant). Nivea's sun care range was one of the earlier extensions, launched multinationally in the late 1950s. Over time, Nivea Sun had extended its original oil and cream products to include lotions with a variety of sun protection factors (SPFs), a specific range of children's products, sensitive gels and after-sun products. The sun care range represented the most extensive product range of any Nivea sub-brand and was one of Nivea's most successful extensions. A major factor for its success was that Nivea's core values of caring, gentleness and family protection could be easily transferred to the sun care category. Another important factor was the choice of multiple distribution channels, which included the grocery trade, giving Nivea Sun wide availability. In 1994, Nivea Sun accounted for more than a quarter of Nivea's total annual sales in the UK (see Exhibit 6.1).

Gilbert's objective was to increase Nivea Sun's market share and profit contribution. She could capitalize on the brand strategy that had evolved over the previous years, which emphasized both Nivea Sun as *the* family protection brand and Nivea's skincare expertise. In addition to this, she had to continue to contemporize the brand's safe but rather old-fashioned image. This had to go hand-in-hand with reinforcing Nivea Sun's image as an authority on sun care issues. Given these multiple objectives she had to decide how to support the new 1995 product range (see Exhibit 6.2) which consisted of established products, as well as an entirely new range of sports products.

Exhibit 6.1 *Nivea UK sales breakdown, 1994*

	% of total sales
Skin Care (Visage, Body)	54
Sun	26
Personal Care (Shower and Bath, Hair Care, Deo)	20

Exhibit 6.2 *Nivea Sun product range, 1995*

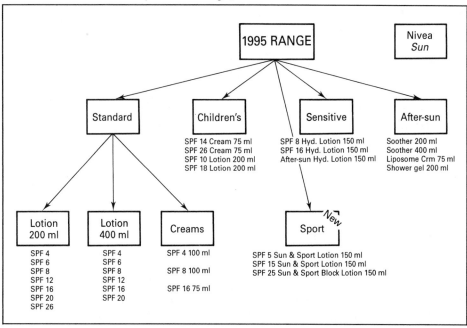

The Sun Care Market

In 1994, it was estimated that the UK sun care market had a value of £129 million at retail prices, a 12 per cent increase on 1993 (see Exhibit 6.3). The total market comprised three product sectors:

Exhibit 6.3 *The market for sun care products, 1991–94*

	1991		1992		1993		1994[a]	
	£m	% change in sales	£m	% change in sales	£m	% change in sales	£m	% change in sales
Total market value	93.2	–	109.2	+17	114.6	+5	129.0	+12
Sector share								
Suntan	80.4	–	80.5	+17	82.8	+8	83.3	+13
After-Sun	13.5	–	14.5	+26	12.6	−10	12.6	+13
Self-tan	6.1	–	5.0	−5	4.6	−2	4.1	−2
RPI[b]		100		105		108		110

[a] Estimates.
[b] RPI Retail price index in the UK.

1. Sun protection/tan promotion products (83 per cent).
2. After-sun skin care/tan prolonging products (13 per cent).
3. Artificial/sunless tanning products (4 per cent).

In value terms, the market had grown by about 300 per cent in the past decade, despite the UK recession from around 1990. This growth was fuelled by consumers' increasing awareness of the risks associated with exposure to the sun. The growth in consumer awareness led to a change in their needs: they still wanted a suntan (52 per cent believed that this was possible without incurring a significant risk), but they were now also actively looking for products that offered protection (75 per cent). The market was projected to continue growing over the next three years at around a minimum of 6 per cent per annum in value terms (versus general retail price inflation of about 3 per cent).

Sun Protection Products

For simplicity, Gilbert decided to focus initially on sun protection products, which accounted for 81 per cent of Nivea's sun care revenues in 1994. Total UK retail sales of sun protection products were valued at £107.5 million in 1994.

Despite the buoyancy of the market as a whole, there was a decline in sales of low protection products; new products launched focused increasingly on ranges with higher SPFs. Products with an SPF of 7 or more had grown significantly to represent almost 50 per cent of sales value in 1992, compared with around 10 per cent in the mid-1980s. The trend from low SPFs towards higher SPFs had been even more marked over the past year (Exhibit 6.4).

There had been a similar trend away from oils, which were less protective, towards lotions, milks and creams, which offered greater protection from both UVA and UVB rays (see Exhibit 6.5 for explanation of UVA and UVB). This trend had further intensified in 1994, when sales of lotions and milk formulations in groceries and pharmacies increased by 47 per cent while sales of oil products decreased by 2 per cent (see Exhibit 6.6). Gels, sprays and sticks were new application formats with low consumer awareness.

Exhibit 6.4   *Sun protection sector by SPF, 1993–94*

	1993 %	1994 %	% Change
SPF 0–3	11.1	7.3	−19
SPF 4–6	37.2	28.5	−6
SPF 7–10	22.5	26.4	+44
SPF 11–14	3.0	3.8	+54
SPF 15+	26.2	34.0	+59

Exhibit 6.5 *Sun and skin*

Sunlight

The sunlight reaching the skin consists of visible light, infrared (IR) rays and ultraviolet rays (UVA and UVB radiation). UVC rays are also emitted by the sun but they are filtered out by the ozone layer in the stratosphere before they reach the earth. However, the thinning ozone layer means that increasing amounts of UVB radiation may get through. Experts believe that for every 1 per cent fall in ozone, there is around a 2 per cent increase in the amount of UV radiation reaching the earth and a 3 per cent increase in non-melanoma skin cancer.

When skin and sun meet

- UVB rays penetrate into the epidermis and can cause sunburn. The length of time this takes depends on the skin-type of the individual. UVB rays are considered to be the most dangerous of the UV rays. They are present whenever the sun shines but are most intense in summer, especially around midday.

- UVA rays penetrate even deeper than UVB rays, into the dermis. The cumulative effect of UVA rays over one's lifetime can lead to wrinkles and signs of premature aging. UVA rays are present all year round.

- Free radicals are formed. These reactive oxidizing molecules can damage cells and tissues in the skin if left unchecked.

The body's response

The skin's exposure to UV rays speeds up the production of the skin's epidermal cells. The epidermis, including the horny layer, becomes thicker as part of the body's natural defence mechanism against the sun. Hence the skin feels tighter and drier after exposure to the sun.

When UV rays penetrate the skin, cells in the epidermis (melanocytes) react by producing melanin – the brown pigment which forms a tan and acts as part of the skin's natural protection barrier against the sun. A tan is therefore a sign of skin damage. Different skin-types produce different amounts of melanin, with the fairest skin producing the least.

Over-exposure to the sun causes the skin to burn (erythema) and peel. Increasing evidence also suggests that prolonged and unprotected exposure to UV rays throughout one's life can cause skin cancer and skin aging. Short, intense bursts of unprotected sun exposure – especially during the early part of a lifetime – is being linked to malignant melanoma – a specific and very dangerous type of skin cancer.

Source: Nivea Market Report 1994.

Exhibit 6.6 *Sun protection sector by formulation type, 1993–94*

	1993 %	1994 %
Lotions and milk	56.2	62.7
Creams	34.3	29.4
Oils	5.9	5.2
Other (gels, sprays, etc.)	3.6	2.7

Niche Products

Another market development was a growing trend towards niche products formulated for specialist use. The key segments were children and babies, sensitive skins and sport.

1. *Children and baby segment.* The children and baby sun care market was a recent development. The high number of new entrants into this category contributed to the growth of 125 per cent in 1994. This segment represented 5.7 per cent of the total sun protection market and in 1994 was already larger than the artificial tanning segment.

2. *Sensitive skin segment.* Products developed for this segment were designed for sensitive and easily irritated skin and contained few, if any, irritant chemicals or perfumes. The top five brands had all developed products for this segment.

3. *Sport segment.* The most recent niche to emerge was for products aimed at sportspeople. Pioneered by L'Oréal's Ambre Solaire UV Sport, these products targeted the 60 per cent of the UK population taking part in outdoor sports and activities. This segment had shown sustained growth since its emergence in 1993. Products targeted mainly men who traditionally showed no or low consumption of sun protection products, offering high-protection, highly water-resistant, long-lasting formulations.

It was expected that throughout the 1990s innovative products with specific targets, such as these, would continue to add value to the sun care market.

Consumption Patterns

Consumption patterns in the sun care market are highly seasonal, related to the peak holiday season of the summer months (May to August). Most UK purchases of sun care products were for holidays abroad. Typically, consumers bought sun care products a week or two before their summer holiday, although they might keep some at home and replace it when finished. Gilbert was not sure if consumer inventory was a significant factor.

Women under 55 years were the main buyers of sun care products, with a peak for those aged 35–44. Purchases by men were lower, with a peak among 25–34 year olds (Exhibit 6.7 for information from a consumer survey). Usage, as opposed to buying, was spread somewhat more evenly across all demographic groups.

Competition

At the end of 1994, L'Oréal's Ambre Solaire was the value (in £ sales) leader in the UK sun care market. However, it was facing growing competition from Boots' Soltan, which was already the volume leader (Exhibit 6.8).

Exhibit 6.7 *Consumer survey*

Consumer data
Sample: 19,916 adults.
Users of suntan lotions, oils and creams were defined according to product use:

- Heavy users: use three or more tubes, bottles or other containers a year.
- Medium users: use two tubes, bottles or other containers a year.
- Light users: use one or less tube, bottle or other container a year.
- Non-users: do not use suntan lotions, oils or creams.

Penetration levels of suntan lotions, oils and creams: usage among women by demographic subgroup, 1992 (base: 7,199 women)[a]

	All users %	Heavy users %	Medium users %	Light users %	Non-users %
All women	63	17	20	26	37
15–19	70	15	20	35	30
20–24	68	18	21	29	32
25–34	71	21	23	27	29
35–44	75	25	27	23	25
45–54	67	23	21	23	33
55–64	50	10	14	26	50
65+	32	2	10	20	68
AB	71	18	23	30	29
C1	71	20	22	29	29
C2	63	18	20	25	37
D	58	17	18	23	42
E	33	4	12	17	67
London	69	21	18	30	31
South	64	18	18	28	36
Anglia/Midlands	58	11	24	23	42
South west/Wales	59	17	23	19	41
Yorkshire/north east	60	16	17	27	40
North west	63	18	23	22	37
Scotland	60	11	19	30	40

Most popular attributes looked for when choosing sun creams or lotions: by demographic subgroup, November 1992 (base: 1,639 adults)[a]

	Protection from UVA rays %	Well-known brand %	Appropriate sun factor %	Value for money %	Protection from UVB rays %
All	40	36	29	27	26
Men	34	24	27	21	19
Women	45	46	30	31	32
15–19	39	35	29	33	29
20–24	39	36	37	29	28

Continued over ▶

Exhibit 6.7 *Continued*

	Protection from UVA rays %	Well-known brand %	Appropriate sun factor %	Value for money %	Protection from UVB rays %
25–34	45	47	35	25	31
35–44	55	44	31	31	31
45–54	46	41	28	31	29
55–64	38	35	24	23	18
65+	11	11	16	14	9
AB	50	41	34	18	32
C1	47	44	33	29	29
C2	42	39	34	32	31
D	28	26	23	28	16
E	19	17	13	29	13
London	46	32	32	27	29
South	43	40	40	28	26
Anglia/Midlands	44	43	43	27	25
South west/Wales	37	46	46	26	27
Yorkshire/north east	33	41	41	27	24
North west	32	33	33	7	25
Scotland	31	9	9	32	24
Working	44	34	33	26	27
Not working	34	39	24	29	25
Married	42	40	35	33	31
Not married	38	33	26	24	23

[a] Row percentages may total more than 100% as respondents could list more than one attribute.

Exhibit 6.8 *Value brand shares, 1992–94*

Brand	Manufacturer	1992 %	1993 %	1994 %
Ambre Solaire	L'Oréal	19.8	19.7	19.6
Soltan[a]	Boots	17.2	18.1	18.2
Nivea	Beiersdorf	10.3	10.7	12.6
Avon	Avon Cosmetics	10.5	11.8	11.0
Piz Buin	Ciba	4.1	5.3	4.5
Hawaiian Tropic	Warner–Lambert	3.7	3.5	2.8
Solait[a]	Superdrug	3.4	2.9	2.8
Other		31.0	28.0	28.5

[a] Own labels.

L'Oréal

L'Oréal, the world's largest cosmetics company, is jointly owned by Gasparal (France) (51 per cent) and Nestlé (Switzerland) (49 per cent). It markets Ambre Solaire through its Laboratoires Garnier division. L'Oréal has interests in most sectors of the global cosmetics and toiletries markets. In addition to its Garnier Division, L'Oréal operates through three divisions in the UK: Salon, Perfume and Beauty (e.g. Cacharel, Armani, Helena Rubinstein) and Active Cosmetics (e.g. Vichy). Ambre Solaire had previously been associated with oil formulations (as opposed to creams and gels) for deep tanning and self-tanning products. L'Oréal is very active in research and development and is perceived by customers as inventive and at the forefront of technology.

Boots Company Plc

Boots is one of Britain's major high street retailers and has interests in both the retailing and manufacturing of sun care products. In 1994, Boots was by far the largest retailer of sun care and other toiletry products. Its Soltan brand accounted for about 40 per cent value share in its 1,100 outlets. Soltan benefited from Boots' skin care and pharmacy heritage, and was especially strong in the after-sun sector, with roughly a one-quarter share by value. The strength of Boots was highlighted in March 1992 when it introduced a star-rating system that indicated how much protection a product provided against UVA rays in proportion to the amount of UVB protection offered. While its introduction created some uncertainty in the industry, virtually all manufacturers accepted the new system.

Avon Cosmetics Ltd

A subsidiary of Avon Products, Inc., Avon Cosmetics is the oldest beauty company in the USA and one of the world's four largest cosmetics companies. It entered the UK market in 1957. Avon sells its cosmetics, toiletries and fragrances to individual consumers. The bulk of its business comes from its sales representatives ('Avon Ladies') selling to women in their homes and workplaces. Avon employs some 100,000 representatives in the UK alone. In the 1980s it increased its market share in line with the growth of home shopping; however, its sales in the early 1990s have been sluggish owing to its inability to match retailers' product ranges and prices. Nevertheless, Avon accounts for around 11 per cent of all sun care sales.

Ciba Consumer Products

Ciba Consumer Products is a subsidiary of the Swiss chemicals giant Ciba–Geigy.

Ciba's core consumer business was in over-the-counter (OTC) health care. In the UK toiletry sector, its main product was Piz Buin, the number five sun care brand.

Warner–Lambert

Warner–Lambert's Hawaiian Tropic was, in 1994, in the process of shaking off its association with the deeply tanned look, having recently repositioned itself through relaunches and repackaging.

Superdrug

Superdrug is the number two UK drugs and toiletries retailer, with seven hundred stores emphasizing everyday low pricing (EDLP). Its sun care sales grew by about 20 per cent in 1994. Whilst most of its sales are of manufacturers' brands sold at highly competitive prices, it also has an own-label brand, Solait.

Bayer

The German company Bayer entered the UK market in 1992 with its Delial brand. Bayer expected Delial to grow rapidly owing to high awareness amongst consumers who had heard of it while abroad. Delial was aimed primarily at 18–35 year old women.

One notable development was the long-term growth of the own-label sector. Boots' Soltan and Superdrug's Solait alone accounted for 21 per cent of the 1994 market. In 1993, all own labels – including Body Shop, Avon and Marks & Spencer's own brand – captured 37.9 per cent of the market, representing a market value of £43.6 million. This trend was expected to continue in line with the emergence of own-label dominance in other consumer packaged goods categories.

Distribution

In the past decade, the distribution of sun care products had widened, with growing distribution in multiple grocery stores. However, the grocery multiples had not threatened the dominance of chemists in the distribution of sun care products as much as they had in other toiletries markets such as toothpaste and hair care. This was partly owing to the seasonal nature of the sun care market, as well as the more specialized nature of its products. Exhibit 6.9 highlights the continuing dominance of the pharmacy sector, especially the market power of Boots.

Exhibit 6.9 *Retail distribution of sun care products: percentage value of sector*

	1992 %	1993 %	1994 %
Boots	46	44	44
Other chemists	16	15	12
Grocers	8	9	12
Drugstores[a]	8	11	10
Department stores	4	3	3
Other retail	6	5	6
Non-retail[b]	12	13	13

[a] Mainly Superdrug.
[b] Mainly Avon.

Boots' strength lay in its prime high street locations, excellent logistics and ability to carry all key brands as well as its highly successful Soltan own label range. Additionally, Boots benefited from its ability to offer the specialized advice associated with pharmacy outlets.

Sales

Smith & Nephew's sales department sold the whole Smith & Nephew product range, including Nivea Sun. It was divided into account representatives and national account managers. The account representatives worked at the fieldforce level, liaising with independent chemists in their regions. For the sun care products, they visited accounts at the end of each year to take orders for delivery around Easter in the following year. Independent chemists who committed themselves to this ordering system were given a discount or special promotion for the forthcoming season. Most of these accounts, whilst visited directly by the account managers, had their stock delivered via a third party on a transfer order to a wholesale chemist. The national account managers were responsible for establishing and developing relationships with major accounts on a more continuous basis throughout the year.

Prices

Between 1988 and 1994, the retail price of toiletries had increased faster than retail prices in general. This reflected the fact that the market had changed, emphasizing added-value products in premium and niche segments. In the case of sun care, higher protection factors commanded higher prices. Most major brands sold at a lower price in the big retailers (e.g. Boots, Superdrug) than in, for example, the independent chemists. Exhibit 6.10 shows average retail selling prices for a range of sun care products.

Exhibit 6.10 *Retail selling prices of main brands, 1994*

	Average price (£) per 100 ml
Nivea Sun	
Cream F4	4.94
Cream F6	5.16
Cream F12	6.99
Lotion F5	3.00
Lotion F8	3.33
Lotion F10	3.88
Lotion F15	3.38
Sensitive Children Cream	7.99
Sensitive Children Lotion	4.00
After-suns	2.57
Ambre Solaire	
Oil	3.42
Cream F2	5.99
Cream F4	5.99
Cream F6	6.29
Cream F8	6.79
Cream F10	6.99
Milk	3.50
High Protection Kids Cream	7.49
High Protection Kids Milk	4.20
After-suns	2.25
UV Sport	4.12
Soltan	
Oil F2	2.99
Lotion F2	2.95
Lotion F4	2.89
Lotion F6	3.48
Lotion F8	2.65
Lotion F10	3.40
Lotion F15	3.70
Lotion F20	3.85
Cream F2	3.15
Cream F4	4.05
Cream F6	4.32
Cream F15	6.29
Children Cream	5.99
Children Lotion	4.75
After-suns	1.95

Source: company records.

Prices for Nivea Sun were approved by Beiersdorf UK in discussion with the Hamburg head office and the Smith & Nephew sales director, with the aim of profit improvement and European harmonization. The main factors in setting prices were general price increases in the market and cost developments owing to changes in the product line and exchange rates. The recommended retail price (RRP) of Nivea Sun products had remained unchanged in 1993 and 1994 against cumulative retail price inflation of 4.8 per cent over the two years.

For 1995, it had been agreed that Nivea Sun RRPs would be increased by 3.5 per cent. This increase had already been negotiated with the main trade accounts. The production cost per unit (strictly, the cost in sterling to Beiersdorf UK) was expected to increase by 3.8 per cent. Beiersdorf UK executives believed that the main competitors would again increase prices roughly in line with the forecast general inflation of about 3 per cent.

Marketing Expenditures

The four principal areas of Nivea Sun marketing expenditure were advertising, consumer promotion, trade promotion and public relations. Direct salesforce expenses were treated as a divisional overhead and not allocated between sub-brands.

Advertising

Both the level of expenditure and the number of advertised brands had increased in the previous three years. Having peaked at over 6% in 1986, the ratio of advertising to retail sales had fallen to 3.8% in 1991; this level had, however, since risen (see Exhibit 6.11).

Advertising was primarily on TV and in the women's press. In 1994, TV accounted for 52 per cent (1993: 47 per cent) of all advertising spent, press 44 per cent (46 per cent), outdoor 4 per cent (5 per cent) and radio 0 (2 per cent). The recent increase in sun care advertising was driven largely by the leading brands like Ambre Solaire, Nivea Sun and Soltan spending more on TV advertising. Despite this shift towards TV, press was still a crucial medium because of the complex nature

Exhibit 6.11   *Advertising expenditure on sun care products, 1991–94*

	Expenditure[a] £m	Advertising/sales ratio %
1991	3.57	3.8
1992	4.85	4.4
1993	6.36	5.5
1994	7.98	6.2

[a] Expenditures are at 'rate card' costs; because of discounting of media space/time, actual expenditure was likely to be lower.

of sun care products. Press advertising accounted for most of the advertising by smaller brands with limited budgets.

Ambre Solaire had traditionally been the most heavily advertised brand, but in 1994 was outspent by both Nivea Sun and Soltan. Nivea Sun started advertising in 1993, using advertisements developed by Beiersdorf for the European market with local language adaptations.

Because Nivea Sun was positioned as a brand for all the family, its retail sales were even more seasonal than for the market as a whole, with most consumer purchases in July and August when families took their summer holiday during the school vacation. Beiersdorf had therefore concentrated its 1994 TV advertising into an £800,000 campaign in July, giving it an 84 per cent share-of-voice (SoV) on TV for that month. Luckily, this had coincided with an exceptionally sunny summer which had benefited all competitors but especially Nivea Sun. Overall, Nivea had an SoV of 21 per cent across all media in 1994 (see Exhibit 6.12).

Gilbert's predecessor had done some analysis of the effectiveness of advertising in the sun care market (Exhibit 6.13). As a matter of head office policy, Beiersdorf UK used pan-European TV commericals. Print advertisements were also strictly controlled. At least in the short term, Gilbert's advertising decision would be confined to deciding how much to spend, in which media, when, and how much to allocate to the exisiting product range and how much to put behind the launch of the new Nivea Sport range. This new range was being introduced with its own packaging and positioning to attract new, young, active sun care users to the brand in the teenage/young adult age group.

Beiersdorf's advertising agency had forecast that media inflation would be about 6 per cent in print media and 10 per cent for television.

Consumer Promotions

Promotional activities were widely used in the sun care market. They tended to centre on point-of-sale display, holiday-related competitions and free offers. They also included the provision of information, often in the form of leaflets and sun care guidelines.

Exhibit 6.12   *Share of voice sun protection sector, 1993 vs 1994*

	1993 %	1994 %
Nivea Sun	9	21
Boots Soltan	31	20
Ambre Solaire	33	18
Delial	–	12
Piz Buin	7	4
Others	20	25

Exhibit 6.13 *Internal memo on advertising effectiveness*

To:	Lynn Heard and Mark Paton
From:	Phillip Erickson
Date:	23 August 1994
Re:	EFFECTS OF ADVERTISING EXPENDITURES

Following up on our discussion last Thursday, I have conducted an analysis of the effects of advertising expenditures in the sun care market. I examined the relationship between both advertising and sales, and share-of-voice and market share. Looking at the top 5 brands for the past three years (1992–94), the correlations are 0.87 and 0.84, respectively.

I also computed these correlations at the brand level (excluding Nivea, since we only started advertising last year). They are as follows:

	Correlation between	
	Ad. spend and sales	SoV and Mkt share
Ambre Solaire	−0.76	0.30
Hawaiian Tropic	0.49	0.72
Piz Buin	0.98	0.84

I'm not sure how to interpret these correlations; the negative correlation for Ambre Solaire is puzzling. We need to consider the implications of these numbers as we develop the advertising budget for next year.

Nivea Sun had relied mostly on gift-with-purchase (GWP) and occasionally on purchase-with-purchase (PWP) promotions. GWP promotions offered consumers a free gift with either a single purchase or with multiple purchases. PWP offered a second item at a discounted price as an incentive to purchase the promoted product at the regular price. Recent Nivea promotional activities included:

- A free beach ball with any Nivea Sun purchase.
- A free kite with any Nivea Sun purchase.
- A multi-buy offer ('buy any two Nivea products and save £X').
- A 'save one-third on any 400 ml product' offer.

These promotions were usually run for four weeks in the key early season months May, June and July.

Trade Promotions

Trade promotions concentrated mostly on price promotions to the retail trade, especially Boots and Superdrug. Typical price promotions were designed either to drive volume (multi-buy price promotions or special reductions on 400 ml) or to encourage trial through selected price promotions on new product lines.

Public Relations

Liaising with the press was very important in the sun care market. Special editorial coverage ('advertorials') was a widely used public relations instrument. The premium cosmetic houses made particular use of such editorial coverage in women's titles, and often backed this with a sampling campaign conducted through the magazine. (See Exhibit 6.14 for Nivea's public relations activities).

Exhibit 6.14 *Public relations*

---

1   Trade activity

1.1   Press releases

'Que Choisir' French report story
Following publication of the results of the 'Que Choisir' report, VKPR (a public relations company) distributed the press release entitled 'Nivea Sun – Premiere Choice for the French' which was distributed to the trade press, along with copies of the *Daily Express* article. VKPR is currently liaising with the trade press to ascertain interest.

TV advertising schedule
VKPR developed a press release detailing the TV and press advertising entitled 'Nivea Sun makes the sun safer'. VKPR distributed the release to relevant trade press and ensured publication in *Chemist and Druggist* (circ.: 13,000) 'What's on TV'.

2   Consumer activity

2.1   Nivea Future Sun Survey
VKPR developed the results of the survey into a report and distributed them to women's consumer, national and regional press and TV and radio with a press release and a covering letter. An intensive follow-up campaign was conducted to maximize coverage. The survey was picked up extensively in the regional press including:

> *Bath Evening Chronicle* – 20.5.94 (circ.: 26,200)
> *Huddersfield Daily Examiner* – 24.5.94 (circ.: 40,700)
> *Wigan Evening Post* – 21.5.94 (circ.: 62,400)
> *Western Morning News* – 6.6.94 (circ.: 57,200)
> *Lancashire Evening Telegraph* – 7.6.94 (circ.: 51,300)
> *South Wales Evening Post* – 16.6.94 (circ.: 68,600)
> *Oxford Mail* – 20.6.94 (circ.: 44,000)
> *Portsmouth News* – 6.7.94 (circ.: 82,600)
> *Dundee Telegraph and Post* – 16.7.94 (circ.: 41,300)

2.2   Syndicated radio tape
To upweight coverage of the Future Sun Survey, VKPR developed a script for a syndicated radio tape with Dr Antony Young and VKPR. This was distributed to thirty radio stations and has been picked up by the following six stations to date:

> Mercury Radio (wr 103,000) (Reigate/Crawley/Guildford) 7.7.94
> LBC Newstalk (wr 1,030,000) (London) 9.7.94
> Lantern Radio (wr not available) (North Devon) 10.7.94
> Swansea Sound (wr 180,000) (Swansea) no date given

Exhibit 6.14 *Continued*

Mix 96 (wr not available) (Aylesbury) no date given
BBC Radio Bristol (wr 266,000) (Bristol) 17.7.94

2.3 Sock Shop promotion

The Sock Shop competition runs until 31 July 1994, with several stores still carrying the promotional material. Entry levels are high at approximately 30–40 a day. VKPR has placed competitions to support the promotion in ten regional newspapers. The first five winners will receive a Sock Shop swimsuit and a Nivea Sun 400 ml water resistant SPF 15 lotion, with runners-up receiving product only.

2.4 *Today* Advertorial

It was agreed to place the advertorial in the launch issue of *Today*'s 'Saturday Review' section on 9 July 1994 to coincide with the beginning of the school holidays. The launch date included a 32-page full-colour supplement with only six pages of advertising, with a print run of 1 million. The issue featured two fashion spreads and a double page spread on the history of the bikini.

Following publication of the advertorial, VKPR liaised with *Today* newspaper regarding the poor quality of production. *Today* have agreed to run the advertorial again; however, this is to include a transparency of the tan planner rather than a scan.

VKPR is currently liaising with the newspaper for a confirmed appearance date.

2.5 KISS kits

All offers are sold in and confirmed, with the exception of *Essentials* which has cancelled its offer page in the scheduled issue. VKPR is currently sourcing an alternative magazine to feature the offer at short notice. The offers are scheduled as follows:

Chat (circ.: 500,000) July 35 kits
Family Circle (circ.: 339,000) August 35 kits
Prima (circ.: 739,000) August 30 kits
Maternity and Mothercraft (circ.: 150,000) August 17 kits

2.6 Sensitive Souls

VKPR have confirmed placement of the offers in the August issues with Sensitive Souls T-Shirt, black book and product. The promotion in *Chat* (circ.: 500,000) appeared in the July issue and was allocated a whole page.

Best (circ.: 630,000) August 80 kits
Woman's Own (circ.: 728,703) August 40 kits
Me (circ.: 359,498) August 40 kits

VKPR has placed five offers for Nivea Sun Sensitive Hydro-lotions in SPF 8 and SPF 16 and an After-sun Hydro-lotion in the following regional papers:

Eastbourne Herald (circ.: 30,000) – value £200 (10 sets)
Torquay Herald Express (circ.: 30,192) – value £200 (10 sets)
North Cornwall Advertiser (circ.: 35,000) – value £200 (10 sets)
Lytham St Anne's Citizen (circ.: 102,000) – value £200 (10 sets)
Colchester Evening Gazette (circ.: 29,730) – value £200 (10 sets)

2.7 Weather sponsorship opportunities

VKPR has liaised with the Met. Office regarding the sponsorship of their UV weather forecast.

The Problem

Gilbert had quite a few issues on her mind. How could she evaluate the effectiveness of previous marketing expenditures? What further information or analysis would she need in the medium term to make better judgements about marketing resource allocation? What specific marketing activites should she propose for 1995? Were there any other types of activity she should investigate for the medium term? For instance, a friend who worked in ice-cream in the USA had mentioned temperature-triggered radio advertisements. Meanwhile she had to get a draft marketing plan together based on the information available. She had just four weeks. As a start she drew up a broad summary of the 1994 budget she had inherited and a similar pro-forma for 1995 (Exhibit 6.15). Her main task over the next four weeks would be to propose some credible numbers for the blank spaces in the pro-forma.

Exhibit 6.15 *Nivea budget proposals*

	1994 £000	Baseline 1995 £000	Proposed 1995 £000
Sales volume (equivalent units)	100		
Price index	100	103.5	
Gross revenue[a] (1)	6,978		
Production cost/unit	100	103.8	
Production cost (2)	3,069		
Gross contribution before marketing costs (1) − (2)	3,909		
Media:			
TV	1,231		
Press	435		
Other	5		
Total media	1,671		
Consumer promotions			
GWP	468		
PWP	102		
Total consumer promotions	570		
Trade promotions	273		
Public relations	128		
Total marketing expenditures (3)	2,642		
Gross contribution after marketing costs (1) − (2) − (3)	1,267		

Baseline assumptions: Proposal assumptions:

[a] Sales to trade. Previous sales figures represent sales to consumers. Trade mark-ups account for the difference.

GEDAS Ltd

Mike Elsas, Walter van Waterschoot and Liesbeth Wuyts
University of Antwerp, Belgium

Introduction

In the early 1980s, a small group of young, dynamic people decided to try their luck as entrepreneurs and to set up their own planning, design and engineering firm. This was the start of GEDAS Ltd. They planned to offer high-quality engineering services, focusing mainly on such basic industrial techniques as electricity, mechanics, piping, etc. These services would be provided to local industries in the Antwerp region and especially to companies whose activities are geared to the harbour. Examples of services offered are the design of production and assembly lines, of pipelines and of air ducts. GEDAS's customers include several large companies in the Antwerp area, for example General Motors and Sidmar. Up till now, GEDAS has focused mainly on drawing and design. Internally trained employees are delegated to the clients and supported by a drawing and design department.

The business turned out to be successful, and the GEDAS management soon decided to reconsider their original ambition to stay a small local company. They expanded their activities to the field of construction and infrastructure. This move took place in 1984, with the acquisition of half of the staff of the bankrupt study firm Peters, located in Geel. For these activities, a separate corporation was founded: GEDAS CI (Construction and Infrastructure). Initially, most of GEDAS CI's orders came from local authorities (e.g. for the design of sports facilities, roads and sewerage systems).

GEDAS CI still works for several municipalities and numerous government agencies. However, it increasingly accepts assignments from private enterprises, in the more general construction field: stability studies, design of sanitary fittings, etc.

This case was prepared in 1992 in the framework of a case project at the UFSIA MBA programme of the University of Antwerp, sponsored by the National Bank of Belgium. It is intended as a basis of class discussion rather than to illustrate either effective or ineffective handling of an administrative situation.

More recently, GEDAS CI has started operating in the environmental projects sector. Currently, for instance, the firm plays a key role in the planning of a number of projects for Aquafin,[1] not only in the design of waste water collectors but also in the field of water treatment. GEDAS CI executes full projects (price calculation, planning and guidance) as well as partial ones. If desired, its intervention can be limited to technical support and implementation of the studies in the executive phase. In most of the cases, though, GEDAS is charged with the entire coordination of a project.

The GEDAS Group has grown tremendously during its ten-year existence (see Exhibit 7.1). Turnover has increased almost fivefold during this period, from BF56 million[2] in 1982 to BF253 million in 1991 (not including Smits) (see Exhibit 7.2).

Exhibit 7.1   *The GEDAS Group*

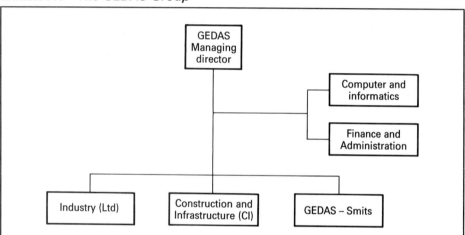

Exhibit 7.2   *GEDAS Group: evolution of turnover*

	GEDAS Ltd. BF million	CI BF million	Smits BF million	Total BF million
1982	56.7	–	–	56.7
1983	69.3	–	–	69.3
1984	91.5	–	–	91.5
1985	106.6	8.6	–	115.2
1986	123.3	14.0	–	137.3
1987	123.0	14.2	–	137.2
1988	129.8	19.3	–	164.9
1989	150.4	28.4	–	193.9
1990	156.2	42.1	–	228.9
1991	166.0	87.5	50.0	303.5

In 1987 this rapid growth forced them to move to a more spacious site where they could group a number of activities. They found a new site in the business centre Galliford in Deurne. At present, the group's headquarters is situated here, as well as all the staff divisions and the entire GEDAS Ltd corporation (Exhibit 7.3). GEDAS CI (Exhibit 7.4) is located partly in Deurne and partly at the company site

Exhibit 7.3 *GEDAS Ltd*

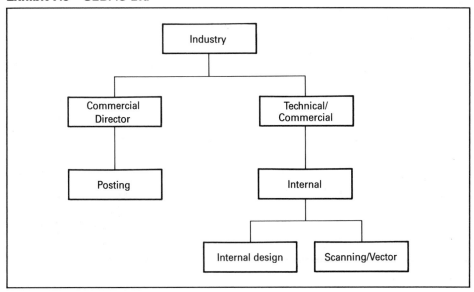

Exhibit 7.4 *GEDAS CI*

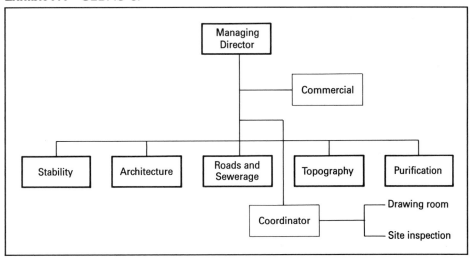

in Kortenberg. In early 1992, the staff of GEDAS Ltd numbered 80. GEDAS CI employed about 30 people, divided into 'responsibility centres'.[3]

From very early on, GEDAS Ltd, as well as GEDAS CI, started using CAD software (computer-aided design) for drawing and design. In 1990, because of the increasing computerization within the sector and the experience accumulated by GEDAS in the field of CAD applications, the company was asked several times to accept CAD consultancy assignments. The GEDAS management saw these requests as a unique opportunity for expansion that they could not afford to pass up. One of GEDAS's most important competitors had already decided to expand in the field of CAD, and GEDAS did not want to risk lagging behind. Out of three options (do nothing, start a CAD department within the existing GEDAS structure, or take over a software producer), the management chose the last, and in 1991 GEDAS purchased Smits Soft, a company located in Ghent.

GEDAS–Smits

Smits Soft was a reasonably well-known software and hardware supplier. It had developed its activities in two main fields: custom-made software and CAD application software (see Exhibit 7.5). All the packages developed by Smits Soft were developed as applications for the AutoCAD program, which was known as the industrial standard (the producer of AutoCAD, Autodesk, was the market leader). Smits Soft had succeeded in developing a program, Mechmenu, that increased the performance of AutoCAD by 20 per cent. (Before the takeover, GEDAS did not use AutoCAD, but Avill which performed 15 per cent faster than AutoCAD.) The combination Mechmenu and AutoCAD still turned out to be 5 per cent faster.

GEDAS was interested mainly in the CAD application software developed by Smits and wanted to run down the production of custom-made software. However, GEDAS still wanted to offer turnkey projects (i.e. advice, training, soft- and hardware, etc.) based on these CAD applications. The management realized that this would entail a comprehensive training programme for the staff. The turnkey approach means that clients should be able to consult GEDAS for all kinds of problem: 'We have always aspired to be a partner for our clients, rather than being an occasional supplier. A partner who comes up with solutions, who talks his client's language.'

By March 1992, GEDAS–Smits had already succeeded in refining the existing software and in increasing its performance. Around that time, they were also adjusting the existing programs to meet the requirements of the diverse fields of CAD application (mechanics, electronics, piping, etc.) In the meantime, they changed the name Mechmenu (this software package initially served only mechanical applications) to Multimenu, since the first name was too much associated with the mechanical applications, while it was now possible to run other packages on this menu as well.

Exhibit 7.5 *Supply-side of the CAD market*

Product supplier	Connected with a system	Independent of any system	Software Standard (adapted for <25%)	Software Application (adapted for >25%)	Consultancy
Type 1	✔		✔	✔	
Type 2	✔		✔	✔	
Type 3	✔		✔	✔	✔
Type 4		✔			✔
Type 5	✔		✔		

The supply-side of the CAD market can be divided into different segments, distinguished by the kind of supply:

Type 1 Hard and software suppliers that are specialized in one particular system. They focus mainly on one kind of computer, database and/or application. Some packages, for instance, work exclusively with DB 2.

Type 2 Suppliers of turnkey projects who supply hardware as well as software. The role of general supplier can be assumed by the hardware as well as by the software supplier.

Type 3 Suppliers of CAD applications who sell software that is developed by adaptation of a standard package that was supplied by a third party. These firms are often affiliated to suppliers of CAD packages.

Type 4 Consultants in the field of CAD systems who render support for an entire project – for the hardware as well as for the software. These firms are mostly independent of any hardware or software.

Type 5 Suppliers of CAD software who adapt a standard package to a particular industrial application and subsequently market it under their own name.

Software

The supplied software can also be divided into several types:

• *CAD packages.* These include (original) standard packages or standard packages which are adapted for, at most, 25 per cent of the specific customer's requirements. In most cases, these packages are not restricted to one supplier. AutoCAD is an example of a widespread standard package. Almost 50 per cent of all companies work with this software.

• *CAD basic packages.* These are packages used as a basis for the development of CAD applications. These are supplied mostly by hardware suppliers who develop specific hardware for CAD applications. The hardware and the basic package are usually purchased together.

• *CAD applications.* This is software developed especially for a particular company or industry.

Besides Multimenu, GEDAS–Smits had developed a mechanical application program, Mechsoft (consisting of a number of libraries, a toolkit and automatic part list creation) and they had reached the final stage in the development of Elsoft, a program for electro-technical applications. Moreover, plans existed for the development of Pidsoft (piping applications).

At the end of March 1992 GEDAS–Smits had not yet succeeded in fully exploiting the intended synergy between Smits Soft on the one hand and GEDAS

Ltd and CI on the other. Smits' customers were mainly smaller firms, and the company was less known by GEDAS's target group, which consisted of larger firms. Moreover, Smits did not appear to project the expected quality image. On the contrary, the name Smits tended to be associated with down-market products. Therefore, the GEDAS management decided to change the existing name. Initially, the name Smits had been preserved because the previous owner and founder, Mr C. Smits, still worked in the company and still owned a 10 per cent share. Later, however, Mr Smits had left the company and had sold his share to GEDAS.

To strengthen the association with the GEDAS Group, GEDAS–Automatisering (Automation, in translation) was considered a plausible name. Indeed, when Smits Soft had been presented as GEDAS–Smits in October 1991, this had almost immediately resulted in an increased interest from the larger companies. However, the outcome of the change of name could not be predicted because the management did not know how the existing customers of Smits Soft would react if confronted with a new name. Still, the decision had to be taken soon, all the more so because an advertising campaign for Multimenu had been planned for April.

The structure of GEDAS–Smits (Exhibit 7.6) had not been fully defined by March 1992, but the intention was to divide the commerical department (under the direction of Mr Ludo Smans) into direct sales (to end-users) and indirect sales (to distributors or dealers). Two salespeople were available full-time for direct sales. For indirect sales, Mr Smans planned to hire someone new.

Products and Competition

At the end of March 1992, GEDAS–Smits sold two types of product – turnkey projects and CAD software – each of which needed a different marketing approach.

Exhibit 7.6   *GEDAS–Smits organizational structure*

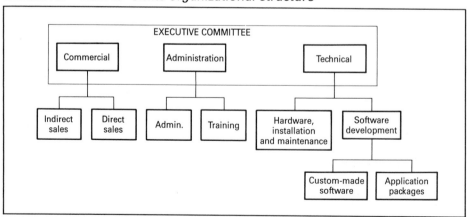

Turnkey Projects

Turnkey projects include the supply of particular CAD hardware and software, attuned to the specific needs of the client. They also comprise training of the staff, technical support, maintenance of the installations, etc. The existing know-how of the planning, design and engineering firm (GEDAS Ltd) is a major competitive advantage in this respect. Other important advantages consist in their expertise in the use of CAD software and in their internally designed software products. If, for example, the client is a planning and design firm in the construction sector, GEDAS can compare the needs of this client with their own needs and experience, and they can start from their own CAD applications to meet the client's needs.

CAD (Application) Software

These are universal CAD software packages, focused on one specific area like mechanics, electricity or piping. They are all designed to fit the basic program AutoCAD, and can be used by everyone who possesses this program and the appropriate hardware. Besides their internally designed packages Multimenu, Mechsoft, Elsoft and, in the near future, Pidsoft, GEDAS–Smits also distributes AED (which transforms two-dimensional into three-dimensional drawings) and GTXRasterCAD (scanning of existing drawings). Moreover, GEDAS–Smits is an authorized AutoCAD dealer.

The software package Multimenu consists of a large number of modular drawing routines and standard libraries. It makes use of the user-friendly tablet menu and is designed to be applied in combination with AutoCAD. It has an open structure, so that all application programs sold by GEDAS can make use of the Multimenu facilities (Exhibit 7.7).

Multimenu is quite unique. In March 1992, there were only two other packages which approximated to it in terms of functionality: Genius, a product developed by the German engineering factory and software developer Baumann GmbH, and Mechslide, a product of the Swedish Company EMT BA. Both these products had been developed shortly before as mechanical CAD applications for AutoCAD, and they quickly succeeded in building up a broad client base. However, they both show one or more shortcomings compared with the combination of Multimenu and Mechsoft. Of the three products, only Multimenu offers extended layer possibilities as well as standard project management and an open structure.

GEDAS made Multimenu and Mechsoft as two separate products, because the first one is a basic package that can be used not only for mechanical but also for other applications. Mechsoft is a mechanical application program that makes use of the facilities of this basic package. It consists of two components (toolkit and part list generation) and a number of libraries.

Elsoft is a revolutionary package for electro-technical applications and, like all other GEDAS packages, it is based on AutoCAD. It is fully compatible with Multimenu and its libraries. Elsoft was still not available in March 1992, although it had already been presented to the public in 1991, at a CAD/CAM exhibition. Despite its not yet being fully developed, the package has been generally admired. Elsoft has two rivals: SchemaCAD from BNS (which is the market leader with this program) and Elschem from the Dutch company TOPCAD. Elschem, however, is largely outdated.

Prices and Discounts

Most producers of CAD (application) software apply fixed dealer prices and recommend end-user prices. Distribution margins are traditionally quite high. They are expressed mostly as a discount on the recommended end-user prices. The distributor/wholesaler's margin amounts to 20 per cent, and that of the dealer up to 40 per cent. Consequently, per unit sold, the producer receives only about 40 per cent of the end-user price. The size of these margins is based on those for standard packages like Autodesk (AutoCAD). Autodesk uses a system of functional discounts. This means that the margins vary between 15 and 50 per cent, depending on the service level of the different dealers. Also the yearly turnover as well as the cumulative turnover will explain differences in margins (see Exhibit 7.8). The overall magnitude of these margins is the result of the considerable added-value that retailers have to provide (training, support, etc.). Sometimes a part of the margin is transferred to the customer by way of a discount on the purchase price.

Exhibit 7.7   *Multimenu*

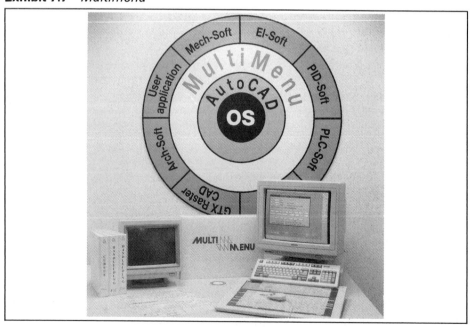

Exhibit 7.7 *Continued*

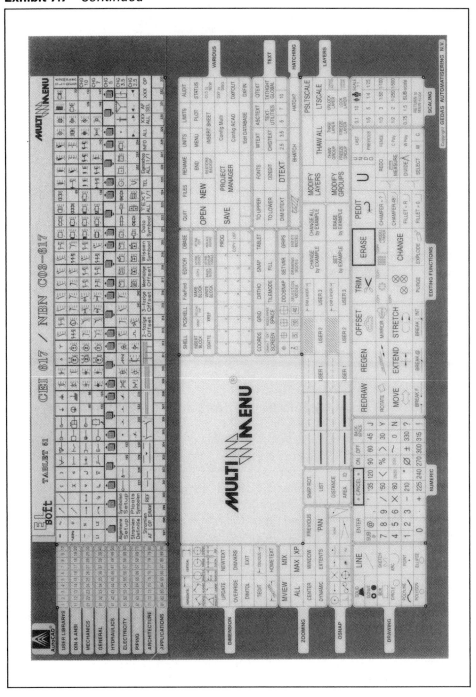

Exhibit 7.8 *Functional discount system AutoCAD*

Type of dealer	Commercial %	Education %
Aspirant	15	0
Authorized AutoCAD	30	20
AutoCAD System Centre 1	40	40
AutoCAD System Centre 2	45	40
AutoCAD System Centre 3	50	40

In spite of the generally supposed margin structure, GEDAS knew for sure only the end-user prices of its competitors. At that time, Genius (BF105,000) and Mechslide (BF95,000) were offered at comparable prices. GEDAS sold the combination Multimenu/Mechsoft at a price that was about 50 per cent higher than that of its competitors (BF150,000). Mr Jan Smans[4] justified this difference by the greater technical possiblilities offered by GEDAS's software package. GEDAS did consider offering cheaper varsions, possibly with a smaller number of libraries, according to the specific needs of the client. Elschem (competing package for Elsoft) was sold at a retail price of BF90,000, Schemacad at a somewhat higher price of BF130,000. For Elsoft, GEDAS considered a retail price of BF175,000. This price difference was also explained by the greater technical possibilities of the program.

Distribution Strategy for the Netherlands

At the end of March 1992, GEDAS–Smits was still seeking a suitable distribution strategy. It was especially looking for the best way to distribute its products on the Dutch market. The decision regarding distribution in Flanders had already been made: the products would be supplied directly to the end-user from GEDAS's own outlets.[5] It was not possible to supply the Dutch market directly from the Belgian outlets simply because it was too far away. A survey of the Dutch CAD market in 1990 showed that 60 per cent of the end-users were willing to travel up to twenty-five kilometres to purchase hardware and software. Thirty per cent would go fifty kilometres and only 10 per cent would travel one hundred kilometres.

The figures of this survey confirmed the impressions of Jan and Ludo Smans after talks with clients and dealers at a CAD/CAM trade fair about five months previously. For the two brothers, these figures constituted an important point to be considered in setting up a separate distribution network for the Netherlands. Besides that, they also had other kinds of information on the Dutch market, its distribution structure, consumer behaviour and the distribution strategy of GEDAS's competitors. See Exhibit 7.9.

Exhibit 7.9 *Composition of the sample in the Dutch CAD survey, 1990*

		\multicolumn{5}{c}{Number of employees}				
		10–20	20–50	50–100	100+	Total
Metallurgical/metal-using industry	N	–	819	393	193	1,407
	n	–	20	20	15	55
Electro-technical industry	N	–	97	65	34	196
	n	–	20	10	10	40
Engineering and architectural firms	N	229	267	84	52	632
	n	27	20	10	10	67
Construction and installation firms	N	1,250	1,733	688	291	3,962
	n	32	25	20	15	92
Utility companies and communalities	N	–	201	135	160	496
	n	–	20	21	10	51
Total: N		1,479	3,117	1,365	732	6,693
n		59	105	81	60	305

N = Population; n = Net sample.
Only companies with a computer system of their own are included in the sample.

Existing Distribution Channels

At first sight, the Dutch market shows a classical distribution structure. The top of the distribution channel consists of a large number of importers. Underneath is a limited number of distributors: Topcad, Pollux and Datech, who in turn sell their products to a large number of dealers and subdealers. At present, there are about fifty possible dealers of CAD products in the Netherlands, fifteen of which are large companies representing about 60 per cent of total turnover. This results from the fact that larger CAD users use mainly the large dealers; sometimes, they even buy directly from the wholesaler/distributor. Smaller users of CAD soft- and hardware make greater use of local dealers or subdealers.

However, this distribution structure is not clearly defined. Some of the distributors also act as importers for some of the products in their product range, and some dealers also develop software packages themselves. Moreover, groups and holdings are intertwined: Teser, one of the larger dealers, for example, belongs to the same group as the distributor TopCAD. Another dealer, Greenock BV, is a part of the holding that also controlls Pollux.

The function of distributor is currently under a great deal of pressure. Within the sector, the future of this function is increasingly being questioned. Traditionally, the distributor has always supplied standard software packages, like the AutoCAD program, hardware and diverse application software. Yet, for a good while now, most large dealers have bought all hardware directly from the importers. Moreover, the producer of AutoCAD, Autodesk, whose policy is seen as authoritative within the sector, has recently decided to change its distribution strategy. During 1992, Autodesk will introduce the AutoCAD System Centre program. Based on a number of selection criteria concerning quality, service and added-value (training, support and development of program), the company will select about ten large dealers who will be offered the chance to place their orders directly with Autodesk instead of with a distributor, with considerable discounts of up to 50 per cent. Moreover, these dealers can supply directly to the major accounts and will have priority for information about products and pre-release software. All these changes are certain to have a considerable impact on the future of the distributors in the Netherlands.

Two of the typical functions of a dealer are training and support for the products that he or she supplies. Consequently, the products must be known in detail. Autodesk has made a classification of several types of its dealers (aspirant, authorized, System Centre 1, System Centre 2 and System Centre 3 – see Exhibit 7.10) and has matched this to a system of functional discounts. In that way, all dealers are rewarded according to the level of service that they provide.

The typical product range of a dealer is quite limited. They usually sell only a few software packages and a small hardware range. Many dealers divide the CAD hard- and software into the following three groups:

1. Products whose functioning the dealer knows in detail and for which he can provide training and support. Often, these products are also used internally.

2. Products of comparable quality to those above but less known by the dealer. These are supplied on specific demand from a client, but the service level cannot be as high as for the first category.

3. The remaining products which are considered to be of insufficient quality. They are not included in the product range and are never supplied, not even on specific demand from the client.

Concerning the range of products sold, a distinction can be made between large and small dealers. Since the dealer is expected to render additional services for each package from the range, only the large ones can afford to carry several standard packages and hardware environments, whereas smaller dealers have to confine themselves to one of each. A typical example of a large retailer is Greenock BV, the exclusive dealer of the Genius program in the Netherlands. As far as hardware is concerned, Greenock confined itself to MS-DOS, OS/2 and Unix; with respect to CAD software, it supplies only AutoCAD, CADAM (IBM) and CATIA (IBM). In addition, Greenock carries a broad range of application software. Through its subsidiaries in Utrecht, Eindhoven and Enschede, it takes care of the entire implementation, service and support of the systems. For the Genius-package, Greenock supplies the complete CAD system, including AutoCAD and Genius, the installation and implementation, support and the necessary courses. Moreover, it offers assistance in adapting Genius to the specific demands of the client.

According to Ludo and Jan Smans, a typical distribution policy for the

Exhibit 7.10 *AutoCAD System Centre program (extract)*

Selection criteria and conditions for authorized AutoCAD dealers

Authorized AutoCAD dealers have to:

B1. Sell at least 8 full commercial copies of AutoCAD per twelve months.
B2. Employ at least 1 qualified and trained sales assistant and 1 qualified and trained support assistant, who can:

- demonstrate Autodesk products and applications;
- compose, test and demonstrate configurations;
- explain installation and service requirements.

B3. Finance the training of their personnel themselves.
B4. Be able to offer, sell and support at least 1 specific software complement of AutoCAD.
B5. Offer sufficient space for the display and demonstration of Autodesk products.
B6. Take care of a demonstration system that is permanently available and operational.
B7. Be an authorized dealer of an acknowledged hardware supplier.
B8. Submit a yearly business plan.
B9. Be able to mention at least 2 names of companies where the dealer has delivered products to the client's satisfaction.
B10. Be prepared and able to deliver installation services to the client, before as well as after sales.
B11. Be prepared and able to offer training to the client, before as well as after sales.
B12. Be able to submit a written recommendation from one of the Autodesk distributors.
B13. Have their own administration, as well as procedures for purchase, sales, marketing and support activities.

Selection criteria and conditions for AutoCAD System Centres

C1. Meet the conditions for authorized AutoCAD dealers.
C2. Have been an authorized dealer for at least twenty-four successive months.
C3. Sell at least 32 full commercial copies per twelve months.
C4. Employ at least 2 sales assistants and 2 support assistants per location.
C5. Be able to offer, sell and support at least two specific software complements to AutoCAD.
C6. Be able to mention at least 20 names of companies where the dealer has delivered products to the client's satisfaction.
C7. Be prepared and able to offer installation services to the client, before as well as after sales. The dealer has to do this indpendently and from his or her own financial resources.
C8. Have a telephonic support facility during working hours.
C9. Be prepared and able to offer training to the client (independently and from his or her own financial resources), before as well as after sales.
C10. Possess permanent training facilities under his or her direct control.
C11. Be able to adapt or extend Autodesk software to the wishes of the client (independently, from his or her own financial resources and with his own people).

Selection criteria and conditions for AutoCAD System Centres Level 2.

D1. Fulfill all the conditions of B and C.
D2. Sell at least 60 full commercial copies AutoCAD per twelve months.
D3. Fulfil one of the following conditions:

Continued over ▶

Exhibit 7.10 *Continued*

- more than 50 per cent of the AutoCADS are sold in combination with an application program;
- more than 50 per cent of the AutoCADS are sold together with another Autodesk product;
- more than 50 per cent of the AutoCADS are sold on a platform different from MS-DOS;
- development of ADS application under the dealer's own control;
- growth of turnover in Autodesk products is more than 35 per cent per year.

D4. Be able to submit an elaborated plan for the acquisition of an ISO-9000X certificate.

Selection criteria and conditions for AutoCAD System Centres Level 3

E1. Fulfil the conditions of B, C and D.
E2. Sell at least 150 full commercial copies of AutoCAD per twelve months.
E3. Try to acquire an ISO-9000X certificate.
E4. Be an associate member of the Belgian Software Association (BSA).

---

producers does not exist. Most of them make use of a distributor, who supplies the products to a number of dealers that have been chosen by himself. Other producers skip the wholesaler's/distributor's function and supply directly to a limited number of carefully selected dealers. Another frequently used policy is exclusive distribution.

Other Market Characteristics

Besides these data, GEDAS possessed information about the CAD market in the Netherlands. It knew for instance, that about 50 per cent of all computer systems on which a CAD package is implemented are purchased as turnkey projects, i.e. computer, software and terminal equipment together (see Exhibit 7.11).

From the market survey from 1990, the Smans brothers knew that 25 per cent of users in the Netherlands intended to invest in CAD software within the next three years. The average amount of money that they expected to invest in this period was DFl41,000[6] per subsidiary. In large companies (100 staff) these investment plans amounted to DFl63,000 (see Exhibit 7.12).

The same survey also mentioned the criteria and influences that are important in choosing CAD hardware and software. The most important criterion turned out to be the user friendliness offered by the system. The purchase price appeared to be of less importance than expected (see Exhibit 7.13). According to the survey, the employees have a considerable impact on the choice of a system, as does word of mouth communication regarding the experiences of other companies. Other influencing factors are advertisements and visits to computer exhibitions (see Exhibit 7.14).

Exhibit 7.11 *Purchasing context of CAD systems*

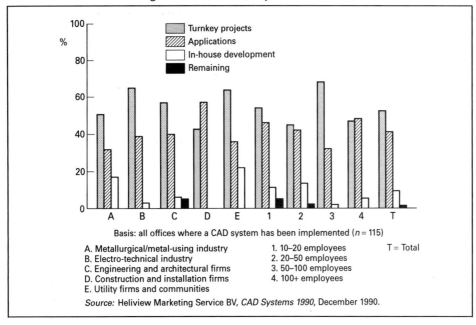

Basis: all offices where a CAD system has been implemented (*n* = 115)

A. Metallurgical/metal-using industry   1. 10–20 employees   T = Total
B. Electro-technical industry   2. 20–50 employees
C. Engineering and architectural firms   3. 50–100 employees
D. Construction and installation firms   4. 100+ employees
E. Utility firms and communities

Source: Heliview Marketing Service BV, *CAD Systems 1990*, December 1990.

Exhibit 7.12 *Investment plans with regard to CAD software*

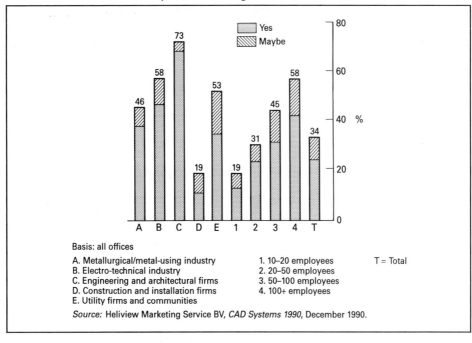

Basis: all offices

A. Metallurgical/metal-using industry   1. 10–20 employees   T = Total
B. Electro-technical industry   2. 20–50 employees
C. Engineering and architectural firms   3. 50–100 employees
D. Construction and installation firms   4. 100+ employees
E. Utility firms and communities

Source: Heliview Marketing Service BV, *CAD Systems 1990*, December 1990.

Exhibit 7.13 *Selection criteria for the purchase of CAD applications*

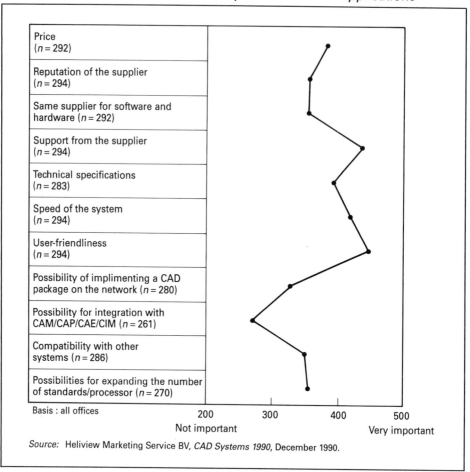

Price
(*n* = 292)

Reputation of the supplier
(*n* = 294)

Same supplier for software and
hardware (*n* = 292)

Support from the supplier
(*n* = 294)

Technical specifications
(*n* = 283)

Speed of the system
(*n* = 294)

User-friendliness
(*n* = 294)

Possibility of implimenting a CAD
package on the network (*n* = 280)

Possibility for integration with
CAM/CAP/CAE/CIM (*n* = 261)

Compatibility with other
systems (*n* = 286)

Possibilities for expanding the number
of standards/processor (*n* = 270)

Basis : all offices

200   300   400   500

Not important   Very important

Source: Heliview Marketing Service BV, *CAD Systems 1990,* December 1990.

Exhibit 7.14 *Factors influencing the decision to purchase a particular software package*

Other companies	37%
Consulting agencies	9%
Educational institutes	2%
Wishes of the employees	72%
Training	14%
Advertisements, exhibitions, etc.	34%
Software supplier	35%
Hardware supplier	19%

TopCAD's Proposal

Although the Smans brothers had a substantial amount of information, their choice of a suitable distribution strategy for the Netherlands was not made easier. Numerous questions kept them busy, until the Dutch company TopCAD made GEDAS an attractive offer for the distribution of Elsoft.

TopCAD was the owner and distributor of the Elschem program. It had purchased this program from the dealer/producer Teser, which belonged to the same group as TopCAD. However, Elschem had been developed quite a few years previously and was now outdated in terms of functionality.

The management of TopCAD had first noticed Elsoft at the CAD/CAM exhibition in October 1990, where the program had been presented to the public for the first time. The management of TopCAD was so impressed by the possibilities of Elsoft, that they had decided to make GEDAS an exceptional offer.

Ludo and Jan Smans were surprised when they heard of this offer, since TopCAD was a widely known distributor of CAD products in the Netherlands and cooperated closely with a number of large (e.g. Teser) and smaller dealers. TopCAD proposed to distribute the Elsoft program exclusively in Benelux, under the name Elschem, as an update of its own outdated product. Per package sold, GEDAS would receive about 40 per cent of the end-user price as a compensation.

This would mean that GEDAS would be assured of a market of some three hundred end-users, and hence immediately obtain a considerable market penetration which would normally take months or even years to achieve. Moreover, the presence of this 'installed base' ensured GEDAS ample coverage of the development costs of the program. The program would be sold for BF55,000, which is remarkably less than the BF175,000 that GEDAS had considered. The reason for this is that the price of an update can be maximally 60 per cent of the price of the original product (the original Elschem's price was BF90,000). Although this price seems low, a 40 per cent margin on a total of three hundred packages sold still means an income of BF6,600,000, which greatly exceeds the development costs of Elsoft.

Accepting the offer would imply that GEDAS need no longer search for suitable dealers. This would mean a substantial decrease in personal sales effort. Moreover, promotion and publicity efforts would be reduced, since TopCAD proposed to handle all the promotion and publicity costs for launching the program (BF3 million during the first year and BF1.5 million during the following years). The TopCAD proposal also implied a possible entry into the CAD market in the UK, since TopCAD had a subsidiary there.

The Smans brothers wondered whether they should accept TopCAD's offer. What about Multimenu? They also needed to work out a distribution strategy for this latter package. Ludo Smans knew a number of dealers from the Netherlands that were interested in purchasing Multimenu directly from GEDAS, but he wondered if it would not be better to distribute all software through the same dealers.

In the meantime, GEDAS had already initiated a publicity campaign for Multimenu. Because of this, they had to make a decision about the change of name:

in the future, GEDAS–Smits would be called GEDAS–Automatisering. The campaign was meant firstly to create product familiarity for Multimenu, and secondly to generate a number of leads by means of an information slip that has to be filled in and sent back to GEDAS. In addition, perhaps some dealers would turn out to be interested after reading the advertisement.

Notes

1.   Aquafin is a holding which deals with water treatment in Flanders. Participants in this private holding include the English company Severn Trent.
2.   In 1992, the average exchange rate was BF1 = £0.0176.
3.   GEDAS CI is organized as a number of substructures, each focused on a particular application and managed as a separate organization, which explains the name 'responsibility centres'.
4.   Jan Smans is the younger brother of Ludo Smans (the managing director of GEDAS). He joined GEDAS a few years ago to assume the financial and administrative control. Before, he had used his training as a commercial engineer in diverse administrative and informatics-orientated functions in an important electronics multinational.
5.   The GEDAS Group has four outlets: Deurne (Antwerp), Geel, Ghent and Kortenberg.
6.   In 1992, the average exchange rate was DFl1 = £0.323.

CASE 8

Marks & Spencer

Maureen Whitehead
Manchester Metropolitan University, UK

Company History

Marks & Spencer started in Leeds in 1884 when Michael Marks, a Russian immigrant, set up a penny bazaar from which no item cost more than one penny. Ten years later, Tom Spencer joined Michael Marks in partnership. By 1901 the business had twelve shops and two dozen stalls in covered markets. This growth continued until 1926, by which time the business was operating from 125 stores. At this point the company changed its status to that of a public company. The families of the founding members played a key role in the development of Marks & Spencer for the next fifty-eight years until, for the first time, in 1984, a non-family chairman and chief executive was appointed as successor to Lord Sieff (Michael Marks' grandson). By the 1980s the company had more than three hundred thousand shareholders and was one of the UK's leading retailers of food, men's, women's and children's fashion. These products formed the core business together with home furnishings, accessories and financial services which were introduced in 1985.

Marks & Spencer has been built on a philosophy of:

1. Offering customers a selective range of high-quality merchandise.
2. Encouraging suppliers to maintain high-quality standards in production and working environments.
3. Store expansion planned for the convenience of customers with a greater width of product choice.
4. Simplified operating procedures.
5. Fostering good human relations with customers, staff, suppliers and the community.
6. Supporting British industry and buying abroad only when new ideas, technology, quality and value are not available in the UK.

All merchandise sold through the UK operation carries the brand name St Michael. Whilst own-label is the key element of leading UK retailers' merchandise offering, no other company brand name has been as successful. City analysts see the company as the most financially solid of the UK retailers and it is the only retailer in the world to carry a triple-A rating.

Marks & Spencer UK and Eire

Merchandise Mix

Fashion
Although declining as a percentage of total turnover, clothing accounted for 49 per cent of domestic sales in 1990[1] and has traditionally been the company's core business. The merchandise ranges are based on quality and fashion content which lasts for more than one season, aimed at a broad consumer base. Quality and value for money is the consumer image of the company's merchandise. Product ranges cover all age groups from babywear upwards. The company faces little competition from other UK variety chains such as British Home Stores and Littlewoods, but individual departments face competition from speciality retailers such as Next for Men and Burton Group's Principles.

Food
Marks & Spencer is the sixth largest food retailer in the UK according to analysts Smith Barney,[2] operating a high margin, low market share business in food. Few basic commodities are on offer, but a quality range of fresh produce, together with an innovative range of chilled convenience foods (ready prepared meals) and a narrow selection of wines form the basic merchandise offer. Food accounted for approximately 38 per cent of total turnover in 1990.

Other areas
The mid-1980s saw the company develop a new strategic direction in the UK through its diversification into financial services, home furnishings and the launch of a physical modernization programme adding close to one million square feet in selling space between 1986 and 1988. The end of the 1980s saw a move to out-of-town developments. Increasing competition amongst UK food retailers for sites within the UK resulted in the development of cooperative joint agreements for site development with Tesco for edge-of-town sites. The first joint site opened in Cheshunt, Hertfordshire, in 1987. The stores share parking facilities but compete with one another on-site.

Organizational Structure

Marks & Spencer conforms to the typical centralized structure which is a feature of UK multiple retailers. The business is highly centralized. Buying decisions are made centrally and goods then distributed to stores. A uniform pricing policy exists in the UK which supports the company's returns policy whereby goods purchased at one store can be returned to another store. The company has no manufacturing capacity in the UK and is a pure retail business. The strength of its relationships with suppliers, many of which are UK-based, enables Marks & Spencer to operate on the lines of a vertically integrated company.[3]

International Strategic Development

Having reached a position of dominance in the UK market after almost nine decades of trading, Marks & Spencer was faced with three strategic options for future business development:

1. Creating new formats.
2. Diversifying into other business areas.
3. Expanding overseas.

Creating new formats appeared to be the least attractive strategy, as diversification had already taken place in two new product areas: financial services and furnishings.

Any diversification into new business areas unrelated to the core business would be a high-risk strategy as the company's strength lay in building on the existing core business. Consequently, the outcome of this search for new growth was that in the early 1970s the company chairman at the time, Lord Sieff, decided to commit Marks & Spencer to a policy of further growth based on overseas expansion and the international development of the St Michael brand.

Development of an International Operation

Canada

The first steps in developing an international operation took place in the early 1970s, when Marks & Spencer acquired a 50 per cent shareholding in three Canadian chains: People's budget priced general merchandise stores, D'Allairds selling clothes for women over 40 and Walkers Clothing Stores which were redeveloped as smaller versions of Marks & Spencer UK stores. Three years after the initial share acquisition the company acquired controlling interest. By 1990 there were 76 Marks & Spencer, 80 People's and 119 D'Allairds stores in operation.

The Canadian operation consisted of three divisions, only one of which operated under the Marks & Spencer fascia selling Marks & Spencer merchandise. These stores were on average ten thousand square feet in size. Early attempts were made to expand the D'Allaird's division by opening four new stores in New York

State, but this proved unsuccessful. Subsequently, the trading performance of the Canadian division became the subject of press criticism. In 1989 the Marks & Spencer division made an operating loss of C$9.7 million, operating profits at D'Allaird's fell by C$5 million and operating losses increased in the People's division. In response to this poor trading performance, plans were introduced to broaden the divisions' ranges to appeal to a wider group of customers. This operating loss had followed a fourteen year period of slowly improving performance by the three divisions.

In the Marks & Spencer division of the Candian operation, productivity in some of the stores was poor because of the high rentals charged by most of the malls in which the company traded. Plans were also made to introduce UK software into the Marks & Spencer division in order to improve stock replenishment. At the same time, stores were being refurbished and new merchandising techniques were introduced. Two new stores opened in 1989 and two more were re-sited. The location of some of the Canadian stores was, in retrospect, less desirable than originally anticipated and the company adopted a policy of damage limitation in the Canadian market in the short term.

The decision to expand into the Canadian market had seemed a sensible decision at the time. In the UK, the stock market was low, the oil crisis had taken place two years earlier and prominent members of the Labour Party were suggesting that leading retailers would be an appropriate target for a future nationalization programme. The need to move funds to outside the UK appeared to be critical and Canada was seen to fulful many needs, being in the western hemisphere and having good labour relations, political stability and oil. Furthermore, a Canadian operation could be used as a springboard to the American market.

Development of Marks & Spencer Europe

Following the Canadian acquisitions, the company decided to turn its attention to Continental Europe and develop its own stores. France and Belgium were chosen as the countries from which to develop a European operation, as they were geographically close and stronger control and communication links could be maintained. The first store was opened in Paris in 1975 in one of the best known shopping streets in Paris, the Boulevard Haussmann, opposite two of France's leading department stores, Galerie Lafayette and Printemps. The merchandise mix in store consisted of core ranges of food, fashion, toiletries and gifts. Food ranges of typically British goods such as tea, marmalade and biscuits took up approximately 20 per cent of selling space.

In the same year a new store was opened in Brussels. European expansion continued slowly, with further stores opening in the French provinces and, seven years after the Brussels store opened, a second Belgian store was opened in Antwerp. Further stores were opened in the Paris area, some of which were located in commercial centres. This period of steady expansion continued throughout the

1980s and was followed by a more rapid rate of international growth, both across existing markets and into new markets.

In 1989 a decision was made to accelerate expansion of the French operation with more stores in the provinces, and to develop new stores in Spain and Holland. Prompting this expansion were three major factors:

1. The corporate ambition to become a more international retailer.

2. The belief that European harmonization was bringing about significant changes.

3. The success of the existing European stores.[4]

Market Entry Planning

In the planning stage of European expansion, the development team conducted an analysis of the strengths and weaknesses of the French operation which was then followed by an examination of the demographics, income levels and retail structures in potentially attractive markets, in particular Holland, Spain and Germany. The development team needed to assess the extent to which the Marks & Spencer corporate values would fit into the operating environment of these markets, the suitability of Marks & Spencer merchandise to the marketplace and the levels of customer service offered by existing and potential competitors.

Having conducted a strategic analysis in potential markets, a decision had to be made as to which was the best route by which to enter new markets which would sustain development on a wider European basis. Two main options were available: either to use the franchise group or to develop the company's own stores. In Spain there was a clear need to work with people with a good local market knowledge both for site selection and store operations.[5] This resulted in the agreement with Cortefiel, one of Spain's leading retail chains, to develop Marks & Spencer jointly in that country, thereby enabling the company to expand more rapidly in the Spanish market.

For the Dutch market, organic growth was identified as the mode of expansion most suited to the company's corporate objectives as, in part, the widespread use of the English language in Holland reduced any possible language problems and the business operating environment was believed to be more similar to that of the UK than were those of other European markets.

Having made the decision to accelerate European growth, the largest expansion programme to date for Marks & Spencer Europe was undertaken, creating 170,000 square feet of new selling space, bringing the total area to 535,000 square feet in seventeen stores.[6] Two new provincial stores (the first since 1982) were opened in France, a new store was opened in Liège in Belgium, the first Dutch store in Amsterdam and a second in Spain opened, followed by an additional store in Holland in The Hague. This brought the total number of stores in France to eleven, with the Haussmann store as the European flagship. Since first opening, the Haussmann store had been extended and modernized with a third floor being added, allowing the company to expand its product ranges, in particular home furnishings and certain food products.

Store Development Teams

The identification of new markets had been carried out by a team of senior managers whose role was to identify suitable sites by spending time in target countries in the major shopping areas, observing consumers' shopping habits and examining competitors' stores. Typical tasks in this process were to identify and understand any existing legislation, local customs and social legislation which would affect retail operations, for example in Holland, store opening hours are subject to regulation with a maximum of fifty-two hours a week trading. Once a new store had opened, multinational teams were then used to carry on its development. The need to understand national labour laws in practice has resulted in indigenous personnel managers being used in various parts of the European operation, as in Holland, France and Belgium.

Far East

The opening of the first Marks & Spencer store in Hong Kong in 1988 took place a year after the formation of the Far Eastern Development Group, whose objectives were:

1. To set up and run profitable stores in Hong Kong and other parts of the Far East.
2. Servicing Far East export customers.
3. Sourcing and buying merchandise to supplement existing supplies.[7]

The head of the development group was reported at the time as saying:

> The Marks & Spencer Far Eastern buying and sourcing team in close liaison with the UK, Canada and Europe is able to take advantage of the massive manufacturing capacity to supplement our existing sources servicing an ever widening catalogue to our expanding international business.[8]

By 1992 four Marks & Spencer stores were in operation.

Alongside the company's international pre-planned strategic growth in Europe, America, Canada and Asia – areas which had been identified as potential growth areas – the Marks & Spencer export group was at the same time increasing the volume of its exports in response to unsolicited orders from overseas businesses.

Financing International Growth

In order to support a strategy of international growth, a holding company had been set up by Marks & Spencer in the Netherlands in the 1970s. This holding company has controlled each overseas venture, with the exceptions of the USA and Spain. The benefit of the holding company was that it allowed dividends from various territories to be mixed in Holland before being repatriated to the UK: a standard procedure for managing tax liabilities and one used by most UK companies with international subsidiaries.

Major considerations in determining the most appropriate methods of financing international growth for Marks & Spencer have been:

1. The UK tax position.

2. The overseas tax position.

3. The tax position of the vendor (as in the case of the American acquisition of Brooks Brothers)

4. The potential earnings in each company.

Financing of the first stages in international expansion differed significantly from that of the European and American operation. Although entry into both the Canadian and American market was by means of acquisition, the methods of financing these acquisitions differed significantly. At the time that the Canadian operation was first established, the Canadian government insisted that 45 per cent of the company's shares were held by the Canadian public. At this time, Canada had strong restrictions on inward investment in order to protect domestic businesses from hostile acquisitions by American companies. The government also insisted that products were locally sourced. Twelve years later restrictions were relaxed and Marks & Spencer bought back the shares which were in public ownership at a cost of £54 million at 1986 exchange rates. These government restrictions constrained the early development of the Canadian business.

European expansion, based on organic growth, was financed from a combination of internally generated funds, initially from the UK and local borrowings. Internally generated funds could not be used as the sole means of finance owing to government restrictions in the French and Belgian markets. Additionally, the UK government at the time was operating a policy of exchange controls which restricted the flow of funds out of the UK. Under the prevailing restrictions in the French and Belgian markets, the company was able to use 90 per cent of local borrowing to establish the Belgian operation, but in contrast, the French government insisted on the company using 50 per cent of its own capital to establish the French operation. These local borrowings were supplemented by the despatch of goods from the UK on a two to three year extended credit basis.

Marks & Spencer Export Group

The export side of the Marks & Spencer business started with lend-lease agreements during the Second World War, which gradually grew into an export group, particularly for textiles. At this stage the company exported to almost any one who wanted to buy St Michael products. By 1962 the first St Michael (not Marks & Spencer) shop opened in Vienna. This was a shop within a shop, as with other major brands such as Gucci and Dior. At this time, the structure of the export group was narrowly focused on the sale of merchandise, i.e. seeking to increase volume sales to add to the total turnover of the domestic business. During the 1960s, merchandise began to be exported to Guernsey and Jersey. Growth was determined by customer demand as the business took no active steps to promote international developments through exports. As the volume of exports was a response to unsolicited orders it was not until the 1970s that a formal recognition of export activity through the establishment of a buying office resulted in a scrutiny of the number of overseas clients and the subsequent introduction of a policy aimed at rationalizing the number of small accounts. In one year alone, the number of requests for merchandise had reached three hundred.

Increasing demand from overseas businesses for Mark & Spencer merchandise meant that a greater priority had to be given to the development of the export group. In order to begin to formalize this export activity there was a need to concentrate on fewer accounts to which higher levels of service could be offered. The need for improved service levels stemmed out of the demand for seasonal merchandise at times which did not correspond with the UK business' seasons. At the same time, relationships were developing with retail organizations in Nigeria, Iran, Eire, Australia, Hong Kong and, in 1977, Japan. None of these companies were St Michael shops, they were department stores in which St Michael merchandise was displayed alongside other merchandise. The value of this business to the company by 1977 accounted for a total of £10.5 million as follows:

	£m
Australia	2.5
Hong Kong	1.5
Iran	2.5
Nigeria	4.0

Throughout the 1970s the company continued to upgrade its service to account customers through the creation of a sales office and showroom in its London headquarters, where overseas buyers could view merchandise and place orders, which were sent direct through to manufacturers. Growth on this basis continued until 1985/86 when further changes were introduced and the number of export accounts was reduced from sixty to forty-five. If the export business was to survive at the same time as the company was developing its own stores internationally, the two parts of the business could not run in parallel with differing corporate objectives. The export activities of the company had developed outside the mainstream business in response to unsolicited orders. Throughout the growth of the export group's activities, the focus of the group's business was in the UK, the point of enquiry. Orders were placed and negotiated in the UK, where merchandise was examined and selected. No attention was paid to the point of sale or the conditions under which St Michael products were sold. By the mid-1980s there emerged a corporate belief that this focus should move away from the point of enquiry and towards the points of sale across the different international markets. To bring about this shift required a change in the structure of Marks & Spencer's export group and the development of guidelines under which St Michael merchandise could be sold. For exisiting account customers, a change in culture and operating procedures was necessary. Many of these account customers were traditional family-run businesses with whom the company had had business links for many years, for example the Bastos family in Portugal have had links with Marks & Spencer for over three decades. By 1986/87 Hong Kong had become the largest export account, which in retail terms was worth over £7 million. The consumer perception of the company was that Marks & Spencer and Dodwells, who was selling St Michael merchandise, were one and the same. As Dodwells had different corporate objectives from Marks & Spencer, Dodwells did not want to be brought within the tighter company guidelines introduced by the export group. Exports to Dodwells were therefore discontinued. Six months later, in 1988, the company opened its first Marks & Spencer store in Hong Kong.

Since the mid-1980s, Marks & Spencer has worked more closely with export customers, setting performance targets for the business. This has resulted in a further reduction of accounts. In 1985/86 there were forty-two accounts, by 1990 this had been reduced to twenty-five. Accounts which were eliminated were those which were too small or where the focus of the business was not felt to be compatible with plans for potential future development, for example Swiss department stores, where little potential for expansion existed. The change in strategic focus from the company's London headquarters to the international store units themselves put an increasing onus on these export account customers to upgrade and modernize their stores. In order to support this development, the international franchise manual was developed.

St Michael from Marks & Spencer

Creation of International Franchise Units

In contrast to previous export accounts where companies sold St Michael merchandise, franchisees began to trade under the 'St Michael from Marks & Spencer' fascia. As these businesses develop, the St Michael name is removed from the fascia, which then becomes the same as the UK operation, Marks & Spencer. A major force in the development of franchise agreements has been the growth of the company's international business development and the need to establish a more uniform international corporate identity so that international consumers do not perceive any difference between Marks & Spencer's international business and Marks & Spencer export accounts. This has resulted in the export group having dual objectives:

1. To convert existing businesses from informal agreements to formal agreements (export to franchise).
2. To develop new franchise units.

Existing International Franchises

None of the early export ventures described earlier was still in existence by the 1990s, by which time St Michael goods were being sold in over twenty countries and, by the end of 1992, through sixty-five St Michael franchise shops and franchise shops within department stores with retail sales exceeding £100 million and trading from over 250,000 square feet of selling space.[9] In 1992, Marks & Spencer had franchises in the following countries: Hong Kong, Portugal, Spain, Norway, Israel, Greece, Jersey, Guernsey, Singapore, Canary Islands, Bahamas, Bermuda, Indonesia and Hungary.

The aim of the franchise systems has been:

> to establish the Company in important new markets without an M&S capital investment and to work much more closely with existing customers to maintain the Company's standards without damaging long established relationships.[10]

The majority of the franchise units are in prime locations in capital cities, for example Vienna, Athens, Lisbon. These franchise units do not stock a full range of St Michael merchandise but select from a core catalogue of products; the stores in Jersey and Guernsey stock the widest range. Other units stock lingerie, toiletries and a limited selection of ambient (i.e. long-life, risk-free) food products. Portugal, Norway, Bermuda and some of the Singapore units have food sections, whilst other franchised units are predominantly clothing. Pricing policy is determined by market factors and the local franchisee's knowledge of the market, together with guidance from head office in London. Intensive research is conducted before prices are set. Physical distribution of the product is the franchisee's responsibility once the merchandise has been shipped out of the UK.

Franchise Agreement

The franchise legal agreement is made initially for five years. A franchise partner must be able to achieve a turnover of at least £2 million retail UK equivalent in the early stages of development, with potential for growth in subsequent years. To attain these targets, a minimum store size of 6,000 square feet in a prime location is necessary. The franchisee pays for the franchise in two ways: first through the purchase of merchandise and secondly through a franchise fee based on a percentage of turnover above an agreed limit. The store interior is sourced from Marks & Spencer who provides fascias, panelling, ceiling tiles, floor coverings, in-store display equipment and promotional material. A detailed operating manual is provided which sets out the systems required to run the store to Marks & Spencer standards.

In return, the franchisee has the benefit of proven systems and the support of one of Britain's major retailers. This managerial support continues once a store is operational. The major benefit to the franchisee results from the increased volume of sales; for example, the Cyprus franchisee doubled its turnover in three years. Additional benefits arise from the Marks & Spencer systems, including stock control, warehousing, staff training and administrative systems. These systems have played a key role in the company's development as the UK's leading retailer.

The benefits to Marks & Spencer are that growth through business format franchising allows the company to establish a presence in countries where population size or per capita spend may not be sufficient to support the development of wholly-owned Marks & Spencer stores. The use of franchising also is of strategic benefit in testing consumer reaction to the company's merchandise before establishing a larger-scale operation.

Transatlantic Growth

North American Market

The international growth strategies pursued by Marks & Spencer under the chairmanship of Lord Sieff were also continued by his successor Lord Rayner who, in 1987, outlined company plans for transatlantic development, when a project team of senior managers established an office in New York. The team's brief was to investigate the US clothing and food retailing industries, with a view to identifying the most effective way for Marks & Spencer to enter the American market.[11] Two separate teams were then formed, one responsible for analysing the food sector, the other fashion, each team aiming to identify possible gaps in the market. After extensive research, collaboration with trade associations and consultants, acquisition was identified as the most effective means of establishing a US presence. Organic growth in the USA would require significant changes to the company's merchandise mix, reducing economies of scale and scope. These changes would have to be made in terms of both fabrics and styling/cut, many of the UK fabrics being too heavy for the US market. On the food side of the business, the lack of a developed cold food chain for chilled foods in the USA could result in difficulties in terms of the supply base. More easily transportable into the American market were Marks & Spencer systems, skills and corporate values.

Identifying Possible Acquisition Targets

US Clothing Sector
An extensive screening process based on store visits and desk research was carried out which reduced the number of potential targets to ninety-one retail companies

in the north east. This number was then reduced to thirty-two and, following store visits, a final sample of eight companies was selected.

The final eight companies were believed to be in the right market segment, profitable and running quality businesses with expansion potential. Following a scrutiny of these eight companies, Brooks Brothers was identified as the most suitable acquisition target.

Brooks Brothers

Brooks Brothers was founded in 1818 and is to the American consumer synonymous with tradition and conservatism.[12] Theodore Roosevelt and Woodrow Wilson both wore Brooks Brothers suits to their inaugurations. The Brooks Brothers name is associated with the American 'preppie' image and traditional merchandise such as button-down collars on its shirts. At the time of the acquisition, a former Brooks executive was quoted as saying. 'This is not a retail store, it's an American institution and anything remotely revolutionary will destroy it.'[13]

Concentration of merchandise was predominantly menswear with a small percentage of womenswear. The company was purchased in 1988 by Marks & Spencer for US$750 million. Under the terms of the agreement, forty-seven Brooks stores in the USA (totalling 550,000 square feet) and twenty-one stores in Japan (three of which are between 4,000 and 7,500 square feet free-standing units and eighteen of which were shops within shops, under 2,000 square feet) were acquired.[14] The purchase agreement also included two special clauses, which gave Marks & Spencer a five year non-competition agreement with the Canadian Campeau organization (the vendors), preventing them from establishing a speciality menswear chain which would compete against Brooks Brothers in the USA or Japan. Secondly, for three years Marks & Spencer would have the right to rent space in any of Campeau's 740 department stores for a St Michael food operation. At the time of acquisition, Brooks Brothers also had three factories in Long Island City and North Carolina which supplied over one-third of the store's requirements. The US business also operated its own profitable charge card. In addition to its manufacturing operation, Brooks Brothers operated a direct marketing arm of the business through its catalogue, from which customers could order seasonal merchandise by mail or telephone.

Prior to the acquisition, the company had been run autonomously with little investment (in systems) by the parent company. At the time of the acquisition, much press speculation was centred around whether the Brooks concept would be expanded in the USA or whether it would be introduced into Europe. Brooks Brothers enjoyed good sales and profit margins which also promoted some speculation that Marks & Spencer, in purchasing the company, were buying a cash cow[15] (Exhibit 8.1).

The profitibility was in part due to the credit size of the business which accounted for 87 per cent of all sales, 54 per cent of which were on the in-house card in 1988.

Exhibit 8.1   *Brooks Brothers: sales and margins pre-acquisition*

	January 1984	January 1985	January 1986	January 1987	January 1988
Sales ($m)	216	236	247	268	290
PBT ($m)	32	35	34	41.7	41.8
Margin (%)	14.8	14.8	13.8	15.6	14.4

Source: Barclays de Zoete, 5 May 1988.

Post-acquisition   Although some changes have been introduced to Brooks, Marks & Spencer did not seek to change the business merely to bring in the benefits of its systems and skills. Some womenswear ranges have been strengthened and the flagship store on Madison Avenue refurbished at a cost of $7 million.

Kings: A Small Strategic Acquisition
In August 1988, Marks & Spencer followed its acquisition of America's oldest clothing company with the acquisition for $108 million of a family-owned chain of sixteen food stores in New Jersey which had built a reputation for quality and customer service.[16] Although a small state geographically, New Jersey is the most densely populated state in the USA. The sixteen stores had an average sales area of 17,000 square feet and were located near centres of population in 'strip shopping' centres. The company's basis of differentiation lay in the preparation of fresh foods, produce, meats, seafood and delicatessen.

At the time of the acquisition, the company chairman Lord Rayner stated that, 'The acquisition of King's will enable us to build a significant food retailing operation in the United States.'[17] No plans were made to change the management of the company, as Marks & Spencer wanted to build on existing expertise as a means of introducing Marks & Spencer to the US food industry. The margins that had been achieved by the company were approximately 2–3 per cent, which was high for a US food chain.

The acquisition of King's, together with the agreement with Campeau made at the time of the acquisition of Brooks Brothers, meant that significant potential existed to roll out a more widespread food chain. The acquisition of Kings came one year after Sainsbury's purchase of Shaw's supermarkets, a group of sixty New England stores.

Post-acquisition, some St Michael lines have been introduced into the King's merchandise ranges, in chilled foods and toiletries. At the time of the acquisition, the company felt that this was the only route of entry to the US food market. Organic growth would not have produced sufficient volume to make production in the USA feasible. Additionally, it was felt that there was a need to be able to trial products, which would have been more difficult in newly established company own stores.[18]

Major differences exist between US and UK food markets. In the USA there are no national food chains, and branded manufacturers labels dominate the market. Net margins of 1–2 per cent are the norm and the cold chain hardly exists.

Impact of International Growth on the UK Business

The overall effect of internationalization was to broaden the company's sourcing policy. International growth resulted in increasing depth with existing suppliers and at the same time a wider search for new suppliers. The original Marks & Spencer principle of purchasing UK products for the UK operation had started to decline. All purchasing remained centrally controlled but whole new areas of the business were developed on the strength of overseas purchasing.

The influence of international styling also developed from an involvement in both European and Japanese trade fairs and brought the company into contact with new suppliers. Selling merchandise across different markets reinforced the company's market intelligence through the company's employees in stores in Eire, France, Belgium, Hong Kong, Japan, Spain and North America. From this market knowledge, a picture could be built up first-hand of the demands of the international consumer, local preferences and international operating procedures. The Hong Kong operation provided an important source of market intelligence for the textile side of the business. Singapore provided a site for trialling lightweight fabrics irrespective of the UK domestic season.

By 1990, there was no other UK fashion retailer with the same depth of international operation. In the year ending March 1990 sales rose to £5.6 billion, whilst pre-tax profits increased by 14 per cent to £604 million, in excess of market estimates of £595 million, at a time when many other UK retailers were suffering from the effects of interest rate rises (Exhibit 8.2). Three years later the company entered the UK's top ten companies in terms of market capitalization for the first time in its history (Exhibit 8.3).

Exhibit 8.2 *Group operating summary: geographical contribution to turnover*

	1992 £m	1991 £m	1990 £m	1989 £m	1988 £m
UK and Eire	5,014.7	5,037.7	4,844.8	4,518.1	4,247.5
Continental Europe	195.0	149.9	121.1	99.2	103.7
Rest of the world	521.0	528.2	592.9	458.4	179.9
Export	62.7	59.0	49.3	45.8	46.5
Total	5,739.4	5,774.8	5,608.1	5,121.5	4,557.6

Source: Company Facts 1992.

Exhibit 8.3 *The UK's top ten companies, 1993*

British Telecom	£26.04 bn
Shell Transport	£21.68 bn
Glaxo Holdings	£19.40 bn
HSBC Holdings	£17.59 bn
British Petroleum	£16.31 bn
British Gas	£14.29 bn
BAT Industries	£13.87 bn
BTR	£13.70 bn
Hanson	£12.18 bn
Marks & Spencer	£10.85 bn

Source: Sunday Observer, 12 September 1993.

International Development in the 1990s

By the early 1990s, the position of the international division of Marks & Spencer was one of consolidation in the USA, downsizing in Canada and expansion in Europe, with signficant growth potential in the Far East (see Exhibit 8.4). In 1992 the company had announced that it intended to sell the People's business in Canada and reduce the number of Marks & Spencer stores substantially, bringing the Canadian division closer to a breakeven situation.[19] Post-acquisition, the company admitted that it paid too much for its North American businesses, which have now

Exhibit 8.4 *Marks & Spencer's international operation: number of stores*

Continental Europe			
	Marks & Spencer	France	11
		Belgium	3
		Spain	2
		Holland	1
USA			
	Brooks Brothers		54
	Kings Supermarkets		17
Canada			
	Marks & Spencer		68
	D'Allaird's		116
	Peoples		81
Far East			
	Marks & Spencer Hong Kong		4
	Brooks Brothers Japan (shops within shops)		39
Exports			
	St Michael franchise shops and franchise shops within department stores		65

Source: Marks & Spencer Annual Report 1992.

to prove themselves in one of the most difficult world retail markets plagued by price-cutting, overdevelopment and fierce competition. In Europe an aggressive phase of expansion was continuing with potential to achieve future sales of £1 billion by the end of the decade. A solid base of four Marks & Spencer stores had been established in Hong Kong. Company chairman Sir Richard Greenbury was confident that there were many opportunities for Marks & Spencer as a retailer abroad, and that under his chairmanship all future expansion would be by means of organic growth.

Summary

The growth and expansion of Marks & Spencer in international markets highlights the nature of international development in the service sector, starting with unsolicited export requests through to the development of a formal franchise structure. In contrast to entry strategies in service industry organizations, where factors determining market entry strategy are related to following the customer, this example of international retail franchising as a first stage in international growth, leading to more active exporting and full-scale market involvement, follows more closely the traditional models of export activity in the manufacturing sector. International franchising holds certain unique advantages over other types of business. For the franchisor it is less prone to economic and political risk, requires fewer financial resources and has less negative impact on the recipient country than other forms of international business expansion. The disadvantages occur when there is a lack of suitable prospective franchisees, loss of control and difficulties which may arise in supporting foreign market operations, for example logistics and maintaining stock replenishment.[20] Critical factors in developing this form of business growth are size of the target market, the existing competition, level of demand, the ease with which the business format can be replicated outside the domestic market and the degree of managerial resources required to support growth.

The inability to maintain control over operating standards severely weakens a company's overall corporate image. Holland & Barrett and Sock Shop have, in the past, withdrawn franchises owing to control problems and McDonald's has retained, until 1993, ownership of its UK franchises. Maintaining a uniform corporate image is critical not only to customer perception but also to attracting new franchisees.

The benefits to Marks & Spencer of the use of business format franchising in international markets are that it has allowed the company to expand its global presence and establish the St Michael name in new markets with minimal capital investment at the same time as creating the opportunity to test consumer reaction to merchandise before undertaking further market development. The major benefits are high returns on investment, rapid accumulation of market knowledge and strengthening of the company's international corporate image. Franchising acts as a means of taking revenue in low-risk countries where development of Marks & Spencer stores would not be feasible.

Marks & Spencer has adopted a portfolio of entry strategies from which to enter new markets, involving differing degrees of organizational and financial risk, dependent of prevailing market conditions and opportunities. The use of this diverse portfolio – franchising, acquisition, joint venture, organic growth and export – has significant implications for the structure of the international division, the learning curve which the company must undertake and the adaptation of sourcing, merchandizing, operational, personnel and finance policies; each strategy bringing with it different degrees of risk. In moving along the international learning curve, several operational and strategic issues have been addressed and policies developed to support the long-term development of the St Michael brand in world food and fashion markets. The basis of the company's competitive advantage in the UK food market lay in convenience and temperature-controlled foods. Replicating this success outside the UK has been a long-term objective. Closely linked to this objective is the need to develop the supply chain for the international sourcing of food products. Key difference in international markets are time differences, geographical distance and climatic variations. Major differences can exist within one national market, for example in the USA or in Europe where significant differences in climate exist between northern and southern France. In order to overcome these differences, developing the supply chain through close collaboration with manufacturers and logistics suppliers is essential. In transferring products across boundaries, critical operational adjustments need to be undertaken. What the company has been able to transfer without adaptation are the principles which underpin the Marks & Spencer corporate culture of quality value and good human relations, the major benefits of which are an increasingly attractive international corporate image in terms of attracting both employees and investors.

Several significant strategic challenges remain in order to establish the St Michael brand name in food markets such as the USA which are dominated by manufacturers' brands and at the same time to develop in fashion markets a catalogue of merchandise which forms a core range capable of being sold across world markets with minimum adaptation. These strategic choices are those of greater penetration of existing markets, for example more rapid expansion across Europe; new market development, as in perhaps the former West Germany where consumers have a favourable level of disposable income through a high propensity to save. Additionally, the changing political face of Germany may result in an expanding demand for quality products which offer value for money.

In just over twenty years of international growth, several stages of development have taken place: rapid market entry to Canada and North America, slow gradual expansion in Europe, followed by accelerated growth almost two decades later and a reorientation of the international business. As yet, the international business remains a small but growing part of the total business. The future challenge will be to balance and integrate the demands of this business portfolio as a means of developing the St Michael brand as the most widely known retail brand in world markets.

Notes

1. *Marks & Spencer Company Facts 1990.*
2. Retailing/International (Research Bulletin), Smith Barney, 19 May 1988.
3. K.K. Tse, *'Marks and Spencer: A Manufacturer without Factories'*, Arthur Andersen series, Chicago, 1987.
4. 'Going Dutch', *Marks & Spencer World*, winter 1991/92.
5. *Ibid.*
6. Marks & Spencer plc, Annual Report and Financial Statement 1989.
7. *Ibid.*
8. 'Going for Gold in the Far East', *Marks & Spencer World*, 1988.
9. *Ibid.*
10. 'Franchise look for export', *Marks & Spencer World*, Autumn 1989.
11. 'Marble Arch to Manhattan', *Marks & Spencer World*, 1988.
12. *Barclays de Zoete World Research*, 21 June 1988.
13. 'An escalator? In Brooks Brothers?' *Forbes*, 9 July 1990.
14. Charterhouse Tilney, Retail Research Report, 5 May 1988.
15. Ibid.
16. Charterhouse Tilney, Retail Research Report, 15 August 1988.
17. Marks & Spencer press bulletin, 5 August 1988.
18. 'Marble Arch to Manhattan', *Marks & Spencer World*, 1988.
19. 'North America restrains overseas growth for Marks & Spencer', *Financial Times*, 13 May 1992.
20. N. Sanghavi, *Retail Franchising in the 1990s*, Longman, 1990.

ABB Transportation Ltd

Waiting for a Train

Richard Blundel

Harper Adams College, UK

Introduction

ABB Transportation Ltd (ATL) is the 85.4 per cent owned subsidiary of the Swiss/Swedish engineering group Asea Brown Boveri Group (ABB), one of Europe's largest industrial companies. ATL's managing director and chief executive officer Bo Södersten is Scandinavian, as are four of his seven boardroom colleagues. ATL is seeking contracts as far afield as Hong Kong and Thailand. Surprisingly, then, this company was until recently a minor subdivision within a major British nationalized industry; it was a wholly-owned subsidiary of British Railways Board (BRB).

History

In 1993, ATL was located at three operational centres: Crewe, Derby and York. Each town has a long and proud railway tradition. Derby Locomotive works, for example, celebrated its 150th anniversary in September 1989. Crewe works had commenced production in 1843, building and repairing locomotives and rolling stock for the Grand Junction Railway; over seven thousand steam locomotives were built there in the years up to 1958. At its peak, the Crewe site covered almost 140 acres (57 hectares). A reorganization in 1964–68 reduced the site to 90 acres (36 hectares). The 1980s saw further downsizing at Crewe and the closure of a number of other railway engineering works (including those at Swindon and Eastleigh).

Leaving the Public Sector

During the 1980s, the Conservative government under Margaret Thatcher required BRB to operate on a more commercial basis. This included both the passenger and freight transport businesses of British Rail and support services such as British Rail Engineering. In October 1987, BRB announced that British Rail Engineering's new construction and maintenance/repair businesses, together with associated assets, would be offered for sale as a single entity. The assets were transferred into a company named BREL (1988) Ltd. A number of large UK and overseas engineering companies expressed an interest. Potential bidders included a management-led employee buy-out team. The successful bidder comprised two major corporate shareholders (Asea Brown Boveri and the UK-based transport and construction company Trafalgar House plc) plus individual shareholders, including senior British Rail Engineering executives and over 7,500 other employees who acquired shares through an employee share ownership plan (ESOP). On 18 April 1989, BREL (1988) Ltd was acquired by the bidders' newly formed holding company, BREL Group Ltd, and became its sole operating subsidiary.

Operations

Following the acquisition, BREL (1988) Ltd was reorganized into eight business units, five in New Construction Group and three in Manufacture and Repair Group. Marketing and product strategies were developed and coordinated with both ABB and Trafalgar House. A total quality management (TQM) programme was established and the company secured the quality standards BS5750/ISO9000, British Railways Board Certification and the British Ministry of Defence standard AQAP1. A computerized manufacturing, planning and financial control system, Protos, was introduced, and a system of team briefings was instituted to improve internal communications. Comprehensive training and development was seen as a vital part of the change managment process. The TQM initiative was launched with a mission statement, delivered by the managing director and circulated in various employee communications. The statement included the following commitment:

> We are dedicated to the achievement of the highest standards of quality and reliability in order to serve our customers' needs. The commitment of each and every employee to these endeavours will ensure the total success of the company.

Acquisition by Asea Brown Boveri

In 1992, following approval by the European Commission, ABB acquired Trafalgar House plc's 40 per cent interest in BREL Group Ltd. By 31 December, ABB had increased its holding to 85.4 per cent of the issued share capital of the holding company (i.e. 4,254,309 £1 ordinary shares out of an issued share capital of £4,979,898). The other issued shares were, for the most part, held by current or former employees as a result of the ESOP. Reflecting this change of ownership, the sole operating subsidiary, BREL (1988) Ltd, was renamed ABB Transportation Ltd and BREL Group Ltd was renamed ABB Transportation Holdings Ltd. (For the purposes of this case, these two companies may be treated as synonymous. The single abbreviation ATL is used throughout.) Exhibit 9.1 is an extract from Bo Södersten's review of the year, published in ATL's 1992 annual report.

Exhibit 9.1 *Extract from ATL Annual Report 1992:*
chief executive officer's review

1992 has been a year of improvement and a year of change. Our streamlined decentralised organisation is operating well and has enabled everyone in the Company to focus on the 12 steps we set ourselves in our Operation Recovery plan which we have now renamed Operation Improvement. There is no doubt that 1992 has been a tough year and my thanks go to all of our employees for their cooperation, hard work and dedication as we strive to achieve our three main objectives:

- To be a profitable company, to reach a return on assets to enable growth and to operate at minimum risk.

- To satisfy customer needs by producing and developing quality products and services – at the right cost and at the right time – with first class after sales service.

- To employ a highly motivated and performing workforce.

A new name for a new era
In September 1992 a new image for the Company was successfully launched, with our name change to **ABB Transportation Ltd.** This was well received by our employees and customers and heralded a new era for the Company. During the year, improved team working was high on our list of priorities and one of the most vital tasks to which we are committed is to try to achieve the Cultural Vision we have set ourselves for the Company.

Our efficient facilities need orders
Despite all of the improvements and achievements we continue to make daily, we do have one great problem – a lack of orders. The much reduced workload on offer from British Rail (BR) and London Underground Limited (LUL) and the continuing debate and uncertainties surrounding the privatisation of British Rail have meant that all of our factories in York, Derby and Crewe are not working at full capacity. The winning of orders is crucial to the employment of our workforce and the future of our factories. We are fighting every inch of the way to secure the orders we so desperately need and will use every weapon at our disposal. In the UK we are in active discussion with the Government, British Rail, London Underground Limited and other transport authorities and we will leave no stone unturned.

Focus on exports
A major export drive was also begun in 1992 and our strengthened marketing, sales and commercial teams have been very active, particularly in South East Asia. I am very pleased that BR and LUL have given their full support in our quest for export work. You can be assured that without this we would stand no chance of securing any overseas business as the client will always seek references from home-based customers.

Delivering successful products
During the year major milestones were reached in many of the Rail Vehicles Group projects:

- The last of the 447 Class 158 diesel multiple units were handed over to Peter Field, Divisional Director, Network South East. Despite the Class 158's earlier problems, they are now recognized as one of the most efficient and reliable trains in BR with passenger revenues well up for the lines on which they operate.

Exhibit 9.1 *Continued*

- The last Network Turbo number 165137 was also delivered to Network SouthEast. The handover ceremony at our York works coincided with the opening of the new state-of-the-art production facility, which was designed by a number of employee taskforce teams. This facility is being used to manufacture the air conditioned Class 166 diesel multiple units.

- The Class 465 Networker electric trains were launched into service in December by the Secretary of State for Transport, John MacGregor. The introduction of these trains is part of an £800 million modernization of Europe's busiest commuter railway and these energy efficient, high quality trains will gradually replace the 30–40 year old slam-door fleet of trains presently serving the North Kent suburban routes to London.

- The first of the Central Line tube trains for LUL were delivered at the end of 1992 to undergo trialling and testing at LUL's Ruislip Depot. Passenger services will commence in 1993.

New divisions to suit customer needs
Our philosophy is one of deep vertical integration and to add to previously new divisions of Bogies and After Sales we have created two further divisions – bodyshells and Interiors. Whilst this increases our risk exposure, it does, at the same time, improve our ability to meet the changing demands from the marketplace quickly.

Innovation through evolution
We believe it is essential to improve our products by evolution and not revolution, working with our customers and suppliers to change products gradually, combining innovation with well proven and documented reliability. A strong after-sales feedback on the effectiveness of our own and supplier's designs, quality and reliability and maintainability will ensure continuous improvements for both new and existing vehicles. This helps avoid making the same mistake twice.

The customer comes first
Despite the severe recession our Customer Support Group has had yet again another successful year, with budgeted profits exceeded and net inventories in line with budget. Customer focus continues to be the Group's main thust with on-time deliveries continuing well above 95 per cent and quality complaints minimal. Rapid response to enquiries continued to give the Vehicle Repairs Division the marketing edge, resulting in consistent success in winning crash damage, modification and refurbishment contracts, one of the key orders being for the refurbishment of 452 vehicles for London's Metropolitan Line.

Empowerment of our employees
Time Based Management (TBM) has been a major focus for the Equipment Division which is now consolidated into our Crewe Works, with employee involvement and empowerment being a key feature. Whilst the benefits of this will be seen in 1993, already throughput time reductions of 50 per cent are being achieved in some areas, resulting in further inventory reductions. Other TBM schemes are now under way in different parts of the Company. Although we have concerns over delays in investment that the current debate on BR privatization is causing, we see that this could present a significant opportunity for growth in the maintenance, spares and repair market. We have formed a taskforce to develop this.

Exhibit 9.1 *Continued*

> **Broadening our customer base**
> Market and product development work by the Customer Support Group in 1992 has helped to generate opportunities in the Ministry of Defence, general utilities and bus markets. The Bogie Division has continued to perform well and as a result of creating this fully autonomous division we have had great success in attracting orders from other manufacturers, the most recent being a £12 million contract from GEC Alsthom for bogies for the Channel Tunnel Night Trains. A £2.5 million investment programme for the Bogie Division was approved during the year and, when completed, the Division will have one of the most modern and efficient factories of its kind in the world.
>
> Whilst acknowledging that we have come a long way in 1992, we should be under no illusion: the year ahead will be extremely tough with the order situation in the UK looking bleak. I can only stress yet again the importance of continued investment in the UK rail network while the issues around its privatization are resolved.
>
> **World class ambitions**
> I know that we have the full backing of our management team and workforce as we continue our journey to get the Company in shape to face whatever the future might bring. I am sure that if we can weather the storm ahead we are on the right track to reach our long-term ambition to be a world class company.
>
> Bo Södersten
> Managing Director and Chief Executive Officer
> ABB Transportation Ltd

Products and Services

ATL's main area of activity is the construction of new railway vehicles and the repair and maintenance of railway rolling stock (including engines/power cars, passenger coaches and, to a lesser extent, freight waggons). They also produce some rail vehicle components, such as bogies (i.e. wheels and axles), for use by other manufacturers.

New Vehicles

In the past, the company has produced many of the large steam, diesel and electric locomotives used on long distance routes. However, ATL's current rail vehicles projects are limited to the following areas:

1. Electric trains for suburban/inter-urban routes (e.g. class 465 Networker).
2. Diesel multiple units for suburban/inter-urban routes (e.g. class 158, class 166).
3. Electric trains for underground routes (e.g. London Underground: Central Line).

4.   Light rail vehicles and trams (e.g. Eurotram for the city of Strasbourg).

ATL has secured a number of contracts from British Rail and London Underground Ltd. However, there is considerable uncertainty over future orders. ATL's chairman John Darby made the following statement in the company's 1992 annual report:

> We now have very effective production units at Crewe, Derby and York. None are fully occupied as the proposals by HM Government to privatize British Rail, together with the Government's economic policy, have precluded either British Rail or London Underground putting orders for new rolling stock out to tender for which we could compete. I must tell you that, without new orders, Derby will run out of new construction work at the end of 1994 and York by mid next year.

The company recognizes the urgent need to supplement its order book with overseas business. ATL has experience in many countries, ranging from Malaysia to the USA to Congo, West Africa. Since 1992, south east Asia has been the focus of an intensive marketing effort. Typically, contracts are won in competition on the basis of detailed tenders submitted by local and other overseas manufacturers. Tender documents make considerable demands on technical and management staff resources, with no guarantee of a successful outcome. Exhibit 9.2 considers the post-privatization future for suppliers of rolling stock.

Repair and Maintenance

In 1989, the company relied on British Rail for over 90 per cent of its repair work. Other customers included the British Ministry of Defence (repair of railway shunters, generators, gearboxes and axles; overhaul of Land Rover engines) and London Underground. Some overseas contracts were awarded by the Crown Agents, a governmental procurement agency acting on behalf of developing countries. One of the business' strengths may be its breadth of operations. Few other engineering companies have the facilities both to manufacture and to repair such a wide variety of heavy mechanical and electrical products. This means that ATL can compete for the repair and maintenance of non-railway equipment. However, as British Rail and its successor(s) search for more competitive tenders, this core repair business is vulnerable to competitors. For example, power units on the high speed train are not dissimilar to marine diesel engines; the newly-privatized Royal Dockyards have already won contracts for some of this work. Similarly, a bus engine repairer has secured diesel multiple unit (DMU) repair contracts. Other factors affecting the repair and maintenance business include the introduction of new, reduced maintenance, rolling stock and the provision of original equipment manufacturer (OEM) warranties on new power units. By retaining control over the sourcing of components, the OEM can generally secure a cost advantage over its competitors. Life-cycle maintenance contracts, where the manufacturer is responsible for all aspects of maintenance and modification (from the moment a new train

Exhibit 9.2 *Press report 1: 'Hard-pressed train makers encounter leases on the line'*

Every time you fly there is a better than even chance that the aircraft you sit in will be owned, not by the airline whose colours adorn the fuselage, but by a bank, finance house or leasing company. By the end of this decade much the same will apply to rail travel in Britain.

On Wednesday British Rail's Network SouthEast division broke with tradition by signing a £150m deal to lease 41 Networker Express trains from the Derby-based train builder ABB Transportation. It is the first time BR has not bought passenger rolling stock outright. It is also the shape of things to come.

Provided the impending privatisation of BR does not go disastrously off the rails, Britain's hardpressed rolling stock manufactures will no longer have one monolithic customer bankrolled by the Government to deal with but an assortment of private rail franchisees and leasing companies.

Since the average length of the franchises will be seven years and since a class 465 Networker, for instance, is built to last 35 years, there are unlikely to be many private operators interested in investing directly in new rolling stock.

Leasing also has strong political attractions in the current economic climate since it is a neat way of transferring risk to the private sector while spreading public expenditure over an extended period.

Instead of having to find £150m up front to finance the Networker order, for instance, BR will pay ABB for its trains over the period of the lease, in this case a minimum of 12 years and a maximum of 25.

But not just new rolling stock will be leased. From next April BR's passenger fleet – 11,000 locomotives and carriages with a book value of £2bn – will be divided up between three new rolling stock leasing companies whose job will be to lease trains to the new wave of franchisees. Initially they will operate as BR subsidiaries, but the eventual aim is to privatise them.

Since these leasing companies will also be responsible for the vast bulk of future rolling stock orders, they have the potential to become even bigger businesses. Network SouthEast alone estimates that over the next 15 years 25 per cent of its 6,000 carriages will need to be replaced – an investment programme amounting to about £1bn.

The Networker orders offers a lifeline for the 1,000 workers at ABB's York factory. But for the company, and Britain's other big train maker GEC, it also marks a watershed in the way they do business.

Bo Södersten, chief executive of ABB, said: 'For the operators of the trains it will be pay as you go or pay as you get the revenue, and that entails quite a major transfer of risk to the supplier and quite a number of complications. An outright purchase is a much cleaner arrangement.'

The reason that the risk has been tipped firmly in the direction of the rolling stock manufacturers is that the type of agreements they will be obliged to enter into involve operating leases rather than finance leases.

Under an operating lease the supplier is responsible for maintenance of the rolling stock throughout the lease period and, since it will still own the asset at the end of the lease, determining a residual value and finding a new lessee.

As well as imposing a strain on suppliers, the leasing mechanism selected by the Government looks like posing a challenge for the established leasing market.

Christine Fowler, of Babcock & Brown, one of the country's principal arrangers of lease financing, said: 'Within the UK there must be £800m to £1bn worth of funds available each year to support the leasing of big-ticket items like aircraft ships and trains. The problem, therefore, is not lack of finance but the terms on which the Government wants it to be provided.'

Because of the sheer complexity of the leasing model adopted by the Treasury and the degree of risk transferred to the private sector, Babcock & Brown had to work with

Exhibit 9.2 *Continued*

ABB for more than a year to put together a workable deal.

The concept of lease financing rolling stock is well established in the US. But there it is largely restricted to freight trains which, because of their standard design, can be used almost anywhere in the world. So there is a healthy secondhand market and it is possible to determine residual values.

'The problem in the UK is that rolling stock is specially designed for parts of the network and doesn't work elsewhere,' Ms Fowler said.

Babcock & Brown has already approached a number of the big US rolling stock leasing companies, such as GE Railcars and GATX, to test their attitude to the potential on this side of the Atlantic. Ms Fowler said: 'They are interested but, not surprisingly, they are also cautious because the market is new and quite restricted.'

In framing its rail privatisation bill the Department of Transport has gone some way to meet the more obvious worries of rolling stock manufacturers and would-be lessors. Where a passenger franchise is handed over from one operator to another,

for instance, the Government-appointed franchising director will have power to require the successor franchisees to use the same rolling stock.

BR, meanwhile, is designing rolling stock that can be used on virtually any part of the network. The Networker Expresses that will begin service in 1995 on Network South-East's Great Northern line routes and Kent coast services can, for instance, run on all electrified lines.

But it is a brave new world for the rolling stock industry. Much remains in the realms of the unknown – the precise type of leases the new leasing companies will offer, how these companies will be capitalised and how quickly ownership can be transferred to the private sector.

As Mr Södersten put it: 'It is not easy to forecast what is going to happen. We will have to use maximum imagination to find ways of securing the finance because Britain has a competent rolling stock industry, and I would hate to see it not being properly developed.'

Source: Independent, 15 October 1993.

---

is delivered until finally it reaches 'the end of the line'), are likely to become standard in the industry. ATL has formed an after-sales division to exploit this. The company believes it will appeal to customers whose main objective is to run an efficient and reliable service without building up substantial in-house maintenance resources.

Railways in Britain

Background

The privately financed railway companies developed rapidly, if rather haphazardly, from the mid-nineteenth century, their (sometimes overlapping) networks extending to cover most parts of the country. However, with the growth of motorized road transport after 1900, the railway companies entered a long period of decline. By the 1930s, ownership of the railway industry had become concentrated into four large companies operating on a regional basis: London, Midland & Scottish; Great

Western; Great Eastern; Southern. These, by now ailing, companies were taken into public ownership in 1948 by Clement Atlee's Labour government. A coordinated national network was maintained, under the control of the British Railways Board. However, in the early 1960s a governmental review of commerical viability (the Beeching Report) led to the closure of many local stations and branch lines.

Finance

British Rail is financed by a mixture of sales revenue (from passengers, freight and parcels business users) plus government subsidy. Central government support for the railways totalled £2.1 billion for the financial year 1992–93. Public service obligation (PSO) funding is a special category, designed to support 'socially necessary' rail services (e.g. those serving remote rural areas) which would not otherwise cover operating costs. PSO funding has been reduced progressively during the 1980s. At regional and local levels, there are a number of additional funding sources. Passenger transport executives (PTEs), such as Metro which operates in the Birmingham conurbation, are financed by local authorities and seek to support and coordinate rail and other transport services in their areas. County councils and regional development organizations also provide some support.

Restructuring in the 1980s

Since nationalization in 1948, British Rail had been organized on a geographical basis, with five regions (Western, Eastern, London Midland, North Eastern, Scottish) echoing the former private company names. In 1982, this structure was replaced by a number of strategic business units, each of which became responsible for its own assets and operation. The principal units were: InterCity, Network South East, regional railways, railfreight, parcels.

The 1980s also saw the disposal of a number of non-core businesses, such as shipping, hotels and catering. The 1989 privatization of BREL was a further example of this process. Some asset sales made significant, albeit short-term contributions to net income, notably the sale of land adjacent to urban stations which was used for 'fill-in' commercial and residential property developments. In 1989–90, British Rail is reported to have earned £412 million from property, although in the following year this figure declined to £233 million. The parcels business Red Star was also sold at this time.

Underinvestment or Inefficiency?

Both opponents and proponents of privatization have used underinvestment to argue their case. Rightly or wrongly, the 1988 rail disaster in Clapham, south

London, was seen as a symptom of under-resourcing, as are the routine delays due to mechanical and signalling faults. InterCity services have shown a profit in recent years. However, Network South East (NSE) has made increasing losses, reflecting a reliance on London's peak-time traffic demand for approximately 75 per cent of its income. The recession of the late 1980s and early 1990s has led to reduced passenger numbers and a fall in NSE's receipts from property sales and lettings.

Privatization of British Rail

In late 1993, British Rail was a nationalized industry on the verge of privatization. In the meantime, its various operating units were accountable to the British Railways Board (BRB). The Railway Privatization Bill began its committee stage in the House of Commons in June 1992, and became law, after much debate, in November 1993 (Exhibit 9.3). This legislation brings to an end British Rail's forty-five year

Exhibit 9.3 *Press report 2: 'Rail sell-off bill to become law today'*

The railway privatisation bill was expected last night to become law today. Its passage was cleared when the Lords shied away from a constitutional clash with the government.

The Lords' final decision yesterday to back down means that British Rail's opportunities to bid for franchises to run services will be restricted to routes where no credible bidder emerges.

Ministers were visibly relieved by the bill's successful passage through the Lords, which ended more than 190 hours of debate in both Houses. The bill is expected to receive royal assent a few hours before the end of the parliamentary session today.

However, the frantic manoeuvring which preceded the final stages undermined the goverment's recent attempts to suggest that the difficulties of the past 18 months are over.

The government was seriously embarrassed on Wednesday when it was forced to interrupt Commons business to reverse three defeats inflicted in the Lords.

The defeats – and the uproar which followed in the Commons – threw doubt on claims that the Conservative party had united in the wake of ratification of the Maastricht treaty.

Mr John Major, the prime minister, told MPs at question time that the rowdy scenes on Wednesday night were 'a disgrace to parliament.'

Officials said the prime minister was particularly upset by Labour's whips, who challenged the count on a division reversing the Lords defeats, in effect accusing the Conservative tellers of lying.

Conservative MPs said Labour had indulged in a number of unparliamentary tricks, including jamming the doors open in the division lobbies to delay the vote, switching tellers halfway through, and deliberately miscounting.

Opposition MPs said the unparliamentary behaviour was not one-sided. Mr. James Wallace, a Liberal Democrat MP, said he was jostled by a Conservative whip as he tried to vote.

Labour leaders were unrepentant about the unruly scenes. Mr. Brian Wilson, deputy transport spokesman, said it was one of the few occasions when the opposition had been able to make procedural tactics work against the government.

Mr. John Prescott, the shadow employment secretary, said Labour had 'done a marvellous job' in delaying the bill. 'The government got everything they deserved,' he said.

Mr. Prescott said a few private sector companies were likely to bid for franchises. He claimed that the government would quietly drop the bill, but warned that a Labour government would recreate a publicly-owned national rail network.

Mr. John MacGregor, the transport secretary, said he expected at lease seven of the proposed 25 route franchises to be awarded by 1995.

Source: Financial Times, 5 November 1993.

monopoly in passenger and rail freight provision. The anticipated benefits of privatization are seen to include access to private sector finance and a stimulus to more efficient and innovative management. Critics argue that an 'open access' system, with rival operators running trains on the same lines, is unworkable, and that only the most profitable routes will be attractive to private sector investors. The so-called cherry pickers will grab the profitable intercity routes, leaving the heavily subsidized commuter and rural services to be operated by a rump British Rail. It is estimated that (excluding the franchised rolling stock) track, signals and other fixed assets could still make up 60 per cent of railway costs. From April 1994, a state-owned track authority, Railtrack, has managed (and charged for) the use of these assets by franchisees and the remaining British Rail businesses.

Other Brtitish Railways

British Rail is Britain's largest railway operator, in terms of track miles, stations and rolling stock. Other operators include London Underground, the Newcastle Metro, British Coal, the Ministry of Defence. A number of small private companies, such as the Severn Valley and Llangollen Railways, run restored steam locomotives on scenic branch lines. Light rail systems (a modern equivalent of the tram) are being considered by some major cities.

Asea Brown Boveri: The Parent Company

In August 1987, Europe's largest ever cross-border merger was announced. The new Asea Brown Boveri group (ABB), comprising Asea (Sweden) and Brown Boveri (Switzerland), had combined sales of US$18 billion (approximately £10 billion) and 180,000 employees. This place ABB amongst the top thirty European companies. The merger was based on a careful analysis of overlaps and complementary areas in both product and geographical terms. In some cases, overcapacity has been eliminated by closing factories. However, the stated objective of the merged group was to invest in and to develop their successful core businesses. In 1988, ABB chief executive Percy Barnevik commentated that: 'We are making a firm and long-term commitment toward electrical utilities, industry and railways. We intend to remain at the technical forefront, and there are within the electro-technical industry important growth niches, such as combined cycle power plants and district heating, our new clean coal technique, high voltage DC transmission, urban transport and high speed trains.' Exhibit 9.4 looks at the possible future for railway companies.

ABB's Business Organization

Before the merger, Asea was already a growth-orientated international business. Its long-term objective was reported to be annual volume growth of 10 per cent, of

Exhibit 9.4 *Press report 3: 'Next chapter of the railway children'*

If Mr Claude Darmon is right, the world's railways may be entering a new golden age. The head of transport operations at GEC–Alsthom has a vision of sleek high-speed trains running at more than 300 kph (212 mph) between many of the world's largest population centres, cutting journey times and curbing pollution.

'We are looking at one of the biggest ventures of the next century,' he says, comparing the new generation of high-speed railways to the development of international highways and telecommunications.

From Europe to Asia, Latin America and the US, the growth of urban populations, national wealth and rail technology lend weight to his view. But if the potential is great, so is the competition.

Mr Wolfram Martinsen is Mr Darmon's greatest competitor and rival as chief executive of Siemens Transportation Systems. His group, with Daimler–Benz's subsidiary, AEG, leads the consortium behind the InterCity Express (ICE) train, which is seeking to erode the lead enjoyed in the world market by GEC–Alsthom's Train à Grande Vitesse (TGV). It is a classic tale of European rivalry.

Mr Martinsen is slightly less sanguine than Mr Darmon in his assessment of the market. 'Within the whole world market for railways, the high-speed market accounts for a maximum of 15 per cent,' he reckons.

The clearest example of the high stakes involved in the industry rivalry has come from South Korea. In August, GEC–Alsthom beat off a furious challenge from Siemens–AEG to win sole negotiating rights to build a high-speed link between Seoul and the south-eastern port of Pusan. Final details of the $2.4bn (£1.61bn) contract to supply the trains and technology are now being hammered out.

Siemens is still protesting at the decision, as is the Japanese consortium led by Mitsubishi, which manufactures the Shinkansen, or bullet trains; but their chances of a Korean change of heart appear slim.

The battle for the Korean contract, however, is just one round of the fight for dominance between the three principal players in the industry. Already, they are preparing to fight for the next contract. First is a possible project to link Taipei with the southern Taiwanese port of Kaohsiung. Bids are expected to be invited towards the end of 1994.

Also on the drawing board are plans for high-speed rail links in Canada, possibly linking Toronto and Quebec via Ottawa and Montreal; in the US, between Washington, New York, and Boston, as well as in Texas (from Houston to Dallas), Chicago, California and the north-west; and between Sydney and Melbourne in Australia.

Siemens and AEG have just spent DM17m (£6.7m) sending a full ICE train to the US, first to undertake a coast-to-coast promotion trip ('Ride the ICE train, the hottest thing on rails' goes the blurb), and now to run for a three-month trial period on the Amtrak lines from Washington to New York.

Both sides have taken in US partners: GEC–Alsthom has linked up with Morrison–Knudsen, and Siemens–AEG with General Motors. Even so, Mr Martinsen believes, 'the US market will develop quite slowly.'

In Europe, therefore, the potential may be greater. At the moment the economic environment is difficult. The effects of recession and the constraints on government budgets have forced the postponement of several TGV orders. Last month, GEC–Alsthom was forced to announce a cost-cutting plan which includes the loss of 660 jobs from its French workforce of more than 9,000. But the first steps of a significant expansion in European high-speed rail links are under way.

The decision by the French government in September to build a new high-speed line between Paris and Strasbourg raises the prospect of the TGV travelling across the border into Germany. It will already do so on the planned Paris–Brussels–Amsterdam and Cologne route, for which 27 trains have been ordered.

Exhibit 9.4 *Continued*

The French authorities have also authorised an extension of the south-eastern line from Lyon to Marseilles and to Montpellier. That would all appear to be to the clear advantage of the TGV.

In Germany, however, the ICE consortium has just won the DM2.2bn next-generation contract for an ICE-2, half the size of the original train, but capable of being linked in pairs to provide greater flexibility. ICEs are now running between from Hamburg in the north and Berlin in the east to Frankfurt, Munich, Stuttgart and Zurich in the south and west. In its 1994 summer timetable, the German Bundesbahn plans to extend the ICE to Vienna.

While the prospects for demand appear healthy, the competition to supply high-speed rail contracts is likely to remain fierce. This is largely the result of the nature of the industry. The market for such networks is comprised of a relatively small number of large projects which come up only every few years and which last for many years. The South Korean contract, for example, is not expected to be completed until 2002.

For GEC–Alsthom and its rivals this time lag makes each contract critical. The experience acquired on one puts the manufacturer in a stronger position for the next. Similarly, the economies of scale obtained by winning several contracts allow cheaper pricing in future bids.

German industry is still reeling from its setback in what Mr Martinsen calls 'the Korea shock'. The final decision in favour of the TGV was said to be because the French train had proved itself for more than a decade, whereas the ICE has only been running since 1991.

Government support is essential to win such massive prestige contracts, Mr Martinsen says. 'It is a question of lots of money, and long-term co-operation. This is only possible if the political will exists.'

Yet he admits that in the US market, for example, the successful contractor will be decided on the basis of 'technology, price and local content. It won't help us much if Chancellor Kohl goes over there.'

Two crucial developments lie ahead. The first is the need to develop multi-system, cross-border trains. If the European links are to become reality, the trains must be able to deal with a host of electricity voltages, signalling systems, and safety standards on different national rail systems. They must also become decidedly cheaper.

This all adds up to good news for the consumer. But for the producers, it raises the question of whether all can survive.

Mr Darmon believes not. 'I doubt very much there is room for three high-speed train manufacturers in Europe,' he says, referring to GEC–Alsthom, Siemens–AEG, and the five-company Trevi consortium, the Italian high-speed train venture led by Breda. 'The investment in R&D and the cost of developing prototypes is too high if you don't win contracts,' he adds.

The intensity of competition could encourage collaboration. 'We are open to co-operation with anyone, and why not Siemens?' asks Mr Darmon. Such a view is supported by the French and German governments, which last year appointed representatives to examine possible co-operation.

The representatives have a delicate task in accommodating national rivalry. Mr Darmon says co-operation would have to consider the fact that 570 high-speed trains have been manufactured by or ordered from GEC–Alsthom, while the comparable figure for the German consortium is 120. He adds that any partnership between the two groups should be based on cost and efficiency considerations and not national and political splits.

Mr Martinsen seems to be more interested in a link-up with the Italian consortium. 'I am convinced we will have two trains in Europe,' he says. 'There is a big enough market at the moment. Whether we can keep that for good is another matter. But that is a question for the railway companies, and the politicians.'

Source: *Financial Times*, 18 November 1993

which about half was to be through organic growth and half through acquisition. During the 1980s, Asea identified a number of essential requirements for decentralization of decision making, many of which have been incorporated into ABB's long-term management and organizational objectives. They are:

1. To devote central staff functions to distinct profit centres.

2. To encourage managers to regard themselves as running an independent business with their own capital base.

3. To reduce head office staff to a minimum.

4. To encourage collaboration and trading between profit centres.

5. To enhance management development.

6. To strengthen corporate identity in order to ensure that decentralization does not detract from overall corporate objectives.

Following the merger, ABB consisted of some eight hundred companies, divided into four thousand profit centres. A matrix structure was used to cover both product and geographical market management. Product management represented one side of the matrix; railway engineering was only one of many business areas, ranging from refrigeration equipment to power transmission cables. Geographical management, on the other side of the matrix, was also essential; it consisted of a number of country and regional managers supporting all the ABB businesses in their areas. Local political and economic factors tend to play an important part in the award of large capital contracts, particularly where the customer is a public sector body. In this context, an active company presence (i.e. production facilities) in a particular country or region may help with market penetration. Despite its size, ABB's head office (in Zurich, Switzerland) employed only fifty staff. The two sides of the matrix reported to a group executive management board, headed by the chief executive and his deputy. Selected financial results for ATL and ABB Group (1989–92) are set out in Exhibits 9.5–9.8.

Financial Results and Targets

Worldwide revenues for 1992 (US$ figures) rose by 3 per cent to $29.6 billion (1991: $28.9 billion). Operating earnings after depreciation fell by 5 per cent to $1.8 billion (1991: $1.9 billion). The group continued its policy of concentrating on core businesses. Divestitures totalled $274 million, whilst acquisitions amounted to $253 million. ABB continued to invest in research and development at a high rate: about 8 per cent of revenues. The group's net debt situation (defined as cash and marketable securities less short- medium- and long-term loans) improved by almost $1 billion. At the end of 1992, the ABB Group had virtually no net debt. Announcing the 1992 results, Percy Barnevik said that:

ABB will emerge from this recession as a much stronger and more profitable company

Exhibit 9.5 *ABB Transportation Holdings Ltd consolidated profit and loss accounts (summarized)*

	1989 £m	1990 £m	1991 £m	1992 £m	1993 £m
Turnover	**126.0**	**318.3**	**299.5**	**401.2**	**518.4**
Operating costs	120.0	305.1	308.6	412.9	519.3
Operating profit/(loss)	**6.0**	**13.2**	**(9.1)**	**(11.7)**	**(0.9)**
Net interest receivable	1.0	9.2	5.4	4.8	3.5
Profit/(loss) before exceptional items	**7.0**	**22.4**	**(3.7)**	**(6.9)**	**2.6**
Exceptional items	0.0	0.0	37.6	0.0	12.4
Profit/(loss) on ordinary activities before taxation	**7.0**	**22.4**	**(41.3)**	**(6.9)**	**(9.8)**
Taxation/(tax receipt)	0.2	0.0	0.3	(7.5)	(2.8)
Profit/(loss) for the period	**6.8**	**22.4**	**(41.6)**	**0.6**	**(7.0)**
Dividends	3.3	4.0	0.0	0.0	0.0
Retained profit for the period	**3.5**	**18.4**	**(41.6)**	**0.6**	**(7.0)**

Note: Changes in financial reporting periods: 1989 data are for 6 months to 30 September 1989 (i.e. from its effective date of acquisition); 1992 data are for 15 months to 31 December 1992 (new accounting reference date coincides with ABB Group's financial year)

Exhibit 9.6 *ABB Transportation Holdings Ltd consolidated balance sheets (summarized)*

	1989 £m	1990 £m	1991 £m	1992 £m	1993 £m
Fixed assets					
Tangible assets	36.5	40.4	64.7	58.8	62.1
Investments	0.0	0.0	0.0	0.0	0.0
	36.5	**40.4**	**64.7**	**58.8**	**62.1**
Current assets					
Stocks	91.4	95.3	97.3	70.1	41.9
Debtors	65.0	103.6	86.2	70.9	69.8
Cash at bank and in hand	91.1	84.4	50.4	119.1	77.8
	247.5	**283.3**	**233.9**	**260.1**	**189.5**
Creditors					
Amounts falling due within one year	175.0	221.3	202.8	238.2	200.5
Net current assets	**72.5**	**62.0**	**31.1**	**21.9**	**(11.0)**
Total assets less current liabilities	109.0	102.4	95.8	80.7	51.1
Creditors					
Amounts falling due after more than one year					
Loans	26.0	26.0	26.0	26.0	13.4
Obligations under finance leases	15.2	11.9	10.5	9.0	9.2
Provisions for liabilities and charges	59.7	37.6	56.3	42.1	31.9
	8.1	**26.9**	**3.0**	**3.6**	**(3.4)**
Financed by:					
Capital and reserves					
Called up share capital	4.6	5.0	5.0	5.0	5.0
Revaluation reserve	0.0	0.0	17.7	17.2	16.7
Profit and loss account	3.5	21.9	(19.7)	(18.6)	(25.1)
	8.1	**26.9**	**3.0**	**3.6**	**(3.4)**

Exhibit 9.7   *ABB Transportation Holdings Ltd selected notes and detail from the financial statements*

	1989 £m	1990 £m	1991 £m	1992 £m	1993 £m
Turnover by destination: geographical analysis					
United Kingdom	124.2	315.4	281.5	399.9	514.2
Exports	1.8	2.9	18.0	1.3	4.2
	126.0	**318.3**	**299.5**	**401.2**	**518.4**
Gross profit calculation					
Turnover	126.0	318.3	299.5	401.2	518.4
Cost of sales	117.5	302.6	301.9	401.9	488.8
Gross profit/(loss)	**8.5**	**15.7**	**(2.4)**	**(0.7)**	**29.6**
Employee numbers (average for period)	8,452	8,707	8,287	6,477	5,846
Aggregate payroll costs (inc. directors' remuneration)	£m	£m	£m	£m	£m
	57.8	128.4	130.9	131.1	100.8
Tangible fixed assets (net book values)					
Freehold land and buildings[a]	12.4	13.1	33.9	34.3	36.7
Plant, equipment and motor vehicles	23.6	26.4	29.1	22.6	22.8
Other	0.5	0.9	1.7	1.9	2.6
	36.5	**40.4**	**64.7**	**58.8**	**62.1**

[a] Most properties were professionally valued on an existing use basis at 30 September 1991.

	£m	£m	£m	£m	£m
Stocks					
Raw materials, components, manufactured stock	59.7	59.3	57.0	54.8	32.6
Work in progress (*less* progress payments)	31.7	36.0	40.3	15.3	9.3
	91.4	**95.3**	**97.3**	**70.1**	**41.9**
Debtors					
Trade debtors	41.4	45.7	56.8	42.9	50.6
Amounts owned by ABB Group undertakings	0.0	0.0	0.0	3.0	5.5
Loan to related company	20.0	30.0	0.0	0.0	0.0
Advance corporation tax recoverable	0.0	0.3	0.0	0.0	0.0
Payments in advance to suppliers	2.2	22.4	24.3	18.0	5.8
Other debtors and prepayments	1.4	5.2	5.1	7.0	7.9
	65.0	**103.6**	**86.2**	**70.9**	**69.8**
Creditors: amounts falling due within one year					
Payments received on account	92.4	138.8	129.8	164.3	75.6
Trade creditors	56.1	58.6	52.0	62.3	77.8
Advance corporation tax	0.2	0.3	0.0	0.0	0.0
Other taxes and social security costs	13.7	12.1	7.9	3.6	6.3
Leasing liabilities	2.3	3.0	1.3	1.3	1.1
Other creditors and accruals	7.0	4.5	11.8	6.7	25.6
Proposed dividend	3.3	4.0	0.0	0.0	0.0
8% unlisted unsecured loan stock	0.0	0.0	0.0	0.0	0.0
	175.0	**221.3**	**202.8**	**238.2**	**200.5**

Exhibit 9.8 *ABB Group selected results, 1992*

Worldwide operations

Revenues of principal business segments	US$m
Power plants	6,947
Power transmission	5,606
Power distribution	3,345
Industry	4,430
Transportation	2,662

Revenues by region	US$m
Western Europe (EU)	11,147
Western Europe (EFTA)	6,320
North America	4,931
Asia, Australasia, Arabia	4,927
South America, Africa, Eastern Europe	2,290
	29,615

Employee numbers (at 31 December 1992)	213,000
Overall return on capital employed	17.9%

Five year trends	Revenues US$m	Operating profit US$m
1988	17,832	854
1989	20,560	1,257
1990	26,688	1,790
1991	28,883	1,980
1992	29,615	1,810

UK operations(£1=US$1.82)

Revenues by business segment	US$m	£m
Power supply	580	317
Industry	186	102
Transportation[a]	407	223
Environmental control	110	60
Financial services	156	85
Various activites	329	180
	1,767	**967**

[a] ABB Group's transportation segment includes ABB British Wheelset Ltd, ABB Signal Ltd, ABB Traction Ltd and ABB Transportation Ltd (consolidated as of 1 July 1992).

than when the recession began. With higher levels of customer service, lower breakeven points and shorter cycle times, the company is well positioned to reap the benefits of increased demand in the Western world when general economic conditions improve. The investments in Asia and Eastern Europe will also increasingly pay off as these economies expand and adjust. Our goals remain to achieve a 10 per cent average operating earnings margin and a 25 per cent return on capital employed within a few years.

Sport-Trax Ltd

Gareth Smith

Loughborough University Business School, UK

On 15 December 1996, Peter Taylor, the sales and marketing manager at Sport-Trax, was informed that his company had failed in its bid to supply a new 400 metre running track to Loughborough University. The university had decided to place the order with one of Sport-Trax's main competitors, Balsam International Ltd. Needless to say, Taylor was disappointed as he had worked for over six months on the project and felt he was in with a good chance of winning the tender. Apart from the size of the order, Loughborough would have been a particularly important contract because of its reputation for sporting excellence in general and athletics in particular. Taylor knew only too well how much easier it was to gain new running track orders when you had well-known and respected existing customers to refer to.

After a few moments' thought, Taylor picked out his by now bulging file of information on the Loughborough bid. Perhaps somewhere in the file was the answer as to why his bid had failed.

Company and Sector Background

Sport-Trax was formed in 1987. Like several businesses in the sector, it was started by a few managers who broke away from the market leader at the time, En Tout Cas. Sport-Trax concentrates on synthetic running tracks, unlike some in the industry which also supply and lay synthetic football, tennis, cricket and hockey pitches. The management structure of the company is shown in Exhibit 10.1.

This case was written with the cooperation of SPRINT (Sports, Play and Recreation Industries National Training Executive), members of staff at Loughborough University and senior managers from running track companies. It is intended to be used as a basis for class discussion rather than to illustrate either effective or ineffective handling of an administrative situation. The personalities involved, the process described and some of the data relating to both have been disguised.

Exhibit 10.1 *Sport-Trax Ltd organizational structure*

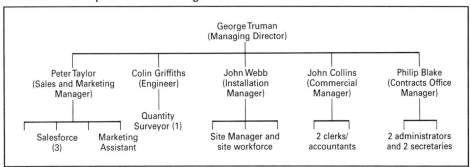

The total workforce is twenty-three employees, which, in the sector, makes it a medium/large size provider. Its turnover in 1995 was £3.7 million and profit levels were 7.3 per cent. Though not massive, this rate of return is seen by commercial manager John Collins as being slightly above the industry norm. Profitability has been relatively poor throughout the synthetic sport surfaces sector (henceforth SSSS) as it felt the draught blowing through the UK economy in the early 1990s. This situation was not helped by the rate-capping of local authorities which directly affected the public sector's demand for running tracks and other large capital expenditure on leisure facilities.

Unlike many other industries, the SSSS is still largely domestic. Some companies will bid for large contracts in the EU, but this is sporadic. Similarly, few European installers compete directly in the UK. Those that do, typically use a British subsidiary for the purpose.

The sector is growing, especially if all synthetic surfaces are included. Most of the competition, like Sport-Trax, are relatively new companies. The only 'old' one, En Tout Cas, was over fifty years old when it was taken over by Balsam in 1993. Other players in this market include Charles Lawrence, Mastersport, Polysport Surfaces and Recreational Surfaces. In the running track market, Polysport and Balsam have approximately the same market share as Sport-Trax. Together they account for 75–80 per cent of the UK market. The UK market for running tracks is the largest in Europe, with between twenty-five and thirty installations per year. The cost of installing a 400 metre track varies considerably. Firstly it varies depending on whether it is a track refurbishment (about £80–100,000), re-laying a new surface on a previously prepared site (anywhere from £180–250,000), or a total 'new build' on a greenfield site (between £400,000 and £500,000). The first option uses existing facilities such as fencing, lighting and even the existing surface, albeit with fairly major repairs and refurbishment. The latter option, the new build, typically includes the new surface, changing facilities, lighting plus basic civil engineering tasks, such as ensuring that the track is not built on top of a natural spring and so on.

The Loughborough contract was for a new surface to be relaid plus upgrading of lighting and perimeter fencing. This was, in fact, the third track that was being laid at the University. The first had been constructed using cinders, followed by an early synthetic 'tartan' track. This last track now was showing its age, and the wear and tear on the more heavily used inside lanes prompted the decision to replace.

The new track surfaces have a rubber base and a polyurethane resin surface. The supply of the raw materials is dominated by two producers, Polytan in Germany and Conica in Switzerland. These two sources supply about 90 per cent of the UK market with the remaining 10 per cent coming from ICI in Holland. The installers buy both the rubber compound and the polyurethane resin from one of these sources. The track is then 'made' on-site by mixing, levelling and then spraying the resin to form the top, running track surface. Although this is a complex task, done to very fine tolerances, it is difficult to differentiate the products of competing installers as they all use similar suppliers. If produced to the correct specification, the surface ought to be identical from all installers. Historically, any differentiation has come from 'augmented' product features (better lighting or changing facility design) or 'augmented' services such as reliability, reputation, warranty provision and so on.

Sport-Trax believed that, given its concentration on running track installation, it was better than the competition and sought to achieve a price premium over its competitors to reflect this.

Peter Taylor often put it this way when selling to potential customers. 'All tracks may be chemically the same, but the way a track performs in use varies depending on who installed it. Our tracks are perfect for those customers who want a long-lasting, trouble-free surface which will satisfy the recreational user as well as the international sprinter. We consistently meet and beat the tolerances and standards laid down by governing bodies of athletics [the Amateur Athletics Association (AAA) and the International Amateur Athletics Federation (IAAF)] and their technical advisers. We don't lay any other synthetic surfaces such as dri-play, and our current list of customers includes some of the most prestigious in the country.' He would then finish off with his favourite line: 'when it comes to running tracks, Sport-Trax has a proven track record.'

In the past six months, Sport-Trax had also begun to promote its product as having a new feature. A research link with a local university yielded a new ingredient which when added during the top coat spraying process improved the durability of the running surface. To support this, Sport-Trax had used laboratory test results to simulate years of wear on the surface. In this environment the life expectancy of the track was increased from ten to over twelve years. The new surface was branded as Sport-Trax W S and sold as resistant to running spike damage. Needless to say, the competition were less convinced about the improvement and they counter-claimed that the benefits were as yet unproven, hinting during sales calls that the 'new' track was something of a risk as the surface had not actually been tested in real conditions.

Purchasing a Running Track – The Seller's Perspective

One of Peter Taylor's salesforce described the buyer segments as follows:

> Our sales tend to split about sixty–forty between the public and private sector. This divide is getting increasingly blurred, however. An increasing number of projects include two, three even four partners from differing sectors. Recently we've seen the effect of the National Lottery as local authorities team up with private clubs or universities to bid for this funding. These groups still act on their own at times too. An interesting link we are increasingly encountering are those builders/developers who have to provide 'sweeteners' in the shape of sports facilities to get permission from the local planners for large housing developments of the new town/suburb variety. In addition, we shouldn't forget the role of the national bodies such as the AAA and the Sports Council which can act not only as paymasters, but also as active initiators of new sports track developments. Finally, there will always be a few developments which are harder to categorize, such as the recent installation of a 100 metre sprint track at Murrayfield in Edinburgh, the Scottish national rugby stadium. This is within a middle distance run from the national athletics stadium at Meadowbank.
>
> All tracks are bought using a formal tendering procedure, though the number of tendering companies can vary from three to double figures at the extreme. They have to budget for their purchase at the beginning of their financial year and, typically, once a budget has been agreed it has to be spent, or at least committed before the end of the financial year.

Peter Taylor, as Sport-Trax's 'expert on universities' and on their buying processes, added the following extra insight:

> When you're selling an expensive piece of kit which will last for a long time, the buying process tends to be very complex. Within universities there are four main groups involved plus other lesser ones:
>
> 1. The Sports Administrators and in Loughborough's case, its physical education, sports science and recreation management department.
> 2. The estates department.
> 3. The finance officers and the bursar.
> 4. Other members of the senior management team of the university such as the vice chancellor (roughly equivalent to the managing director), the senior pro-vice chancellor (read deputy MD), the registrar (read operations director) plus a few others.

Sports administrators are users of the track and trackside facilities. They are typically lecturers on sport-related degrees who split their time between this activity and coaching gifted athletes. To them, Loughborough's sporting reputation and the quality of facilities are inextricably linked. Only with the best possible track will Loughborough continue to attract the best student athletes and continue to host prestigious athletics competitions. Such competitions include national AAA trials and the annual Loughborough students, the AAA and GB students competitions (see Plate 9).

The estates department is staffed by engineers and surveyors who deal with all building matters on the campus. They manage a large number of gardeners, carpenters, electricians, cleaners and so on who maintain the buildings and campus area. The grounds-staff who look after the running track are also based in estates.

The bursar is head of finance in the university. As such, any capital expenditure is controlled eventually by him. As resources are increasingly stretched in higher education, his job is to get ever more from scarce resources. Along with the rest of the senior management of the university, he is concerned about wastage and is keen to increase productivity wherever possible. The finance officers who work for the bursar also have to control expenditures. They tend to have the task of managing individual budgets relating to specific projects when senior management have agreed them. There is a genuine concern about purchasing expensive, state-of-the-art kit which will be superseded in a short time. Like estates, the finance officers are concerned about new, untried technology which may involve unforeseen extra work and expense in the future.

The senior management team of the university is invariably influential in large expenditure decisions but very difficult to influence directly. Individual senior managers are always busy and usually protected from the outside by secretaries or administrators whose role it is to filter out those enquiries and requests which can be dealt with at a lower level. Also, the group is not always made up of the same people. The director of works is involved at the highest level for new building decisions but only marginally when academic matters are discussed. A further complication is that this group, whilst making broad policy decisions, will then devolve the detail elsewhere: having agreed to a running track, the task of awarding the contract falls to others.

On a more personal note, both the vice chancellor and senior pro vice chancellor at Loughborough are keenly interested in sport. They are very aware that in an increasingly competitive market for students it is important to be differentiated in some way. Sport is clearly one way Loughborough can achieve this.

Purchasing a Running Track – The Buyer's Perspective

From inside an organization there is often a different view of the buying process than from the outside. Purchases critical to a supplier may be relatively small to the purchaser and vice versa. To balance the perspective from Sport-Trax, the views and recollections of the director of works and the director of the Centre for Coaching and Recreation Management have been collected. Though not the only university employees involved in the track purchase, they were closely associated with the process at various stages, from its inception through to its formal opening.

Richard Ellison's Story

Richard, as director of the Centre for Coaching and Recreation Management is well positioned to provide the perspective from the sports side. He, in effect, manages the university's sporting facilities and is responsible for the various coaches and ultimately the sporting success of the university as a whole. The athletics coach, Nick Emmett, was the person who informed Richard of the need for the new track. It was Nick's view that, to maintain its current status, Loughborough's track facilities must be at least as good, and preferably better, than the top athletics clubs from which many of the new undergraduates came. As coach to several international athletes and recently England track event coach for a major international competition, Nick travelled extensively and was well aware of current state-of-the-art developments in track and stadia design.

The formal request which Nick had made was not the first that Richard had received. Two years before, a similar request had been passed into the committee structure only to be rejected because of the priority given to spending on new halls of residence to cater for the growth in undergraduate numbers in the early to mid-1990s. As such, Richard was aware that timing and luck played a part in capital expenditure like this. He gauged that the new residence building boom was past for now but was aware that two other large projects in the shape of new buildings for the business school and engineering were being considered. Any new request for sports facilities would also be considered in the light of the new sports centre that had recently been agreed. A final consideration was that there were others in the physical education, sports science and recreation management (PESS&RM) department who wanted improved facilities for their own area, be it a new swimming pool or a new fitness testing laboratory. However, these decisions about how to spend scarce resources were not Richard's to make. He requested information on tracks from his deputy. Given the spread of facilities, he no longer tried to keep abreast of all the latest developments and this task fell to Barbara Smith. Any technical or general sales literature about sports equipment or facilities he forwarded to her to file. Part of her job was to keep abreast of technological trends and developments, so she actively collected any information that might be useful.

The next stage was for Richard to put the proposal forward, in principle, to the rest of the PESS&RM department. It would be for them to do the initial screening of requests for resources. At this stage, Professor Derwyn Jones as head of department, would make known his views on the department's priorities. As the track expenditure no longer conflicted with the new sports hall, he gave the proposal his initial support. Although not all members of staff were enthusiastic about the new track, it was agreed at the staff meeting that it would be a top priority in their pleading for the coming year.

The next stage was for the proposal to go before the working party on sports facilities. The registrar was in the chair with the remit of adding a broader university-wide view on proceedings. Also on this committee were Richard Ellison and Professor Jones. A final member was the director of works, Gordon Walker. As the head of the estates section his job is to look after the university, its buildings and grounds. At this early stage, his brief was mainly one of listening and asking questions about the scope and feasibility of the proposal from a civil engineering perspective: will new roads need to be built, new drainage laid and so on?

Richard recalled that Professor Jones made the case for the proposal at the meeting and it was agreed to forward it to the next rung of the committee ladder, the university facility development committee. From this point on Richard could only report on meetings and discussions where he was not present. Gordon Walker and the registrar were present. Walker provided general support about the feasibility of the new track and the limited amount of disruption to the university's infrastructure. The registrar sought to balance out the need for a new track with the requirements for the two new buildings already mentioned and the refurbishment of the building that the business school would vacate. In addition there were smaller proposals for funds for machinery for grounds maintenance. The committee agreed that the track proposal should go before the senior management committee and that estates should flesh out the practical issues and likely costs.

This was done with the vice chancellor showing his enthusiasm for the proposal while the bursar showed a natural caution about the funding implications for wider university finances. From here, the task of developing a detailed specification for the work to be done was passed back to the estates department. A budget figure for the work was given to Gordon Walker. The guideline figure was £200,000, some £50,000 less than the original approximate costing supplied by estates.

As a final comment on the process of buying the track and those involved, Richard threw the names of the Athletics Union (AU) and Mark Jackson into the discussion. The AU, through its president Alison Woolmer, was surprisingly not too enthusiastic about the track. A new 50 metre swimming pool was seen as more urgently needed, providing greater benefit to a larger number of students. Given the unusually democratic nature of university decision-making procedures, it is likely that Alison or her students' union equivalent, would have been able to make their views known at various committees. Mark Jackson, on the other hand, was the president of the Charnwood Athletics Club which shared the track with the students. Legally the track belongs to the university but Charnwood had just built a new clubhouse next to the track. Also the club has close links both with the local authority and community – both important 'publics' to a university always seeking to improve the town and gown links. To further complicate matters, Jackson was a member of the academic staff at the university. Richard was unsure of the amount of consultation and influence Jackson and Woolmer had had.

Gordon Walker's Story

Gordon's story confirmed the passage of events much as Richard had perceived them. Being on the university facility development committee, he was able to confirm the committee's role in balancing requests from across the university. He also mentioned the role of good fortune in the process. If more capital projects had been before the meeting, the new track would probably have been sacrificed, it being the last of those proposals accepted.

Gordon, as a fellow of the Institute of Chartered Surveyors, is a professional in his chosen area. He defined his job as 'acting as the university's agent when procuring facilities'. To this end he brings his professional expertise and training to bear on all matters involving the fabric of the university. If a hall of residence is being built, he or one of his colleagues will commission architects, choose a builder, inspect progress and generally protect the university's interests until the project is finished.

Although he had been in his current post for nearly twenty years, Walker still faces new problems because of the wide range of areas that estates is asked to manage. The running track is a good example of this. One is bought every ten to fifteen years and the needs of athletes and surfaces change markedly over this timescale. In addition, he and his colleagues are more comfortable with buildings, simply because they have more practical and professional experience of them. As he pointed out, 'a hall of residence is a known quantity. Many builders can handle such a project easily and we have well established links with a number of them. An increasing number provide what is called design and build facility, where they supply the architectural design service as part of the package. Sports facilities, be it an indoor sports hall or a running track, are more tricky. The needs of more people need to be considered, given the range of uses to which they tend to be put. Also the suppliers are more diverse and typically a lot smaller than the building companies we deal with. Add to this the choices of surfaces available which often compete and are difficult to differentiate between except on personal preference and you can see what I mean.'

In fact, Gordon's grounds superintendent, Paul Murray, became particularly involved in the preparatory stages of setting the specifications and managing the actual installation of the track because he had been heavily involved when the previous track had been laid some ten years earlier. His job also meant that he would be directly involved with all maintenance work on the track when installed.

Sensibly, Gordon sought advice on how to proceed, and he talked to Richard Ellison initially. Many questions needed answering, such as who were the main companies in this market? What sorts of surface were available? What type of surface met the requirements of the users and other interested parties? What was the going rate for this sort of project? What actually needs to be provided as opposed to what would be nice to have? Richard was able to furnish Gordon with some of this information but not all. On the more technical side of the track's specification he used the Sports Council and the AAA for guidance. On the more managerial considerations, such as which companies and which surfaces were appropriate for the mixed type of use it would get (serious athletes, fun/fitness runners, the local club – Charnwood Athletic – and local schools), he commissioned a consultancy specializing in sport and leisure artificial surfaces. At the end of the day, Gordon was not sure whether he had got good value from the five figure sum spent in this way. He did, however, have a much better grasp of the main activities required from any installer; what was less critical and the sorts of costs involved.

Gordon went back to the senior management group to inform them of a realistic budget only to be told that this was on the high side of what was available.

The 'realistic' figure Gordon quoted was not totally ruled out but it would eat into contingency reserve funds which had to cover this and other capital projects being undertaken in the next financial year. This put Gordon in the familiar position of looking for value for money with a tight budget. Sometimes he felt that quality was being shaved to get the right price, and that in the longer term it would cost the university more via extra maintenance costs or premature replacement of a facility.

From the above consultations and internal expertise within the estates department a formal tender document was drafted. The external consultants produced the body of this and some amendments were made after joint discussions. Part of this technical specification is supplied as Exhibit 10.2. Also included were requirements for completion and penalty payments for lateness. The deadline for submission of the tenders was Friday, 25 August 1995.

After some debate it was decided to invite five companies to tender: Sport-Trax, Balsam, Charles Lawrence, Polysport Surfaces and a small, new supplier which had recently set up in the locality.

Taylor Tries to Sell a Running Track

Sport-Trax received a call from Paul Murray informing the company of the university's intention to replace its existing 400 metre track. Given the potential size of the job and Loughborough's reputation, it was passed to Peter Taylor rather than to one of the salesforce. Taylor immediately called up the relevant files to see if the company had dealt with the university before. It had not. On the file was some background data on the university, the PESS&RM department and its head, Professor Jones. The latter was described as an internationally regarded expert in the field of sports science. His department had thirty-two academics and full-time coaches as of March 1993. The sports facilities at Loughborough were judged to be somewhat dated and a general process of upgrading and new building had been identified. Observational research in 1994 by one of Sport-Trax's more enthusiastic salespeople had identified synthetic football, hockey and tennis surfaces laid by En Tout Cas and Charles Lawrence. The running track had no corporate identification on view, though, at a guess, it had also been laid by En Tout Cas (now part of Balsam). Also in the file was a copy of a printout which showed that the university had been sent a copy of Sport-Trax's brochure in the autumn of 1993, addressed to the director of the Centre for Coaching and Recreation. They had not received the brochure containing information on the new W S track system.

Taylor kept a diary and notes of his sales visits which chart his experiences from this initial contact. More unusually, he used a tape recorder to capture the views and actions during the tendering process. He justified this by pointing out that a lot of the detail was lost when written into the sales management forms (see Exhibit 10.3). His tapes are transcribed below.

Exhibit 10.2 *Technical specifications*

LOUGHBOROUGH UNIVERSITY OF TECHNOLOGY

400 Metre Running Track – Specifications for Tendering Purposes

1. **General description**
   The university is looking for a new track to replace its existing one. We are seeking a specially formulated spike-resistant two-layer multi-component porous rubber and resin composite system formed *in situ* by mixing levelling and screeding process.

   The base layer to be composed of polyurethane resin bound to black EPDM or SBR granules of a graded size. The surface layer comprises a specially formulated high-grade coloured EPDM granule bound with polyurethane resin which, when mixed, is spray-applied to the base layer.

   Main areas of application: track installations which have to meet regional performance requirements (i.e. local authority tracks, school tracks) attracting 50,000 users per annum.

2. **Surface texture**
   Porous granular finish.

3. **Colour**
   Terracotta red.

4. **Thickness**
   The track is to be laid to achieve a minimum thickness of 13 mm to comply with the current IAAF requirements. The thickness will be measured in accordance with DIN 18035 pt 6. Any adustments required to meet specific contract conditions will be taken up in the base layer of the system (i.e. minimum, maximum or average depths).

5. **Standard deformation**

	Ideal results	*DIN standard*
At 0°C	0.81 mm	0.6–1.8 mm
At 23°C	1.04 mm	(temp. range 0–40°C)
At 40°C	1.35 mm	

6. **Permeability** · 0.24 cm s^{-1} · min. 0.01 cm s^{-1}

7. **Spike resistance** · Class 1 · Class 1

8. **Tensile strength** · 0.65 N mm^{-2} / 68% · min. 0.5 N mm^{-2} / min. 40%

9. **Sliding behaviour** · Dry 0.97 / Wet 0.73 · Dry < 1.1 / Wet > 0.5

10. **Penetration characteristics**
    Residual penetration · 0.65 mm · max. 1.00 mm

11. **Burning characteristics** · Class 1 to DIN 51960 · Class 1 to DIN 51960

12. **Wearing behaviour** · 2.0 · min 1.0

Exhibit 10.2 *Continued*

13. Aging	QZ no value < 0.75	Tensile strength min. 0.75
	QB no value < 0.75	Ultimate strain min. 0.75
	QE no value < 0.75	QE min 0.75
	QE no value > 1.25	QE max 1.25
	No colour value < 3 degrees	colour transfer min. 3 degrees

Comments
The above specifications are such that the tender should comply with the requirements of DIN 18035 pt 6 (draft October 1991) and is suitable as a surface for running track and field event runways.

Wednesday, 10 May 1995

I rang Paul Murray back straight away to thank him for allowing us to tender for the track. I fished for some extra information on who we were competing with but he was unwilling to give the information. I told him that I knew Gordon Walker, his boss, from the days when I was an engineer and he, Gordon, was a surveyor. When I tried to find out who else was involved internally with the project, he suggested that I ring Professor Jones in the PE department. Felt I'd made a useful first impression on Paul.

Called through to Professor Jones' office only to be informed that he was in Hungary at a conference and wouldn't be back this week. Arranged to see him on Tuesday next on his return. His secretary's name is Janet and she talks about her boss with a kind of hushed reverence. I tried to get an earlier appointment on the Monday but she refused, saying he had too many things to catch up with. I asked if there was anybody else whom I could talk to in the meantime, but she thought it better to wait until Tuesday's meeting.

Tuesday, 16 May

Met up with Professor Jones as arranged. He is a man under pressure. He arrived fifteen minutes late from another meeting and it was only 9.45. He briefly ran through the decision from the senior management committee to put the running track out to tender and that funds had been earmarked for the purpose. I didn't fall into the trap of asking him what the budget was and he didn't tell me. When he had recovered from his rush across campus he became enthusiastic about the track. Clearly he is keen on sport as well as a good academic. After giving him my sales pitch on the new Sport-Trax W S product, he asked some very insightful questions, some of which about the technical make-up of the track and its new properties I couldn't answer there and then but promised to send him more information. I also gave him the new brochures on the W S track and noticed that he (a) was impressed

Exhibit 10.3   *Sport-Trax sales management analysis form*

ACCOUNT NAME:

KEY ACCOUNT DATA

Tender request date: _____   Account no.: _____   Type of organization: _____

Main contact: Name _____   Designated salesperson _____ Previous files: *Yes   No*
Position _____   *(If YES append to this)*
Postal address: _____   Telephone: _____ Fax: _____

1. NAME AND ADDRESS OF OTHER PARTNERS IF A JOINT BID:

Partner 1: _____
Partner 2: _____
Partner 3: _____

2. DECISION MAKERS – IMPORTANT CONTACTS

Individuals	Name	Job title/ speciality	General remarks
Influencers			
Decision-makers			
Users			
Initiators			
Buyers			
Gatekeepers			

3. CURRENTLY INSTALLED TRACK

Type	Description	Supplied by	Installation date	Year to replace	Value of potential order

4. PLANNED NEW TRACK INSTALLATION

Type	Quote		% chance	Est. order date		Est. delivery		Quoted price
	No.	Date		1996	1997	1996	1997	

5. TENDER COMPETITION

Company/ product	Strategy/ tactics	% chance	Strength	Weakness

6. SALES PLAN   Product: _____ Quote no.: _____ Quoted price: _____

Key issues	Sport-Trax's plan	Support needed from:	Date of follow-up/ remarks

7. ACTIONS – IN SUPPORT OF PLAN

Specific action	Responsibility	Due dates			Results/remarks
		Original	Revised	Completed	

8. FUTURE MARKETING STRATEGY (FIVE YEAR HORIZON)

Key longer-term issues	Involvement of Sport-Trak personnel	Timings (approx.)	Specific activities	Broad cost implications

at their quality and (b) put them into a file which already contained brochures of at least two of our main competitors, Polysport and Charles Lawrence. He asked if we had installed a running track anywhere interesting of late and so I referred him to the list of our clients in the brochure. I emphasized the number of 'good' athletics clubs we had as clients and again he seemed impressed.

When I asked for more information he referred me to Gordon Walker, the director of works and I told him of our past acquaintance. At 10.30 on the dot his attitude changed and I was aware that he was due at another meeting and ours was at an end. I left, promising to be in touch with the technical information he had asked for. Whilst he hurried off I tried to engage Janet in conversation. She became less cautious as we talked, but she doesn't know much about the running track except that it generated a lot of debate at a staff meeting several months before. I left her after getting directions to the estates office which was on the other side of the campus.

Gordon Walker was out of the university all day so I left a message with his secretary promising to ring the next day.

Wednesday, 17 May

Met up with Gordon Walker this afternoon. It was good to see him again after all this time. He seems to be wearing better than me. We didn't make much progress on the track as he has decided to devolve most if not all responsibility to Paul Murray. He will feed information to Paul from the university and channel Paul's progress to the relevant committees when required. I gained a strong impression that he wasn't as interested in the track project as some other major building initiatives around the university. We agreed that I would keep in touch but that the day to day work should go through Paul. Paul had another appointment so I didn't get to see him. His secretary is the same as Gordon's and she gave me a large file containing all the specifications for the new track.

Monday, 22 May

Used the weekend to have a good look at the track specs. Most of it was as I expected, using AAA and IAAF standards across the board. As the typeface was different in places as well as the style of writing I think some of it was written by a consultant, with the estates department adding the introduction and the conclusion. The specifications do not help us as much as they might because they do not make much of a play on the delivery and service side of things. Also, all of our competitors will be able to meet the minimum technical standards requested.

Tuesday, 23 May

Colin Griffiths and John Webb have looked at the proposal and they confirm my initial reaction to the spec. It looks as if I've got to work hard on selling our benefits which go beyond those minimums required in the tender document. On the positive side, we are selling into an organization which will understand and value the benefits and hopefully will be prepared to pay for them. Although we really need this contract I think that the right approach is to try the premium product, premium price strategy in the first instance. In fact, I talked this through with George [Truman, the MD] over a working lunch and he trusted my judgement on this one, especially when he heard of my prior acquaintance with Gordon Walker.

Friday, 26 May

Eventually managed to see Paul Murray. He is surprisingly young and, reading between the lines, is pleased to be given so much responsibility on this project. While we were socializing at the start of the meeting he told me that he was doing a part-time MBA at the business school. He mentioned this because he planned to use the purchase of the running track as the focus of his final year project. It means he will be keen to do things right, I guess.

I told Paul all about our product features, though at times he looked less interested than I'd hoped. I spent some time talking through some of the technical benefits of the W S system which proved easy now that I'd had to supply them to Professor Jones. I gave him the full range of our brochures, including the technical documentation. I assured him that we not only met but exceeded the technical requirements. I also suggested he asked our competition how they compared on after-sales service, warranty and the overall durability of their track surface. I left him with the open-ended offer to call me at any time if he needed more information or clarification. Given that he will see another four salespeople, the potential for confusion is great and I think he appreciated the offer. I promised I would be in touch again anyway when I returned from my vacation in two weeks' time.

Monday, 12 June

Returned feeling refreshed and anxious to progress things with the university. I rang through to Janet, Professor Jones' secretary only to discover he was out of the country at another conference – not a bad life if you can get it. He is back on Thursday but is particularly busy because it is undergraduate exam time. I booked a meeting for the following Monday in the afternoon. I tried to meet with others from the department about the track but Janet said the Professor might not approve. Luckily I have some work to do on a contract in Norwich over the next few days to keep me busy.

Monday, 19 June

Saw Professor Jones and was pleased to find that he had read and understood the brochures I had left with him. He confessed to reading them on his flight to San Francisco. He also seems to be pleased with what he had read. The only sticky moment came when he asked why we had gone to a competitor university to have the testing done on the new product features. I told him that we were tied in with them because of the overall research project and he let it pass. After more discussion on the track's features he asked about price. I told him that our contracts manager was working on this and that it would be available soon. To pave the way for what I suspect will be a higher quote than at least two of the competition, I reinforced the idea that ours included a better level of service and a unique product. When I told him that, and that we would be sure to provide value for money when the whole package was considered, he smiled.

Tuesday, 27 June

I finally managed to get to see the bursar, Mr Reason. It's always like this when you want to talk to the senior management of an organization, and the university is no different. Knowing that he has no technical knowledge of the product I kept things pretty general and concentrated on what I think is of most importance to him, the cost of the project. He listened politely to my reasons why we had chosen the price and then told him that we would be quoting in the region of £260,000. I asked him if this was in the area they were expecting but he refused to commit himself. He did, however, say that we were expensive compared with other initial prices quoted. I went over the reasons for this and then used my 'secret weapon'. I gave him what my old lecture notes refer to as 'perceived value pricing'. This means putting a price on the benefits to allow differing offers to be compared fairly. For the Loughborough job it went like this:

> *Pricing Structure: 400 metre Sport-Trax W S running track*
> £200,000 is the price if we offered the same as the competition
> £ 30,000 is the price for the longer-lasting product
> £ 20,000 is the price for the more comprehensive warranty cover
> £ 10,000 is the price for the assurance of better after-sales service
> £ 10,000 is the price for better service during the installation
> £ 5,000 is the price for our specialism in running track installation
>
> £275,000 is the price to cover the total package
> £ 15,000 is the DISCOUNT

I sat back to let it sink in. It usually comes as a surprise to customers to realize that a higher quote is actually a discounted price, in this case of £15,000 using the figures above. Mr Reason was quiet for a while and then asked how I had arrived at the figures and how I could justify £10,000 for better service and £5,000 for our specialization in running tracks only. Of course I was ready and explained how we were better than the competition on these dimensions. He spoiled the effect by saying that they were only estimates but I think the point was well and truly made. He asked if he could keep my figures and naturally I agreed. As I took my leave, Reason told me that he was dealing with the pricing side of things through estates and that he didn't want other members of the university knowing everyone's prices before the formal tenders were submitted on or before August 24th. This seemed a little unusual but, given that prices quoted at this stage can still change and thus cause confusion, I said I understood.

I left him with our brochures but he didn't look at them whilst I was there. This, and a few other things he did, make me think he is an old hand at negotiating contracts and didn't want to be seen to be too keen.

Friday, 30 June

I took a file over to Reason which contained more detail on three other universities that already had one of our tracks installed, one of them has the new W S system. There were testimonials from each supporting the level of service received and their general satisfaction with the track in use. Also included were contact numbers for the bursars at these institutions. His secretary told me Reason was busy and I left the material with her. She was very keen to chat and quickly told me that Mr Reason had already seen all of the other companies' reps, as she called them. 'Some of them have been here more than once and one in particular seems desperate for the job. The trouble is that Mr Reason is getting confused because prices vary so much.' At this point she realized perhaps she had said too much and changed the subject. Before I left I managed to discover a bit more about how the decision to buy the track was made. It appears that there is a senior management committee which will decide based on the tenders themselves and the recommendation of estates. 'Maybe you need to talk to the vice chancellor himself,' she joked.

Tuesday, 11 July

I called back on Paul Murray to see if he had read all our material and to answer any questions he might have as a result. He said he had but didn't have any questions to ask. Instead he began to ask me about whether we had BS5750 in Sport-Trax.[1] This threw me a little but then I remembered about his MBA thesis. He was using me as part of his case study. I told him we hadn't but neither did any of our competitors as yet. He started to talk about 'relationship marketing' and the 'supply chain', both of which I had heard of and could talk about as they relate to Sport-Trax. It was difficult to gauge how things went as he did most of the talking. I wish Gordon was taking a more active role in the decision as we understand each other so well.

Back in the office I rang through to the bursar. He was out of his office but Irene, his secretary, did volunteer that he had got some positive feedback from the three universities already using our track. I asked her to send copies of this to Paul Murray and Professor Jones and she said she would. This pleased me because it showed they were interested enough to follow things through and also that there was now evidence to support our product and service claims.

Tuesday, 18 July

Rang through to Professor Jones to check that he had received the endorsements from the other universities and he had. He asked what sort of price we would be asking and I told him of the bursar's request for confidentiality. This didn't go down at all well especially as one of the competition had already quoted a figure of £225,000 to him. This put me in a difficult position and I resolved it partially by saying that we would be competitive given the extra value we were offering. Although he was still clearly annoyed, I was encouraged because his response told me that he wants our track but sees price as a stumbling block. My thoughts about Jones were confirmed this afternoon. I rang through to arrange a meeting when his secretary told me we were the sports administrator's preference. I'm booked to see Reason next week and feeling quietly confident with the way things are going.

Friday, 28 July

After the last meeting with the bursar I thought that I'd take George Truman, our MD, along to fly the flag. Reason still seems stuck on the price. 'Everybody claims to be the best so I can't understand why your quote is so much higher than the rest.' We tried to move the discussion away from price and back to the product, but in the end Reason said 'only a significant reduction will help you I'm afraid.' I asked for some time to talk to George and also requested that Paul be asked to attend. Within half an hour all four of us were back together and I gave our new, lower price. I would have held out, thinking we were being bluffed, but George was keen to get the business and we had no new starts on the order book before November. At least I was able to put in the classic 'if' part of the negotiator's armoury. We were prepared to drop the price to £240,000 *if* the contract was signed before the end of the calendar year and an initial payment of 50 per cent was made in the financial year to April 1996; the balance to be paid on completion. This would help our cash flow position without being too onerous on the university, whose finances could cope with such an arrangement. More importantly, it signalled that we were not caving in on price. Both Reason and Murray were non-committal but thanked us for our time.

Tuesday, 1 August

I left a few days for the news of the price change to filter through to Professor Jones before ringing him. He had heard of the reduction and said, 'perhaps you should have been lower first time round'. He sounded a little angry but asked how quickly we could install. I told him that it was unwise to start before March because of the danger of a hard frost affecting the curing process of the track. After that it should take about three months assuming no unforeseen problems. He didn't comment on this.

Friday, 4 August

During our monthly management meeting I told my colleagues of progress on the Loughborough tender and how things were still in the melting pot. Philip Blake suggested that a site visit for Murray and anyone else interested would be a good idea. Beyond this we had a general chat about our pricing strategy and I told them how difficult it was to sustain our premium pricing strategy given the state of the marketplace.

Monday, 7 August

Rang through to Murray and suggested a site visit. He wasn't enthusiastic even though I promised him a good lunch on the way. He told me that he was very busy now as there was a lot of work getting the grass playing fields and amenity areas ready for the winter. As he was the person most likely to want a site visit I decided not to offer the same to Jones or Reason.

　　Made a casual call to Irene Daley, the bursar's secretary, as she seems to know as well as anyone what is going on. According to her there had been more discussion over the track than over much bigger projects – some of it, she said, had been ill-tempered, though she wouldn't give me any more details on who had been involved. At a guess, Reason and Jones might not see eye to eye on this. I'm not sure where Paul Murray stands or, for that matter, how much influence he or Gordon Walker will have.

Thursday, 10 August

I've pondered what Irene said on Monday and arranged to meet with George Truman about our final position. With the deadline for tenders to be submitted at the end of this month I'm beginning to worry that we might just be pipped to the post. George was concerned that another reduction would send the wrong messages to the university. After quite a discussion, which considered Sport-Trax's wider business position, we agreed to make a final offer with the previous payment conditions of £225,000; this represents a super value package and should be successful. It certainly means we won't make much profit on the deal.

Friday, 25 August

I took our tender in a sealed envelope to Paul Murray's office as requested. He didn't open it but put it with some other envelopes in a cabinet and locked it. He said that he was glad that this part of the process was over. He also said that he had never realized how complex such decisions were and that even though he was writing it up for his thesis he wasn't totally clear on it now. He said it had been a great way of seeing how the culture of an organization and internal politics alters the traditional, rational models of decision-making in some of the more naive textbooks. I just agreed with him.

September 1995

Over the month I've tried to keep my finger on the pulse and gauge how things are moving. Reason doesn't want to talk about it and Murray is always too busy to say more than that things are progressing through the normal channels. Gordon has been more communicative but he doesn't seem to have much to do with the proposal now. Professor Jones didn't seem to be too keen to talk to me but I'm not sure if its to do with the track or because he has a lot of teaching to prepare for in October.

   At the end of the month I received a letter which had obviously been sent to all of the companies which tendered apologizing for the fact that the decision on the track had not been made at a committee meeting recently because of too much on the agenda. A reconvened meeting would take place in December and we would all be notified then.

Friday, 15 December

Received an early Christmas present that I could have done without – a letter from the bursar confirming that we had been unsuccessful and thanking us for the effort we had put in, difficult to make the decision etc.etc. Got my secretary to ring his secretary and found out that Balsam had got the contract for £220,000. Needless to say I'm gutted to have lost it by such a small amount and think the university has made a mistake. This means I must talk through with John Webb and George Truman whether we will have to lay off some or all of the site workers until work picks up.

Note

1.   BS5750 is the British standard for quality as applied to trading organizations.

Guinness Peat Aviation
The Global Flotation that Failed

Brenda Cullen
University College Dublin, Ireland

Introduction

On Wednesday, 17 June 1992, the directors of Guinness Peat Aviation (GPA), the world's largest aircraft leasing group, reluctantly accepted the advice of their financial advisors. The public flotation of GPA would have to be cancelled. Despite great optimism in advance of the flotation, investors had simply failed to subscribe in sufficient numbers on the day. Just hours before shares were due to be priced and trading was to begin, Tony Ryan, GPA's chairman announced, 'It would be unwise to proceed with the offer in circumstances which were adverse to both the company's and the shareholders' interest'.

GPA's planned global flotation had been billed as a unique offering, a simultaneous listing in New York, London, Tokyo and Dublin by tender offer, to give the issue maximum flexibility. A team of the world's most impressive investment banks and security houses were enlisted to ensure the success of the flotation. If the worldwide public offering had gone as planned, a company that started with a $50,000 loan seventeen years previously, would have been worth $3 billion in 1992.

Possible reasons why GPA had not proved a popular stock abounded. Many analysts pointed to the current difficulties faced by the US airline industry, general market conditions and the reluctance of US fund managers to commit themselves to the issue before seeing the response of UK investors. Another view was that the flotation was dogged from the outset by noisy disagreements between GPA and its advisors, relationships with the investors were considered strained and the company's contact with the media was often 'extremely icy'.

GPA and its team of advisors were both surprised and bitterly disappointed with the failure. They urgently needed to consider ways to deal with the adverse public attention which this failed flotation would attract. Furthermore, although they had sufficient financial resources to see the group through the next twelve to fifteen months, they now desperately needed the confidence and goodwill of the financial community which, at some stage, they would have to tap for finance.

Background

Chairman Tony Ryan founded GPA as a private company in 1975 with just $50,000 in equity. At that time Guinness Peat, the merchant banker, and Aer Lingus, the Irish national airline, provided 90 per cent of the capital. In 1980, Air Canada became a shareholder and General Electric took a large stake in 1983. The major Irish institutions became involved in 1988 when they bought 14 per cent of the company for Ir£145 million. Over this period of fifteen years GPA had grown to a company with profits of just under $300 million in 1991 (this could be calculated as an average profit of $1 million per employee).

Tony Ryan, now 56 years old, is the grandson of a station master and the son of a train driver. He began his career at 19 with Aer Lingus as a despatcher at Shannon airport. He quickly moved up through the ranks. It was when Ryan leased two 747s for Aer Lingus in the early 1970s that he discovered there was good profit in jet aircraft leasing. A year later he set up GPA which was to become the world's largest aircraft leasing company.

Much of the success of GPA was attributable to Ryan's tenacity and vision. He bred in his staff an unbridled level of optimism, his attitude was very much 'to hell with the rest of the world, let us show them we can be the best'. GPA executives were driven by a truly amazing appetite for work, for which they were extremely well rewarded. He identified committed and talented people who shared his zeal. An ex-employee remarked, 'The whole ethos of the company was that tucked away in an inconspicuous building in Shannon were the best brains in Ireland.'

GPA's chief executive, Maurice Foley, had been with GPA from 1976 when he joined as an non-executive director representing Aer Lingus. Brokers, fund managers and GPA employees rated him very highly. He and Ryan became a formidable double act. Where Ryan was creative and impulsive, Foley was considered a powerful strategist. It was Foley who sought to expand GPA's source of financing by involving General Electric in a partnership that in effect tripled the company's equity base and subsequently brought in other US and Japanese investors. He also helped to create a highly respected management team. The key players here were Colm Barrington, Peter Ledbetter, Jim King and John Tierney.

From 1987, Ryan began to build a star-studded cast of non-executive directors whose political and economic pedigree would impress financial institutions. These included: Nigel Lawson, former UK chancellor; Garrett Fitzgerald, former Irish prime minister; Sir John Harvey-Jones, chairman of *The Economist* and previous chairman of ICI; Peter Sutherland, chairman of Allied Irish Bank Group, former EC commissioner and Ireland's former attorney general; Shinroku Morohashi, president of Mitsubishi Corporation; Claude Taylor, chairman of Air Canada, and Lord Keith, former chairman of Rolls-Royce and Hill Samuel. Many of these individuals had substantial shareholdings in GPA (Exhibit 11.1).

Ryan's early attempts to interest the financial community in GPA were met with a mixture of bafflement and hostility. Ryan explained in a rare interview with the press:

Exhibit 11.1 *Individual shareholdings in GPA*

	No. of shares 000
Tony Ryan	9,300
Maurice Foley	515
Colm Barrington	538
John Harvey-Jones	40
Garrett Fitzgerald	22
Peter Sutherland	17

This is a new industry, a young industry. I remember when I first went to the City of London, I talked to ten or so banks. We were mainly in Boeing 737s then, and they would ask me two questions. One was how much can you buy a 737 for, which in those days was $3 or $4 million new. And the next question was, what is the scrap value of a 737, and I'd say, well $25,000. They didn't understand that it was a mobile asset that could generate revenues anywhere. They didn't understand the industry. You won't find that question asked today. But it has been a very long, slow educational process.

Current Situation

The headquarters of GPA in Shannon look more like the branch office of a small software company than the nerve centre of a worldwide business. Its main operations room, however, resembles that of a military headquarters. Maps, charts and data can be instantly called up. Information on every jet manufactured in the Western world – maintenance, history, owner, technical data – can be shown in seconds. Simultaneously, maps are displayed showing the locations of individual aircraft types, beside charts of the latest exchange rates in the world's main financial centres. The location of GPA's one hundred marketing agents in the field can be superimposed, and game plans drawn up.

GPA's basic strategy involves purchasing jet aircraft at fairly sizeable discounts (reportedly up to 20 per cent) from manufacturers, attaching a lease to the aircraft and then packaging the aircraft-cum-lease in a tax-efficient way for the investor. The business was based on 'securitization', whereby GPA provides a dollar-denominated investment in aircraft, offering a good yield, which is inflation hedged and asset backed. A typical deal might see GPA acquire a $30 million list price jet for $25 million and then arrange a lease generating income of $3–$3.5 million per annum. The plane would then be sold to the corporate or private investor at a price determined by the yield that the investor required. This yield comprised income generated by lease rentals and expected future residual value of the aircraft. GPA was then frequently retained by the investor to manage the aircraft that had been sold on.

Among global lessors, GPA in 1992 had a 48 per cent share of new plane deliveries and options. In 1991 they delivered 10 per cent of new aircraft or 80 planes. The group earned about 33 per cent of its profits from leasing, 50–55 per cent from sales and 15 per cent from joint ventures and management fees. At the time of the flotation they had 400 planes in their portfolio and orders for 580 aircraft over ten to fifteen years; 300 of these were firm orders, most of them over the three years to 1994. This meant that the company needed to place almost two planes a week over that period. A bull position, it represented $12.1 billion of purchases, including options, to the year 2000 (Exhibit 11.2).

GPA's performance was impressive: it had an unbroken record of annual pre-tax profits, rising from $71 million in 1987 to $281 million for the year to March 1991. The group's phenomenal growth during this period was based on the enormous demand for aircraft financing, prompted by the growth of the airline industry. GPA was forecasting that the airline business, which in 1991 suffered a 1 per cent fall in growth, was able to bounce back to between 5 and 9 per cent growth in 1992. If this prediction were true, and it was no more optimistic than Boeing's forecasts, then there was no reason why GPA should not continue to produce increased profits. This was provided, of course, that the untapped markets in China, Cambodia and other countries in Asia/Pacific proved as lucrative as GPA suggested they would.

GPA had always been keen to separate the turmoil of the US aviation market from the global marketplace in which it operated. This was important, as in 1991 the USA accounted for only 10 per cent of the group's global leading profits, compared with 21 per cent in 1988. Furthermore, GPA had a 32 per cent increase in earnings per share in this market despite the recession in the airline industry (some analysts had argued that this was partly owing to US accounting standards). The group clearly had a sound financial track record behind it; however, they were dogged by the perceived riskiness of the global airline business.

Exhibit 11.2   *GPA's funding requirements*

Due for delivery year ending 31 December	1992	1993	1994	1995	1996	1997	1998	1999	2000	Total
Aircraft on order	85	78	55	30	26	16	11	13	4	318
Value ($m)	2,602	2,640	2,105	1,066	1,083	853	594	822	345	12,110
Aircraft on option	–	–	47	69	48	29	18	16	5	230
Value ($m)	–	–	1,373	2,520	2,032	1,338	953	914	330	9,460

Includes both GPA group and subsidiaries

Global Airline Industry

Many analysts argued that the Gulf War and the worldwide recession put an end to the growth in the airline industry. For the first time since 1945, air travel declined worldwide. This decline was most pronounced amongst US airlines which turned cumulative earnings of $2.3 billion between 1986 and 1989 into a loss of more than $5 billion in 1990. Pan-Am and Eastern Airlines were gone; TWA, America West and Continental were protected by Chapter 11 bankruptcy laws, and 'suicide fares' were squeezing the big three: American, Delta and United. Visibly, approximately eight hundred aircraft (10 per cent of world aircraft) were currently redundant and parked in the Californian desert. Many of these airplanes were more than twenty years old, but included were forty Boeing 727s that belonged to the bankrupt Eastern Airlines, some British Airways Tristars and a couple of 747s belonging to Air Canada which cost $140 million each and arrived in the parking lot straight from the factory.

Aircraft manufacturers were more optimistic than the analysts. On 3 March 1992, Boeing published its long-term market forecast which predicted that airlines will take delivery of nearly six thousand new jets (of all makes) up to the year 2000, valued at some $380 billion. In the following decade Boeing forecast that airlines will spend another $500 billion on new aircraft. The forecasts assume a 5 per cent annual growth in world air travel up to the year 2010 (Exhibit 11.4). Boeing's two biggest competitors – Europe's Airbus Industrie and California's McDonnell Douglas – were equally bullish. Although all three companies had cut the production plans of their 737s they were maintaining their plans for all other models.

Even if passenger volumes were to grow as rapidly as aircraft manufacturers predicted, it was not clear who would provide the enormous sums that airlines needed to purchase these aircraft. Globally, deliveries were forecast to decline from 850 in 1992 to 700 units in 1993 and down to 400 in 1994 before rising again.

Exhibit 11.3 *Global aircraft orders*

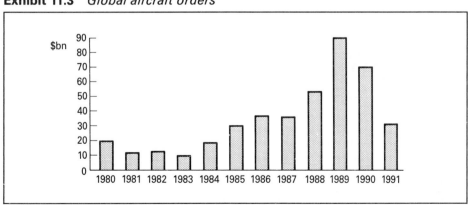

Exhibit 11.4   *Travel demand*

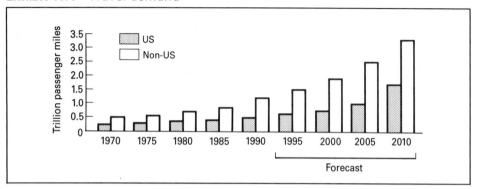

The total required to fund these purchases, according to analysts, was approximately $450 billion. In the recent past, Japanese banks, trading companies and equity investors had provided up to 65 per cent of global aircraft finance. This, however, had fallen to 10 per cent as a consequence of the decline in Japanese share and property values. There was now a need for more innovative ways of financing aircraft purchases (Exhibit 11.5). Leasing offered airlines a cheaper alternative to buying aircraft, particularly as leasing rates had fallen by 17–20 per cent between January 1991 and May 1992. Operating lessors had increased their share of world aircraft finance from 5 per cent to 17 per cent between 1982 and 1991 and market indicators suggested that they would increase further during the 1990s. Manufacturers were also increasingly taking on the burden of financing their own sales; Boeing, Airbus and McDonnell Douglas increased the financing of their customers' sales by about 30 per cent from $6.4 billion to $8.3 billion.

Exhibit 11.5   *Sources of aircraft financing*

	Recent past %	Near future %
Japan (banks, trading companies, equity investors in aircraft leases)	55–65	8–12
European banks	10–20	10–25
Insurance companies and pension funds	10–20	10–20
American banks	3–7	–
Aircraft makers	4–6	5–9
Equity issues	Insignificant	8–12
Bonds	Insignificant	25–35

Source: Boeing

In essence market perception of the future of aircraft was a key determinant of the outlook for GPA and that perception was not clear in the first six months of 1992. Although it was clear that GPA was set to remain a major global player, there was no way to extrapolate from past profits. Furthermore, GPA was a complex and highly individual business and therefore a very difficult company for analysts and investors to understand (Exhibit 11.6).

Corporate Communications and Investor Relations

GPA announced that the reason that they had decided to go public was because some of their shareholders – including Mitsubishi Trust and Banking, the Long-term Credit Bank of Japan, General Electric Capital, Salomon Brothers and Allied Irish Banks – wanted to realize the value of their shares. The view held by the group was that leasing finance would be in tradable liquid securities and a public quote would allow the group to issue bonds at a more competitive rate. Furthermore, whereas in the 1980s banks had plenty to lend, finance in the 1990s was not so easily available from this source, and GPA had an ambitious programme of aircraft purchases ahead (Exhibit 11.7). The company value was estimated then at $2.46 billion.

When Tony Ryan decided to seek a public flotation for his aircraft leasing company, he approached S.G. Warburg, where he received a cautious response from Sir David Scholey, chairman of Warburgs. The merchant bank explained that, while

Exhibit 11.6   *The Lex Column: GPA Group*

How much longer can GPA, the high-flying Irish aircraft financing group defy gravity? The question is more than passing interest. GPA is now a major financial institution in its own right, valued at $4 billion plus; and, judging by the growing number of distinguished names on its letterhead, it is only a matter of time before it seeks a stock market listing. Over the last couple of years, its revenues have trebled to $2 billion, while its after-tax profits last year rose 59% to $242 million. Based on the last private transaction, its shares are selling at 15½ times earnings and yield less than 2%. A typical big US or UK bank is lucky to sell on six times earnings and yields three times as much. However, the bulls argue that this is no ordinary financial institution and that it looks positively cheap when compared with the heady multiple of Boeing.

The force of the latter comparison is that both companies are benefiting from the continued ordering frenzy for new aircraft and have a vested interest in prolonging it. GPA, which makes a third of its profits from aircraft sales, increased its leased fleet by 40% to 240 aircraft last year and has orders and options for another 700. This is all very well when aircraft values are rising; but the question arises of what happens if the 6% per annum industry growth forecasts turn out to be wrong. GPA has been particularly successful in laying off the risk from its own modest balance sheet. But in an industry where a new jumbo jet can cost $120 million, there must be limits as to how far it could insulate itself were there ever to be a sharp fall in aircraft values. Talk of GPA being a recession-proof stock is bunkum.

Source: *Financial Times*, 7 June 1990

Exhibit 11.7 *GPA Group borrowings*

	31 March 1990 $m	31 March 1991 $m	31 December 1991 $m
Short-term borrowings (including current portion of long-term borrowings)	90	419	428
Long-term borrowings secured revolving corporate credit facility	773	1,397	981
Other secured lending and finance leases	144	276	605
Other loans	630	621	1,732
Total long-term	1,547	2,294	3,318
Total borrowings	1,637	2,713	3,746

it was happy to form a relationship with GPA, it could not be certain a flotation was appropriate until it knew the company better. GPA was disappointed, many of its executive directors could not understand Warburg's hesitancy. Ryan decided to go elsewhere. Shortly afterwards they secured eminent advisers: Nomura of Japan as global coordinators, Goldman Sachs, Merrill Lynch and Salomon Brothers in the USA, Schroders and BZW in the UK and Nomura and Yamaichi in Japan.

As the flotation drew nearer GPA became exposed to the powerful role of the media and their influence in the financial community. The culture of GPA was such that its executives had never, to this point, concerned themselves unduly about public image. Therefore when the flotation process began, considerable groundwork had to be undertaken to 'develop relationships' with the media and the investment community. However, a catalogue of events unfolded between January 1992 and the date of the flotation which made the task of courting favour increasingly difficult for the group.

In January 1992 one of the GPA's financial advisors suggested bringing the flotation forward to late March to take advantage of a still buoyant US stock market and prior to the UK general elections on 9 April. Differences of opinion were expressed, but before a decision was made the first of a number of inspired leaks reached *Financial Times* reporter Roland Rudd, who reported that the marketing of the public offer would begin in March and that the sale of shares would take place in April. This caused some uncertainly in the marketplace.

In the meantime there were acrimonious arguments about pricing. When GPA's advisors decided in February that the new ordinary shares should be priced at around $20, GPA executives immediately insisted on flying the bankers to the group headquarters in Shannon. Clearly irritated, Ryan was reported to be even more angry when he learned that Goldman Sachs was proposing to sell shares for as little as $17 in order to be sure of placing $500 million of the stock in the USA. One advisor described the meeting: 'Ryan hit the roof when he heard that. In retrospect, I think we should have realized at that time that the group's way of dealing with problems is best suited to a private company'. Again, details of this row found their way into the *Financial Times* the next day. The negative sentiment that this aroused in the investment community scuppered any plans for a quick flotation.

In March another damaging story hit the headlines, it was revealed through the financial press that major shareholders had been requested by GPA to agree to a 'lock-in'. This agreement required that shareholders with more than 300,000 shares could not sell more than 20 per cent of their holdings before 31 March 1993. This led to natural anxiety among shareholders concerned about implications of a fall in share price following the flotation. Furthermore, the statement led investors to believe that the flotation was essential to fund the group's ambitious development plans and should not be delayed. A period of what the *Sunday Business Post* termed 'bluff and counterbluff' began through the media, with suggestions that GPA might postpone the flotation unless the shareholders agreed to the lock-in proposals. The incident contributed to the impression forming in financial circles of a flotation dogged by controversy (Exhibit 11.8).

Exhibit 11.8 *Press report: 'Company worried by damaging press leaks'*

The recent appointment to GPA of former government press secretary P.J. Mara seems to be part of a plan to limit damaging press coverage about the group.

It was highly embarrassing, and unusual, that the debate between the group and its merchant banking advisers as to the price at which the shares should be placed found its way into the newspapers months in advance of the actual placing. Pricing is one of the last things to be decided at a flotation.

One adviser is believed to have suggested that the shares should be placed as low as $17, but this would appear to have been a gambit by some underwriter who wants to eliminate his risk in addition to receiving a generous underwriting fee.

Other advisers, with similar underwriting considerations in mind, spoke of a price in the $20–$25 range. GPA believes that the discounted value of a recent sale of convertible shares to an American institutional investor puts a value of $27 on the shares.

Last week, the *Sunday Business Post* learned the details of the 'lock-in' arrangements proposed by GPA to shareholders, and that the shareholders had declined to return the contracts presented to them.

The *Financial Times* picked up the story on Tuesday morning and added that a named Japanese investor had no incentive to see the flotation proceed, something which angered GPA who denied this.

However, the *Financial Times* quoted an unnamed adviser to GPA as saying that the Japanese position is causing 'serious concern'.

On Tuesday, a US debt rating agency announced that it was considering downgrading the rating of GPA debt because of concern over GPA's 'need to fund large numbers of new aircraft deliveries and place them in service with airline lessees, considering the reduced levels of aircraft demand'.

The warning does not mean that the down-grading of senior debt and commercial paper will take place. But if it were to, the timing would be inappropriate for the flotation and could make the future issue of debt instruments less attractive to investors.

Source: Financial Times, March 1992

Roland Rudd of the *Financial Times* continued to haunt GPA, as did Kristy Hamilton who wrote on City matters in the *Evening Standard*. What astounded GPA directors was not only the accuracy of Hamilton's and Rudd's stories, but also the speed at which they could report on the internal problems affecting the flotation. Executives became convinced that senior figures in the City of London were deliberately leaking information to blacken the company. They began to feel that they were victims of 'Paddy-bashing' in the City. The influential Lex Column in the *Financial Times* had been critical of GPA, even before the airline industry had been hit by recession.

Apart from the leaks, the financial press subjected GPA to detailed analysis. The company's depreciation policy and their funding methods baffled and worried many. According to Matt Cooper, business editor of the *Sunday Business Post* who followed the GPA story with vigour, 'GPA people were always polite but they often gave the impression that they felt they were having to suffer fools. The management clearly knew their jobs and did not take kindly to having to provide regular kindergarten guides to members of the press.'

In late March the company employed an investor relations and public relations consultant, P.J. Mara (Exhibit 11.9). Mara, a former government press secretary, was considered a strange choice by the media and financial community alike. However, the new recruit had a considerable task on his hands. GPA was being described as 'arrogant' and had a reputation for repeatedly stonewalling questions. Foley was quoted as saying, following a request for an interview by a journalist, 'I am giving an interview because there is probably a legitimate public interest. I am not seeking it. Therefore I don't have anything I want to volunteer'.

A communications strategy, which included an advertising campaign, was put in place to deliver a more positive message to potential investors (Exhibit 11.10). By May 1992 GPA had compiled a prospectus which they wished to present to

Exhibit 11.9 *Press report: 'PJ on board'*

Guess what? Guinness Peat Aviation, the world's largest aircraft leasing company, has added yet another well-connected politico to its pay roll. Not content with signing up such heavyweight names as Nigel Lawson, Garret Fitzgerald, and Peter Sutherland, GPA founder Tony Ryan has just hired Charlie Haughey's old pr man – P.J. Mara – as his new media relations adviser.

As Haughey's press secretary for the past five years, Mara played a key role in Haughey's surprisingly long existence as Ireland's prime minister.

PJ, as he likes to be known, is the consummate spin-doctor. He manages to keep his boss one step ahead of the baying hounds of the press corps, putting them off the scent with humorous, in-depth, off-the-record briefings, and even in Haughey's darkest hours managed to maintain a sense of bonhomie between his government and the fourth estate. He proudly recaps by saying: 'I never told a lie.'

Nevertheless, it's a strange appointment. A bit like putting Sir Bernard Ingham, Mrs. Thatcher's old mouthpiece, in charge of British Airways' public relations.

Source: Financial Times, 1 April 1992

Exhibit 11.10   *GPA press advertisement to encourage investors*

> ### GPA HAS ORDERED 819 NEW AIRCRAFT WORTH $30 BILLION.
> ### THESE ARE THE REASONS WHY:
>
> AIR TRAVEL is fundamental to contemporary life and economic progress. Over one billion people travelled by air last year. That number will double by the year 2,000.
>
> 7,000 new jets and 3,500 turboprop aircraft are needed to meet this growth and to replace older aircraft (one in three jets in the world fleet is over 15 years old). This means that on average more than three new aircraft will be delivered every working day to the turn of the century. At a cost in excess of $425 billion.
>
> As the airline industry matures like other service businesses, there is increasing separation of ownership and operation. Leasing makes this possible.
>
> Nearly half the US fleet, the largest in the world, is on lease. Worldwide, established airlines are improving their balance sheets through a better mix of owned and leased equipment. New carriers entering the industry with leased aircraft are expanding services to the public and demand for the manufacturers.
>
> GPA has defined the concept of the *operating* lease for new aircraft. An operating lease enables an airline to acquire the use of an aircraft without having to finance its full cost. GPA thus provides airlines with access to a pool of aircraft at relatively short lead times and on flexible financing terms.
>
> Our commitment to buy approximately 10% of all commercial jets to be delivered through the mid-1990s helps to underpin production plans for the manufacturers while broadening their market base and introducing new sources of finance to meet the industry's investment requirement.
>
> GPA's aircraft portfolio is deployed on operating lease to 64 carriers in 32 countries. GPA complements this core business by worldwide trading of aircraft and by the provision of financial and technical services to the aviation and investor communities.
>
> A global marketing reach and expert research provide GPA with unequalled industry knowledge. Our $30 billion order for 819 new aircraft is based on a strategy first developed in 1984 and progressively implemented since.
>
> GPA IS THE WORLD'S LARGEST NEW AIRCRAFT LESSOR. WE ARE PROUD THAT THE GREAT NAMES OF AIRCRAFT AND ENGINE MANUFACTURING ARE INCLUDED IN OUR ORDERS:
> AIRBUS, BOEING, FOKKER, McDONNELL DOUGLAS, ATR, BOEING CANADA, FAIRCHILD, SHORT BROTHERS, CFMI, GENERAL ELECTRIC, IAE, PRATT & WHITNEY, ROLLS ROYCE.

institutional investors. The company felt that the news was good; pretax profits had risen to $268 million on revenues of $2.01 billion in the year ended 31 March 1992 compared with a net profit of $262 million on revenues of $1.89 billion in the previous year. This performance was good despite the fact that GPA was operating in the depth of the biggest recession to hit the airline industry.

During the month prior to the flotation Tony Ryan and his team of executive directors began a whistle stop tour, starting in Dublin and going on to eight countries including the UK, USA, Germany, Japan and France, making a total of thirty presentations to institutions who were interested in buying shares in the company. The press were not invited to these presentations. As Ryan began the gruelling tour, he stated, 'I feel a bit like Jesus Christ tying to convert people to this business'. The reaction of the financial media was difficult to measure (Exhibit 11.11 and 11.12).

Exhibit 11.11 *GPA: assorted international media coverage, May 1992*

Values of aircraft will improve over the next five years. The question is whether GPA are strong enough to survive until values improve.

Financial Times, 15 May 1992

Directors of GPA received more than $31 million in salaries and dividends last year when profit growth was flat and the company's value fell by a third.

Daily Telegraph, 15 May 1992

Unfortunately, GPA is more reminiscent of the 1980s than representative of the 1990s' values.

London Independent, 10 May 1992

GPA is generally regarded to have made a good job of educating inexperienced fund managers about the aircraft leasing business.

Airline Business, June 1992

Exhibit 11.12 *Press report: GPA's public relations dilemma*

Scepticism about the flotation of the Irish aircraft lessor GPA is on the increase. That's about the last thing the new issues market wants as it comes alive after the election.

Advisers to GPA, the world's largest aircraft leasing company have decided to change course and actively offer shares to private investors. With the terms of GPA's offer for sale due out on Monday, an advertising campaign will appear this week in the national newspapers. The minimum investment is to be set at £1,400. The shares are to be priced between $10 and $12.50 (£5.50 to £7.00). The new shares will represent 28 per cent of the enlarged capital with GPA valued at some £1.9bn.

Advisers Schroders puts the change down to the unexpected level of enquiries it has had from private clients. There is little question but that GPA is an intriguing business and that it will remain a leading player in its markets. And an initial multiple of 10 compares nicely with a UK market multiple of 16 times earnings. That means the issue can't be sneezed at. But the difficulty of forecasting profits, given massive changes in the industry, and the difficulty of getting a grip on what the residual value of its fleet will be as its leases expire, suggests that the shares are not ideal private client country.

Still, there is no reason to see any direct connection between the new interest in private investors and the difficulty Nomura, the international coordinator for the issue, is reported to be having in marketing the shares to Japanese institutions. Tokyo is already big in GPA stock and is not in the mood to buy more overseas stock in a company it is difficult to understand. But in public relations terms, which count a great deal in new issues, this marketing volte-face is most unwise, as it follows a PR campaign which has already been too low-profile. It gives lots of ammunition to GPA's detractors, irrespective of the underlying reasons for the decision now to target private investors.

Source: Investors Chronicle, 5 June 1992

GPA and its advisors believed that the roadshow presentations went very well, that they had sold the value of the company effectively and that they had overcome any fears that investors might have had about the future. So confident was Goldman Sachs about the US reaction that it suggested an increase of 5 million in the number of shares to be issued, to 85 million. One company source said, 'You have to remember that this was a really small flotation. $1 billion may have seemed like a large amount of money but it's not when you spread it across the world. The attendance at the roadshows and the number of searching questions asked suggested a large degree of interest, enough to make the issue of shares quite easy'.

Global Flotation

Orginally GPA had hoped to sell 80 million shares worldwide: 30 million in the UK and Ireland, 20 million in the USA, 15 million in Japan and 15 million between Continental Europe, the Middle East and Asia. In the end there was demand for only 50 million shares. The problem was that the bids were hopelessly unbalanced in terms of geography and type of investor. Whereas the demand in Japan was greatest at 23 million, nearly all were from retail investors, while institutional interest there was minimal. Demand from other markets was divided as follows: UK and Ireland 7.5 million, USA 6.5 million, Swiss, German and Middle East 13.3 million. The advisors concluded that to float on the basis of such an unbalanced market would not be in GPA's interest. One of the advisors to the issue complained; 'There wasn't any single issue which arose, but it was partly the fact that the US investors seemed to be looking to the UK for a lead, while the UK investors looked to the US for a lead.'

Conclusion

On the week of the failed flotation the main questions being asked were just how the company and their financial advisors could have so poorly estimated market reaction. GPA blamed Goldman Sachs. The financial media speculated that 'The ultimate lack of investor interest was due to the specific handicaps of the company rather than to deeper disenchantment with flotations at this stage of the cycle' (Lex Column, *Financial Times*, 22 June 1992). Meanwhile, a leading London analyst warned that GPA may be forced to cancel orders and options for some new aircraft if it could not arrange funding following cancellation of the flotation. Maurice Foley was considerably more bullish: 'The outcome is disappointing but we are resilient and this is not our only strategy. We'll go back to the market again when a good opportunity arises' *(Sunday Business Post*, 21 June 1992).

CASE 12

Gatorade

Tiziano Vescovi

University Ca'Foscari of Venice, Italy

The Market

In the Italian market, before 1987, there was no ready-made drink specifically for sportspeople, only mineral salts restorers, in powder or in tablets, strongly medicinal in character and sold in modest quantity through pharmaceutical outlets. These products were generally imported from the USA and aimed at users with particular needs rather than at the general public. The market was static, dominated by the big pharmaceutical companies, limited in a single distributive channel (in Italy pharmacies are governed by strict licensing laws) and had poor expectations.

Sportspeople used mainly traditional soft drinks, mineral water, sodas and fruit juice. The size of this market in the food outlets such as bars was reputed to be around 6,300 million litres, or Lira 6,100 billion. In terms of quantity, mineral waters accounted for 57 per cent of the market, and soft drinks 32 per cent. In value, however, soft drinks occupied the first position with 46 per cent of the total; there was parity at 27 per cent of total market value for mineral waters and fruit juices (see Exhibit 12.1).

In Italy, about 12 million people (30 per cent of the population over 15 years old) took part, at least occasionally, in a sporting activity, while 4 million people practised sports regularly. Therefore a robust potential market could be served, provided that the product was perceived as neither highly scientific (connoting medicinal) – so as not to discourage potential consumers – nor too general – so as not be in direct competition with traditional soft drinks, the typical drinks of the average amateur sportsperson.

Exhibit 12.1 *The soft drinks market in Italy, 1988*

	Litres (millions)	% of total	Lire (billions)	% of total
soft drinks	2,000	32	2,800	46
mineral waters	3,600	57	1,650	27
fruit juices	700	11	1,650	27

In the second half of the 1980s the fitness culture exploded in Italy, revealing itself through new eating habits, the diffusion of mass sports and the gymnasium boom, all of which often became transformed into fashionable behaviours, status symbols and lifestyles. The concept of regeneration became an important component of the quality of life. This concept presents two main characteristics: it is not enough simply to have a healthy body: regeneration/well-being can only be realized in the balance between physical and mental states; it is considered actively and planned for on several levels, not only in a curative, therapeutic level. Safe eating and drinking represents one of the routes to well-being and regeneration, together with sporting activity.

The Product

Gatorade is a hydrosaline refreshing and rebalancing drink, aimed at those who practise a physical sporting activity, in order to allow the prolongation of effort. It was developed by a group of researchers led by Dr Robert Cade in Miami, in 1965, for the Alligators, the football team of the University of Florida. Tested during the matches, the new product was appreciated and the Gators (short for Alligators) maintained an excellent efficiency, scoring more than their adversaries in the second part of the game. The tests seemed to confirm the initial hypotheses: the new drink, besides being refreshing, helped to regenerate the energy of the athletes, who declared that they felt less tired when they drank the new product. The Gators won the Orange Bowl, undoubtedly with the help of the drink that they named Gatorade. When it was introduced on the US market in 1967 it soon became the top-rated drink among sportspeople.

Since then Gatorade has been subject to regular research and development to improve the product. At first only the lemon-flavoured Gatorade was available, but in 1979 orange flavour was added, and in 1983 mixed fruit flavour was introduced. Its formula, a well guarded industrial secret, is constantly being improved, although it undergoes some adaptation to cater for national tastes, in order to guarantee greater success in the country in which it is being sold. Given, then, its composition and its uses, a new kind of soft drink, the 'sports drink', was born.

In Italy, the presence of a growing naturalistic conscience generated a greater sophistication in the behaviour of consumers. This led to a reduction in wine-drinking during meals, and people appeared to prefer non-alcoholic to alcoholic drinks; moreover, the preference for carbonated drinks decreased so much that, in 1992, consumption of flat mineral waters equalled that of carbonated ones, and the greatest rates of growth were seen in the markets for fruit juices and tea-based drinks, all 'flat' drinks. The market for and lifecycle of soft drinks in Italy is shown in Exhibits 12.2 and 12.3.

In 1983 the Quaker Oats Company acquired Gatorade from Stokely–Van Camp. Since then, distribution of Gatorade has spread from the USA to Canada and Europe. In Italy, the Quaker Oats Co. is represented by a subsidiary, the

Exhibit 12.2   *Position of soft drinks in the Italian market*

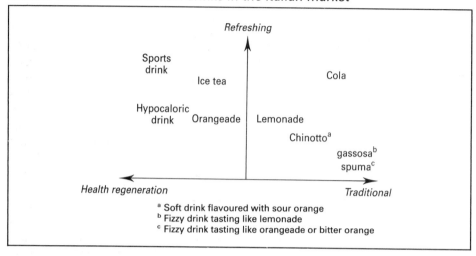

Exhibit 12.3   *Life cycle of soft drinks in Italy, 1992*

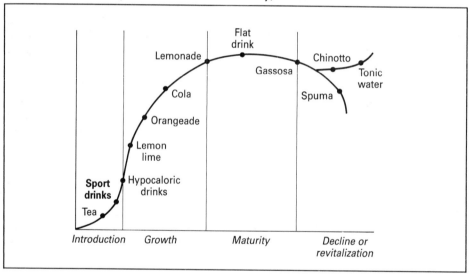

Quaker Chiari & Forti SpA, a well known food company, owner of important brands in the sectors of seed oil, pet food and baked products, and with a strong presence in both traditional and modern food outlets (groceries, supermarkets and hypermarkets). The management of Quaker Chiari & Forti had the task of developing an Italian market for Gatorade.

The Launch

In April 1987 Gatorade was introduced in the test market of Lombardy. It was distributed in 330 supermarkets through the traditional salesforce of the company, and in 250 sporting clubs by means of a special force of agent-merchandizers, supported by a telephone ordering service. The drink was offered at first in orange flavour. The first advertisement timed to coincided with the Stramilano, a marathon which attracts a large number of sportspeople, both professionals and amateurs. An advertisement, printed in the local newspaper, promoted a catchphrase that has ever since been associated with the brand: '*vinci la sete . . . e riparti di slancio*' (beat thirst . . . and restart with a dash). Both before and at the time of the marathon, market research was carried out to discover consumers' attitudes towards Gatorade and to plan the future of the product.

After the first marketing research, the researchers expressed a substantially negative opinion about the future of Gatorade in Italy, to the extent that they advised against the introduction of the drink into the market. However, Giulio Malgara, president and managing director of Quaker Chiari & Forti, decided in October 1987 to launch the product on a national scale, beginning from February 1988. In addition, it was decided to repeat the research considering a further element essential for the assessment of purchase intention: the product had to be proposed and tested in a particular condition, the 'sweat moment', that is, in a situation of notable physical stress and rapid loss of liquids and salts. The moment had to be independent of the external temperature, that would rather be a factor of acceleration of the 'sweat moment' and therefore of the need to use the product.

In the first research, the tests had been made in winter and the sportsperson had drunk Gatorade almost an hour after their physical effort, without considering the possibility that they might have had other drinks in the meantime. In the second research further significant changes to the marketing inputs were introduced. On the management's suggestion, the standard channels for promoting that type of product were put aside and an alternative introduced entailing far greater communication expenditure and distributive effort than usual. The change of such variables was expected to bring about far better results than those seen in the previous research. The risk involved in the launch was quite small. During the summer of 1987 a second test took place in two hundred tennis clubs and in a small number of traditional stores in Lombardy. The results were reassuring: the product sold well, and it met the demands of the consumers.

Competitors

Other sports drinks were launched in Italy at about the same time as Gatorade:

- *Isostad* (Wander), 250 millilitre canned drink (it was the first to appear on the European market).

- *Aquasport* (Also), 500 millilitre PET[1] package.
- *Fitgar Misura* (Plasmon–Heinz), 350 millilitre can and 500 millilitre bottle (this product was launched some time after the other two).

Nevertheless, all the soft drinks (carbonated drinks, mineral waters, fruit juices, tea etc.) commonly drunk during and after a sporting activity must be considered as indirect competitiors of the sports drinks.

While Isostad tried to position itself as strongly specialized and almost medicinal, Aquasport assumed a less clear position, combining a medicinal image with a lower price. Considering the failures of the first two competitors, the strategy used by Fitgar quickly became a typical 'me too'. The packaging, marketing and positioning imitated Gatorade as much as possible, adding the incentive of a lower price (7–8 per cent less, on average). This choice allowed Fitgar quickly to become the second most popular sports drink on the market, even if notably far behind the leader. Exhibits 12.4 and 12.5 show the growth of the Italian sports drink market and the shares held by the various competing brands.

Positioning

The target positioning for Gatorade was defined thus:

> For the physically active persons, Gatorade is the drink to beat thirst and restore the liquids and mineral salts lost by the body during the physical activity.

The product was thus installed on the dietetic/healthy dimension of Exhibit 12.2, its specific double promise (to beat thirst and to resore mineral salts) moving it away

Exhibit 12.4 *Italian market for sports drinks*

	1988	1989	1990	1991	1992
Sold (thousands of litres)	6,700	13,800	22,220	30,500	45,000
Sales (millions of lire)	6,700	27,800	55,000	102,000	145,000

Exhibit 12.5 *Market shares of sports drinks in Italy*

Brand	1989	1990	1991	1992
Gastorade	93.1	91.5	91.0	89.7
Isostad	3.6	3.6	2.5	3.0
Aquasport	1.5	3.6	2.3	2.7
Fitgar	–	0.4	4.0	4.4
Others	1.8	0.8	0.2	0.2

from direct competition with other soft drinks. The target group was identified as people between 14 and 44 years old, physically active and practising an active sport.

A further important element of the positioning was given by the 'alchemistic' formula of the product, secret but strictly 'scientific', with a strong positive perception created by its very technical and scientific qualities. Thus the product was likely to give consumers the idea that they had a modern 'magic potion' enabling them to achieve miraculous results. However, together with these attributes Gatorade, being a food product, had to maintain an image of safety, quality, naturalness.

The sales target, expressed at the beginning of the project, was between 2 and 3 million bottles in the first year, in the most optimistic evaluations, to become 4 million in a steady market. The forecast was made considering conventional situations, it being difficult to predict figures for a completely new market. However, in the event, first year sales reached almost ten million.

Marketing Mix

The Product

One particular strength of the marketing mix was the drink's packaging: it was not only instantly recognizable as Gatorade but also practical. In 1990, because Gatorade and the lifestyle attributes that it implied were very popular, the 330 millilitre can was proposed as the most suitable package for distribution through bars.

The 500 millilitre glass bottle in which it was originally launched gave an impression of confidence about the quality of the product. Moreover, the name of the product was imprinted in the glass itself so as to increase and further consolidate the brand message. A particular milling of the glass communicated a feeling of thickness, together with perceptions of quality and freshness; at the same time the product could be easily seen through the transparent glass bottle. The neck of the bottle was fairly wide, allowing easy direct drinking, which was underlined also by the advertising, and which constituted another of the product's strong points: it could be consumed in 'difficult' situations (lack of glasses), typical of sporting competitions. The resealable cap meant that the drink did not have to be consumed all at once.

The taste of the product was slightly different compared with the original: a bit sweeter and less medicinal, more suited to the taste of Italian consumers.

Distribution

Other interesting innovations concerned the distribution. First of all the foods outlets (supermarkets, hypermarkets, chain stores, cooperative and traditional groceries) were used. Such channels, commonly served by Quaker Chiari Forti, were supplied Gatorade in just the same way as they were supplied any other of the company's commodities. The innovation was represented by the dispersion of the product among 2,500 sports clubs. The so-called 'sweat moments' were spotted: that is, sports clubs in which the need for hydrosaline restoration could arise and the product had to meet the demand for replenishment immediately. The distribution developed by means of a specialized network of agent-merchandizers, a supervisor and twelve salespeople, working with the help of an efficient telephone order collection service. Besides the traditional sales function, the main tasks of the selling network in the sports clubs were the supply and setting up of display materials, credit chasing and the evaluation of proposals of micro-sponsorships of local championships or competitions managed by the sports clubs, for the most part satisfied through the supply of products and other associated materials.

Normal supply to the clubs was satisfied by the telemarketing service, because the characteristics of the channel did not allow large purchases, only frequent, small restocking. The sports channel, after distribution of the product in the mass market and despite the constant increase in sales, became less weighty by comparison with the food channel (if initial phases are compared) and stabilized at around 10 per cent of total sales. Moreover, it must be borne in mind that, because of the widening of distribution, many sports clubs were able to use the normal wholesalers instead of the company's salespeople.

The creation of the sports club channel was possible because the product appealed to the world of sport, and advertising images and words did the same. The strategy resided in the defence of the positioning of the sporting image more than in the real distributive potential. Therefore the company continued to maintain and support the channel, even if its importance in terms of sales became marginal.

The same network of agent-merchandizers sold Gatorade to bars (in Italy bars sell both alcoholic and non-alcoholic drinks, from milk to whisky, and are common throughout the country) through 650 specialist wholesalers. This channel gained 20 per cent of total sales. The product was then sold into Autogrill (a chain of motorway restaurants and coffee shops) and other special customers by means of telemarketing and ordering, managed directly by head office.

Since 1989, distribution has followed the mass market, through the food channel, above all supermarkets and hypermarkets, and these latter quickly became the most important channel (70 per cent of total sales), maintaining an increasing rate of growth. This choice had been considered necessary in order to extend the range of consumers. Exhibit 12.6 illustrates the relative importance of the main distribution channels.

Price

The price level was strongly influenced by the product's uniqueness. For the mass market, the sports drink represented a new product category, more similar to dietetic/health products than to other soft drinks. That made it possible to set the price around three times higher than that of soft drinks.

Exhibit 12.6   *Distribution channels of sports drinks in Italy, 1992*

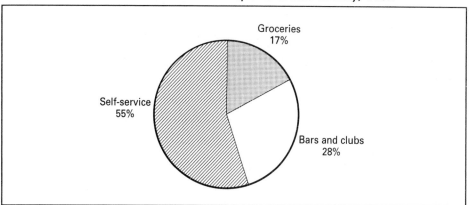

By comparison with the prices of other sports drinks, Gatorade was initially in an intermediate position, while Isostad was in a decidedly higher one, strengthening its predominantly medicinal image, and Aquasport in a slightly lower one. The price of such products has been decreasing in real terms because the strategy of target enlargement and the actions of the rival Fitgar have necessitated price cuts. However, costs have decreased more slowly than forecast, because of the increased costs brought about by widening the distribution network.

Nevertheless, the high price represents one of the most significant differences between the Italian marketing approach and the American. For Italian consumers, Gatorade was not a drink, but a 'magic potion' that would enhance the sporting performances of those who had drunk it. After some years of uncertainty and changes, at the end of 1992 the price ratios among the competitors and stabilized (see Exhibit 12.7).

Exhibit 12.7   *Price ratios of sports drinks (500 ml package) measured against Gatorade*

Brand	Price ratio
Gatorade	1.0
Fitgar	0.7
Aquasport	0.8
Isostad	1.2

Communication

In the sports drinks market, communication is the main marketing tool, especially advertising and sponsorship. Brand preference and brand loyalty have been attained by means of heavy advertising investment, because the product does not have a unique selling point by which to promote itself over its rivals. An important set of advertising options characterized the marketing mix strategy, especially taking into account the effectiveness of sponsorship of sporting events and of individual athletes. For this reason, Gatorade was connected in a limited way to technical/pharmaceutical products, giving it a serious sporting image as well as that of a refreshing drink.

The communication policy supported the launch of the new product. It developed through the combined use of the tools of communication, aiming for significant synergies. The promise of the advertising cmapaign supported the product, emphasizing its benefits; the use of the press and of television had a strong impact, increased brand awareness and enhanced the sporting image of the product; a strong connection with sporting sponsorship linked the success of the athletes with the use of the product.

The particular communication tools used are described below.

Advertising

A strategy 'on a double track' in two parallel logics was used:

1. Thematic campaign, with the task of supporting the product concept, communicating its main benefits. The slogan 'Gatorade, beat thirst . . . and restart with a dash' was directed towards this campaign.

2. Event campaign, with predominantly tactical purposes, complementary to the thematic campaign, with the objective of increasing brand awareness and positioning Gatorade as the definitive sports drink.

Sponsorship

The image of the product was associated with well known professional athletes, with teams of different sporting activities and with specific sporting events. The aim was to characterize with great care the image of the product and to strengthen its positioning among potential consumers.

Public Relations

Gatroade was able to establish itself in the scientific literature as the leading sports drink, thereby gaining significant advocates among doctors and professional coaches. Endorsement by such knowledgeable people implied the reliability and effectiveness of the product.

Sales Promotion

The communication tools were differentiated according to the two targets – consumers and distribution – as follows:

1. *Consumers*. The product test was advertised through the distribution of coupons, of technical leaflets about the product, sampling and with the help of a mailing to sports societies.

2. *Distribution*. Gifts connected with the sport and with the sporting image of the product were promoted; moreover, favourable selling conditions were arranged for the dealers thus encouraging their greater appreciation of the product.

The very use of communication tools was fundamental to success. First of all, the size of the budget was unusual. Under the push of the managing director, the initial level of investment in advertising and sponsorship equalled sales turnover. Moreover, the budget was elastic, since it was renegotiated every month on the basis of the sales of the previous month. This flexibility allowed effective communication strategies to be developed quickly so that advantage could be taken of sporting victories more or less as they happened, utilizing them in subsequent advertising and promotions while they were still fresh in mind.

However, sponsorship of sport represented the most innovative element. The idea of using the image of popular athletes had been considered from the beginning, if not in the manner in which the programme was afterwards developed. In the USA, sponsorship was used only in events and, for the most part, was of whole teams because the association with an individual champion, tied inevitably to his or her personality and lifestyle, was considered too risky.

Nineteen eighty-eight, the year that Gatorade was launched in the Italian market, was an Olympic year, and the company took the opportunity to use images of Olympic competitors, for the most part participants in individual sports. Using specialist sports public relations agencies, the company offered some champions a relatively low payment. The chosen athletes tended to be in the less well rewarded sports; nevertheless, if they won then they would earn much more.

The operation was successful, as many athletes won Olympic laurels (Antibo in the 10,000 metres race, Bordin in the marathon, the Abbagnale brothers in

Exhibit 12.8 *Advertising investments (excluding sponsorships) in the Italian sports drinks market*

Brand	1988 (L. millions)	1989 (L. millions)	1990 (L. millions)	1991 (L. millions)
Gatorade	4,380	16,920	26,641	19,617
Aquasport	2,600	5,430	4,303	2,038
Fitgar	3,225	6,960	5,674	9,974
Isostad	1,060	3,350	2,371	2,085
Others	810	1,240	1,032	2,887
Total	12,100	33,900	40,021	36,601

rowing) and Gatorade used their winning image. Sponsorship widened, always keeping up with the two tracks (sporting events and athletics), until its budget surpassed that of advertising. Alberto Tomba and Deborah Compagnoni, the ski champions, were involved as well as the Milan football team with Franco Baresi, Gianni Bugno, the world cycling champion, and a team of cyclists, the Moro of Venice in sailing (America's Cup), some ATP tennis tournaments, Jennifer Capriati and many others.

The priority accorded to the advertising and sponsorship campaign created the need to reorganize relations between the marketing and communications functions within Quaker Chiari & Forti. The two functions, previously divided, were now integrated under a single product direction. The relationship with the advertising function was also affected by the decision to integrate the communication activities, meetings becoming more frequent and less formal. Besides the traditional annual or seasonal brief in which the objective of the corporate campaign theme was indicated, it was necessary to promote constantly micro-campaigns to take advantage of the opportunity represented by a single sporting event or by a champion's victory.

The integration of marketing concerned not only the communication function but also the sales strategy. One example of this concerned a tennis tournament. Gatorade decided to give major sponsorship to a series of tournaments, applying its own name to the series and providing information about the matches and results day by day. The product was supplied as the official drink to the competitors. The communication activity was completed by the sports press which reported the tournament, by now named Gatorade, on the television, the footage showing Gatorade's eye-catching banners in the sports ground and the players drinking the product between games. Scientific information about the product and its use could be found in the cafés and refreshment kiosks of the sports ground where the tournament was held, and Gatorade itself could be purchased in the same places because the dealers had been given a special introductory offer and expected attractive gains. In this way the sporting public could taste the same drink as their champions were using, thereby simultaneously promoting imitation and reinforcing the identification of the drink with top sportspeople.

Future Challenges

In the autumn of 1993, the management of Quaker Chiari & Forti began planning for the following year, realizing that it would be a turning year. The market had become more mature, the original segment to whom the sports drink had been addressed was growing more selective, and new competitors had appeared on the stage. Moreover, the building of a large new plant necessitated the widening of the market and development of exports. Thanks to their remarkable successes, the senior management of Quaker Chiari & Forti had an additional task: management of the Gatorade brand throughout all Europe.

The Target

The first step was to redefine the target, since the sports market was saturated by then. One idea was to identify people who had a physically demanding job and who would need to restore their body's liquids in order to maintain work performance. This group would include truck drivers, bricklayers and so on. Another possibility, again moving out of the sports market was to enter directly into competition with soft drinks, both in summer and in winter.

Positioning

Redefining the target meant repositioning the product and the brand as less sports-specific, sporting with the risk, on one side, of losing the technical leadership among the sports drinks, and on the other, of opening the product to attacks from competitors that aimed at a higher specificity and qualification. The specificity is typical in every new consumption market: as the product's success curve begins to flatten out, new niches will automatically be sought guaranteeing more specific benefits to more sophisticated and selective consumers.

     The Italian market could in theory absorb another brand leader (there was a rumour that Coca Cola was preparing an anti-Gatorade drink, named Powerade), but in this situation, given the strong concentration of the market shares, the decisive variable could only be a more competitive price; an innovative product formulation would be less important. A new formula did not have to imply a change in the priorities of health care of the original target market of the isotonic drink: during the past year two new Italian brands of sports drink had appeared, increasing the competitive level of the market.

New Products

Should Gatorade, therefore, think of a differentiated product offer? Up to then, the differentiation was only in flavours and package sizes, but now packaging could become larger (cans, PET, cardboard bricks), family sizes were a possibility (1–1.5 litres) and new flavours could be offered (grapefruit, mixed citrus fruits, lemon tea). The product could be sold in powder form for heavy users (especially sportspeople) who might prefer to prepare their drink to a particular dosage that was optimum for them while participating in their sport (long-distance running, cycling, rock climbing, etc.).

New Communication

The same message, the same testimonial, the same level of investment in communication as before was no longer adequate: even if the sporting image was to be maintained, it was still necessary to create a new image of the product in order to hit a larger target or to increase the consumption occasions. Within the company, two strategic hypotheses were in conflict: whether to consolidate the positions now subjected to greater and greater attacks by competitors, or whether to win sales in new markets. Which should be the main message? Which media would be suitable for the purpose? Which protagonists could bear comparison with the winning athletes? What should the advertising effort aim at?

Price

Up to then, Gatorade had enjoyed a high premium price because of its strong market leadership. However, the enlargement of the target would place it in competition with products priced much lower (50–60 per cent less). Could the product then keep the price or would it have to lower it, and how ought it to compare itself with the traditional, more direct competitors?

The European Market

No other country in Europe recorded a consumption of sports drinks as high as in Italy. As a consequence of the success of the national product, the import of rival brands was almost nothing, while the export of Gatorade had started, albeit initially only to Quaker Chiari & Forti branches in neighbouring countries. Nevertheless, the new plant had made a large amount of product available for export and the management was wondering whether the best strategy was to adopt global marketing based upon the Italian model or to differentiate locally. The question was: is there a European consumer of the sports drink, i.e. do sportspeople behave in the same way in all the countries? Professional sport certainly appeared to be uniform throughout Europe; however, were the national culture and habits more important to amateurs or did they imitate their sporting heroes?

The planning meetings would be certainly quite lively.

Note

1.   PET (polyethyleneterephthalate) is the most commonly used plastic bottling material.

Magnum

Frans A. Kense
Tilburg Polytechnic, Holland

The Traditional Dutch Ice-cream Market

About 95 per cent of Europeans eat an ice-cream occasionally. The majority of them, mainly adults, hardly ever have one. These adults are the low users, consuming fewer than up to three ice-creams a year. Until 1989 the purchase decision and time of purchase were not so much decided by the adults themselves as by specific circumstances. Adults apparently do not love ice-creams so very much, but just appreciate them: contrary to children who all tend to love them. So adults, just to be sociable, tend to take an ice-cream when with children or others. The traditional ice-creams just did not satisfy adult taste.

As Exhibit 13.1 shows, ice-cream consumption in Holland at 6.7 litres per person per year is low. Surprisingly, consumption is not related to the temperature of a country. As these consumption figures show, consumption in Norway and Sweden is twice as high as in Holland.

Production

Ice-cream is either home-made or manufactured. In Holland, ice-cream is produced by almost five hundred mostly small traders, half of whom are Italians. The fresh ice-cream outlets are at the shops in city centres and are usually open during the summer period only. The packed ice-cream, produced by a few larger firms, showed little development during the 1980s (Exhibit 13.2).

Exhibit 13.1 *Ice-cream consumption in various countries, 1990*

Country	Ice-cream consumption (litres/head)
Holland	6.7
Norway/Sweden	14.8
Australia	18.0
United States	23.0

Exhibit 13.2 *Relative division of fresh and packed ice-cream in Holland, 1988*

	Fresh ice-cream	Packed ice-cream
Quantity	10%	90%
Value	25%	75%
Number of pieces	40%	60%

Magnum Segmentation Strategy

According to Wouter Koetzier, product group manager of Unilever's Iglo-Ola at Utrecht, the demand existed but the supply was just not adjusted to it. 'We at Iglo discovered an interesting market gap,' he remarked. This gap was reason enough for Unilever to set up a taskforce to develop a suitable marketing programme, consisting of four marketing mix elements:

1. The development and introduction of a product of very high quality for adults.
2. An acceptable price for the market sector.
3. A distribution policy that guaranteed the required availability.
4. A promotion strategy to create sufficient brand knowledge and appropriate image.

Ice-cream can be looked at in different ways. British research findings showed that the eating of ice-cream is experienced as a sensual, even sexual, experience.

Selecting the Product Range

The first Magnum Dark would, according to the press release in 1989, attract the more manly, sturdy, extrovert characters.

New was the fact that the thick layer of chocolate was made of real chocolate, instead of the conventional chocolate substitute. Magnum's flavour set the standard for later introductions: the ice-cream is rich, containing more cream and milk than many other ice-creams. After the success of the Dark, the Magnum White came with 'more female, softer and introvert elements'. Later on, Magnum Almond followed with milk chocolate containing pieces of almond, adding a 'snack dimension' to the product. Magnum Pecan was launched in 1994 (Plate 10).

In short, almost every segment of market is covered. More and more people are eating ice-cream, on more days and at more varied times of the day than was the case previously. People do identify themselves with Magnum which was not possible with previous ice-creams. By 1994, the total demand in Holland had already grown to eight litres per head (from 6.7 litres in 1990) including four pieces of Magnum each.

In Germany, Magnum press advertising extends to the better magazines like *Spiegel, Stern* and *Geo*. This keeps sales stable during the year, even in winter. For the projected European coverage, it was evident immediately that Magnum was introduced that completely new production lines would be required. In view of the plant capacities and the planned requirements both in Holland and in Germany, production was set up in a few European countries.

Distribution Policy

At first the new product was for the male adult. The distribution policy aimed to reach as many sales outlets as possible that were visited by adults. Petrol stations were a major stronghold for this and appeared to be a success. A petrol station owner reported that, 'when we were sold out, disappointed clients drove on to the next station to fill up there'. Soon signs began to appear at replenished sales outlets saying 'Hooray, there are Magnums again'.

Although the ice-cream had been introduced in Holland on a small scale in 1989, Magnum sales made a giant leap forward after two years, by which time the brand had achieved very high brand awareness – 62 per cent of 1,000 people surveyed. A salesman on the Utrecht/Amsterdam highway claimed 'I have Magnum for breakfast, while I used to eat an ice-cream only during a heatwave.'

Students, too, entered the market. Research showed high school students considered Magnum indispensable, in third place after products like LA Gear and Levis.

For home consumption, the supermarkets were provided with specially developed multi-packs. In Germany, where Magnum was introduced as well, housewives in the supermarket soon accounted for 30 per cent of the Magnum sales.

Promotional Constraint

As product group manager Wouter Koetzier explained 'Magnum grew with a minimal sales budget. According to marketing literature DFl3–5 million, i.e. up to $3 million, are needed to introduce a strong brand. Magnum proves that there are other ways.' In spite of little promotion, the introduction was so successful that the promotion strategy had to be adjusted. Magnum's production capacity could not follow demand in 1991 and 1992, and all advertising activities had to be postponed. The ice-cream market, being an impulse-buy market, meant that all that was required was visibility at points of sale. PR and word-of-mouth promotion by satisfied clients was enough to expand demand.

In soft drinks and washing powders there are several global brands. With the introduction of Magnum, a global brand has been established in Europe for ice-cream. The name Magnum, Latin for giant, was to some extent based on the well-known television series of that name, which was intended to give the ice-cream a macho image.

Europe-wide

In Holland, of the total 15 million population in 1993, 6 million had tried Magnum and 2 million eat Magnum several times a week, independent of the weather.

Until 1991 Magnum was sold in Europe only. According to Peter Kool, Iglo's president of the frozen food and ice-cream section in the Netherlands, an international brand manager has been appointed – the Irish lady Jean Callanan, working from Hamburg in Germany, at Unilever's Langnese office. This is because Germany, which also saw the introduction of Magnum in 1989 and achieved sales of 100 million pieces, has been appointed the headquarters for Magnum across Europe. It is here that all new activities on sales campaigns, packaging etc. will take place.

It is certain, then, that Magnum will also be available in far flung countries in the years to come.

CASE 14

IKEA

Maureen Whitehead
Manchester Metropolitan University, UK

Introduction

The IKEA case demonstrates the historical development of a Swedish home furnishings group in world markets, from the creation of its first store in Sweden in 1965 to its current position of trading in twenty-six countries worldwide.

A major feature of IKEA's international corporate development is the extent to which the organization has been able to transfer its operational format across geographical boundaries, irrespective of cultural differences in consumer tastes. The mechanism through which internationalization has taken place has been the replication of a standardized trading format and operational policies across world markets. As such, the company is one of the few retail organizations which have expanded globally without making significant changes to their operational format, merchandise mix and marketing strategy. What the company has achieved is a capacity to tap an international consumer demand for immediate satisfaction, purchasing as a pleasurable experience and good design at affordable prices. The business disciplines on which this success has been achieved are strong cost control across all operational functions, a flat management structure atypical of many leading European retail organizations and high levels of decentralization. According to both classical and neoclassical management theory, cost control is frequently the major cornerstone in the development of highly centralized organizations.[1] The corporate structure of IKEA is therefore one of its most unique features. To avoid bureaucratic structures or bureaucratic tendencies developing, decisions are delegated to lower levels and internal communication channels are short. As a result, decentralization has provided the flexibility to develop in overseas markets through organic growth (the development of company-owned stores) and to learn by growing with the marketplace. Where the company has adopted other modes of market entry in Europe, e.g. franchising, initial success has been more difficult to achieve, as in the Belgian market.

Company History

IKEA is a privately held multi-million pound Swedish retailer of furniture and home furnishings. The company was first registered as a commerical enterprise in Sweden in 1943. Today the company trades in fourteen countries in Europe, in the USA and Canada and with franchise operations in Australia, the Canary Islands, Hong Kong, Iceland, Kuwait, Saudi Arabia and Singapore.

IKEA has been built on the philosophy of:

> Creating a better everyday life for the majority of people through the product range
> the IKEA spirit
> profit which gives resources
> achieving good results with small means
> the belief in simplicity as a virtue
> daring to be different
> concentration of energy
> assuming responsibility
> the belief that most things remain to be done. (*IKEA Facts*)

The company's overall objective is 'to offer a wide range of home furnishing items of good design and function, at prices so low that the majority of people can afford to buy them'.

Early Stages of Company Growth: The Domestic Market

IKEA was founded by Ingvar Kamprad who based the company name on his initials and those of the place in which he grew up, Elmtaryd in Agunnaryd. The company started as a one-man business with a few product lines. These lines were gradually increased until the company had grown into a small local furniture business. Although Ingvar Kamprad believed that his products could be sold more widely, he needed an opportunity to test consumer reaction to his merchandise: he decided to exhibit at the Sankt Erik's Fair in Stockholm, a national fair visited by customers from all over Sweden.[2]

One of Kamprad's guiding principles was maintaining low prices, significantly cheaper than those of traditional furniture dealers. In response to the threat of IKEA, those dealers who also exhibited at the fair began to put pressure on their suppliers to stop trading with Kamprad. The traditional method of merchandizing in the furniture industry had been for retailers to select product ranges from manufacturers who controlled design and production. In response, through collaborating with furniture industry suppliers, IKEA was able to overcome the problem by taking control of its own product designs and designing its own merchandise which the suppliers would then manufacture. This response to competitors' threats ensured that IKEA maintained its suppliers, who in turn could supply both their traditonal customers and IKEA without the danger of losing business.

In taking control of the design function and designing furniture to suit industry production methods, Kamprad could ensure tight control over costs while at the same time developing new ways of distributing the product to the consumer. The supply structure of the industry had previously been such that customers purchased completely assembled units of furniture. These ready-assembled units were costly to the retailer in terms of in-store warehousing and of the number of units which could be transported to a store at any one time.

By 1965 the company had opened its first store in Stockholm. Unlike existing furniture stores located in prime sites on major high streets and stocking a limited line of merchandise, the IKEA store was built out of town where land could be obtained more cheaply. In-store innovations in the form of store design and display were created through coordination of product ranges as opposed to the display of individual items. The use of a large, out of town, warehouse-type store with merchandise displayed in multiple room settings provided the consumer with an opportunity to see how products could look in their own homes.

This first store, then, was built on the basis of careful control of costs by:

1. Acquiring sales space at a low cost.

2. Low transportation costs after sale as the customer carried the goods home.

3. Low handling costs.

4. Cheaper production through cooperation with suppliers.

The opening of the first outlet in Stockholm proved so popular that queues developed in the store. Rather than increasing staffing levels, the company decided to move the cash tills back into the warehouse and let the customers serve themselves. This early trading success resulted in a large volume of customer traffic in-store. Not all customers made a purchase: many also came to look for ideas. In order to benefit from this customer throughput, a decision was made to extend the product mix to small items, mainly low-ticket items such as kitchen utensils and picture frames.[3]

IKEA Trading Format

Within the company's stores, a full range of home furnishings are sold under one roof, from large items such as wardrobes, dining tables and sofas, to wallpaper, pictures and rugs. Shopping at IKEA is meant to be an experience for the whole family. In-store provision is made for children in the shape of supervised playrooms, allowing parents time to browse through the showroom and marketplace. Stores are designed so that customers must pass through all the departments before reaching the sales tills. Each store trades from two floors (the showroom and the market-place), making the most of the available space. On the upper floor, large items of furniture are displayed both individually and in room settings which are built around the perimeter of the upper floor. Smaller items, e.g. kitchen utensils, plants and furnishing fabric, are sold at ground level in the marketplace. Having decided on a purchase, customers collect their goods from the warehouse. The majority of items are flat-packed for the customer to assemble at home; only 4–5 per cent of the product range is not flat-packed.[4] Roof racks are available for customers wanting to take immediate delivery of large items. Outside of the domestic market the stores emphasize their Scandinavian roots through the use of Swedish product names, e.g. Fjord (a chest of drawers) or Nyliden (a glass cabinet). Externally, each outlet is painted in the distinctive blue and yellow colours of the Swedish flag.

Overseas Expansion

In 1973, twenty-five years after the first store opened in Stockholm, IKEA decided to look for additional growth opportunities through overseas expansion and chose the Swiss market for its first overseas venture. This was followed one year later by the development of the first store in West Germany. Prior to these ventures in Continental Europe, the company had focused its attention on neighbouring Scandinavian markets. At the time that company expansion into the Swiss market took place, five stores were operational in Sweden, one in Denmark (1969) and one in Norway (1963).

UK Market Entry

In 1987 IKEA entered the UK market, the first store being opened in the north west of England in Warrington, close to the two major conurbations of Merseyside and Greater Manchester. The store held eleven thousand product lines, one-quarter of which were in the company's catalogue. To support the store, a service office, which also acted as a base for product planners and product range selectors, was established in London. A separate purchasing office was set up in the north west. Goods were despatched to the store from Sweden with very little local sourcing.

In entering the UK furnishings market, the company was faced with competition from MFI and Allied Maples in the volume end of the market and from Habitat in the design-led segment. By 1989, estimates of market share showed the company beginning to make inroads into the UK furnishing market on the strength of two stores, one in Warrington and the other in London at Brent Park, which had opened in 1988. This growth was achieved despite low rates of growth in the UK furnishings market.

By 1991 the company had opened three stores in the UK and made a pre-tax profit of £1.4 million on sales of £91.4 million, achieving sales per square foot of 2.7 times the industry average.[5] The company opened two more stores in 1992, giving a total of five stores in the UK: Warrington, Brent Cross, Birmingham, Gateshead and Croydon.

US Market

'It's a big country . . . someone's got to furnish it' was the slogan used by the company to announce its entry to the US market.[6] The first store in the USA opened just outside Philadelphia, followed by stores near Washington, DC, Baltimore, Pittsburgh, New York City and Los Angeles. Many of the same market conditions existed in the USA as in the UK: poor delivery, high costs and unrelenting demand.[7] When the Philadelphia store opened, 130,000 shoppers made their way to the store. Sales for the first three months totalled $8 million. Subsequently problems were exerienced with warehousing space, as the first US stores were too small and demand outweighed supply in some product categories.[8] In response, IKEA started to build its own distribution centre and review its sourcing policy for the US market.

Acquisition of Habitat UK and France

In 1992, the Dutch foundation, which owns the IKEA group of which the company founder is chairman, purchased the Habitat chain in the UK and France, the US stores having been disposed of separately. At the time of the acquisition, Ingvar Kamprad was quoted as saying that 'Habitat would be run as a totally independent group . . . with a distinct Habitat identity'.[9] The intention was to keep IKEA and Habitat as two separate brands.

Habitat had been the creation of entrepreneur Terence Conran. Founded in 1964, it was to prove a major influence not only on the furnishings market, but also on the ideas of a generation of post-war baby boomers. When the first store opened, it was unlike anything to be found elsewhere. Stores were filled with innovative merchandise and were accessible to the consumer.[10] After a long period of success, the Habitat chain started to change direction, moving away from its high street locations to out of town sites. This move was not successful, and in 1982 the company was merged with Mothercare, the UK baby and childrenswear chain.

In 1986 Habitat was subject to a further merger with the British Home Stores chain, a high street multiple fashion retailer. Throughout its trading history, the French part of the Habitat business had performed better than the UK operation, in part owing to its market positioning and in-store merchandizing techniques.

Post-acquisition

Post-acquisition, some high street Habitat stores were refurbished to make then more distinctive and to create stronger store identities.[11] Additionally, plans were drawn up to open new stores, in contrast to the extensive rationalization which had taken place under The Storehouse group.[12] A major issue raised in the trade press at the time was whether the new management team would be able to revive an ailing concept which had underperformed for years.

Eastern Europe

In 1990 IKEA began a store-opening programme in Eastern Europe. By 1993 four stores had been opened in Poland, the fourth store in Janki near Warsaw being the largest of such stores in Eastern Europe. Twenty per cent of the products in-store are made in Poland by IKEA's own factories.

Also in 1990 the company entered the Hungarian market through a partnership with Butorker. Under the terms of the partnership, IKEA held 50 per cent of the shares, Butorker 45 per cent and 5 per cent were held by the Hungarian Credit Bank.[13]

In opening stores in Eastern Europe, IKEA has had to modify its market offering. Product ranges have been adapted to be multifunctional and, owing to inflationary pressures, prices have been omitted from the catalogue.[14] Lack of consumer spending power has also meant there was not the need to offer the same breadth of product range. Eastern Europe has also been a supply base for the company. When IKEA tried to source products for its Danish stores in the early stages of growth, it encountered the same opposition from Danish suppliers with Swedish customers as it had experienced in the domestic market from its Swedish competitors. In response, IKEA began to import furniture from Eastern Europe.[15] Plans to open stores in Russia were delayed owing to problems between Russian local and national authorities, as well as to demands for payment in Western currency.[16]

International Strategic Planning: Europe

IKEA's market entry strategy in European markets has been based predominantly on organic growth. Small markets adjacent to major markets have been chosen in order to gain market experience and to act as a bridgehead to further expansion: Switzerland, the first foreign venture outside of Scandinavia, because it is adjacent to Germany, and Canada (where franchises were established) prior to entry into the US market.[17,18] The Canadian franchises were subsequently bought back by the company. Cautious development prior to more rapid expansion is a feature of IKEA's strategic planning process. Supporting the creation of new stores in new markets is the market entry planning group, which consists of two subgroups: the construction group and the first year group.[19] The construction group has responsibility for developing a new store and the first year group for the first year of operation. Once operational, high levels of support are maintained from the company's headquarters during the first year of operation; this first store then acts as a pilot for further expansion. Only in the Belgian market has the company adopted a different mode of market entry. In this market, four units were acquired and refurbished in the IKEA style. The outcome of this rapid mode of market entry was that the company's product pricing position in the marketplace was fixed at too high a level and it took two to three years to establish the pricing level appropriate to IKEA's marketing strategy.

International Marketing Strategy:
The IKEA Catalogue

The first catalogue was produced in 1951.[20] This annual catalogue is the company's main marketing tool and serves a dual purpose, introducing the company to new customers and enabling exisiting consumers to decide on a purchase in the comfort of their own homes. The catalogue is used in all markets and varies little between them, adaptation being made mainly to accommodate language and currency differences. IKEA's careful control of costs is also reflected in the production of the catalogue: costs are kept low through the use of idle printing capacity. In 1992, sixty million catalogues were given away free. In the domestic market the catalogue is automatically sent to every household. In total, twenty-seven editions are produced in twelve languages across the global operation. The company's marketing strategy also includes the use of local press and radio campaigns.[21]

International Sourcing

Volume purchases and efficient production are essential requirements of the company's sourcing policy. Since its foundation, the company has refined sourcing policies and developed in line with suppliers' production capacity. Prototypes of new furniture are developed by IKEA employees in conjunction with production engineers and suppliers. Where necessary, support is given to introduce new systems and equipment at suppliers' production units. Products may be made up of parts manufactured by four or five different suppliers. In selecting manufacturers, choice is not restricted to the furniture industry: relationships have been developed with suppliers from, for example, the building industry.[22] Where necessary, the company buys production capacity rather than a guaranteed quantity of products. In a number of countries, IKEA has entered joint agreements in order to develop the supply base through acting as joint owners or financiers to furniture industry suppliers, as in Poland, Slovakia, Russia, Rumania and Bulgaria.

Some factories have also been aquired. A major objective of the company's sourcing policy is to be production-orientated, buying low-cost production capacity. Products are designed with economy in mind, for example the same carcass may be used for kitchen and bedroom furnishings. Usually there is more than one supplier for each article and IKEA's manufacturing requirements do not exceed more than 50 per cent of any supplier's capacity. More than 1,500 suppliers in over fifty countries supply the company's product range, which is purchased through the central purchasing office in Sweden. IKEA usually accounts for a significant share of a supplier's total production, but the supplier provides only a small part of the total IKEA purchases.

Management Structure

Dilution of the IKEA philosophy in overseas units is prevented by the use of Swedish nationals in stores and by visits by store workers to Sweden to look at new product ranges. Tight controls exist in terms of cost control and maintenance of the typically Swedish concept. Outside of the domestic market, responsibility for operational success is then developed to individual operating units/stores. This Scandinavian influence is a cornerstone of the company's trading philosophy. Significant levels of responsibility are devolved to stores, with support from the company's administrative centre in Denmark. The centre exerts incentive controls on stores, for example interest is levied on stock which is held in excess of a specified number of weeks. Stores 'pull' stock rather than the centre pushing stock out. Similarly, the overall business plan for the UK is sent from the administrative centre in Denmark and it is then the responsibility of each store to interpret this into their own business plan. All stores pay interest on merchandise in stock. This interest is paid into the banking side of the business which is based in Switzerland. This levy of interest acts as a management control and also devolves the responsibility of maintaining accurate stock levels to each operating unit. Each store is then subject to the same discipline as if it were buying direct from a supplier. Additionally, stores pay a 3 per cent charge to IKEA for the IKEA copyright.

Within each IKEA store an informal, non-status-orientated structure exists. All staff wear the distinctive red colours of IKEA personnel. Only four levels of responsibility exist in-store: store manager, department head, group leader and co-worker. These functions reflect different responsibilities and skills. The company prides itself on being a flexible organization with little formality.

The Globalization of Retailing

A key difference between the globalization of retailing and that of manufacturing is the number of organizations competing in the global arena. Only a handful of retailers operate across world markets, and those which do so rarely compete in the same markets as other global competitors targeting the same group of customers. Two major forces drive the globalization of markets: the homogenization of the world's wants, and people's willingness to forgo specific function design and the like for lower prices at high quality.[23]

As part of its international success, one of IKEA's strengths has been the ability to gain consumer acceptance of its products, irrespective of culture, owing to its low prices. The scale of company developments in world markets has been supported through a strong product orientation. A major issue facing companies developing across world markets is that of the extent to which they should standardize their product offering and marketing activity or whether significant adaptation to different markets should take place. Global retailers 'essentially target the same group of customers in each country, whose offer varies little across national boundaries with strong central control dependent on excellent information systems.'[24] An industry's potential for globalization is dependent on market, economic, environmental and competitive factors. Market factors determine how receptive consumers are to global products. Economic forces determine the extent to which a global strategy provides a cost advantage, and environmental factors indicate the existence of the necessary infrastructure.[25]

IKEA has sought to influence these factors in international furnishings markets. Through its price-led marketing strategy it has influenced consumers' receptiveness to the IKEA product range; economies of scale in sourcing, marketing and merchandizing provide the company with significant cost advantages which have been unmatched by competitors, and the search for new, non-tradtional supplies from other sectors has created a supply structure in the domestic market which competitors have been unable to replicate as this changing infrastructure has been created over a twenty-five year period in the domestic market (Exhibit 14.1).

In Sweden, the basis of the company's competitive advantage has been careful cost control, price as a major strategic tool and differentiation from the narrow, traditional furniture operating format through the use of broad range of merchandise which was accessible to a wider range of people.

When IKEA began its strategy of overseas development outside Scandinavia, the company had helped to create a supply base in Sweden that could not be copied in the short term without considerable investment. By working closely with manufacturers, it had supported the growth of the supply base and created new suppliers until it had at its disposal a purchasing and distribution system that could not be challenged.[26]

The strategic routes by which companies can develop a global orientation differ. Five main methods of becoming a global player are:

1. Play big in major markets.
2. Standardize the core product.

Exhibit 14.1 *Traditional furnishing industry structure (left) and changes introduced by IKEA (right)*

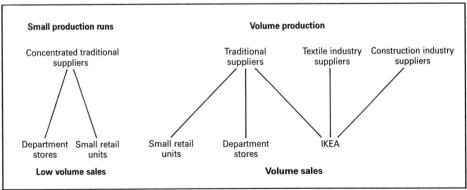

3. Concentrate on value-added activities.

4. Adopt a uniform marketing position and marketing mix.

5. Integrate competitive strategy across countries.[27]

IKEA has, in the course of global expansion, standardized its core product, adopted a uniform marketing position and marketing mix and integrated its competitive strategy across countries. At an organizational level, three major factors support globalization:

1. The need to think of the world as one market, even if this means accepting a low return on investment.

2. The need to make policy and operational changes, e.g. setting financial performance targets that differ across different country operations.

3. The need to view, country by country, positions as interdependent and not as independent elements of a worldwide portfolio. The successful global competitor manages its business in various countries as a single system, not as a portfolio of independent positions.[28]

International Development in the 1990s

By 1993 IKEA had developed from a one-man business into an expanding global enterprise (Exhibit 14.2). Although its initial roots were in retailing and mail order, corporate growth had brought with it increasing diversification, with vertical integration into manufacturing in Eastern Europe through joint ventures and company-owned manufacturing units. In the UK market, one of the company's competitors (Habitat) had been purchased outright by the Dutch foundation which owns IKEA. Additionally, IKEA's company founder had begun to distance himself from operational control of the business and a new company president, Anders Moberg, had been appointed in 1986. Under his management, the company had expanded in the US market. This growth in the USA had not taken place as rapidly as originally anticipated. In Europe, a steady expansion was still taking place, with plans for further store openings. Saturation was beginning to occur in some markets, in particular the smaller ones such as Belgium.[29] Additionally, new Swedish managers were brought into the company from outside organizations, in contrast to the more orthodox route of developing managers through the business.[30] By 1991/92 the company's total surface area worldwide had reached 1,517,200 square metres[31] and the number of visitors worldwide had reached 95,748,000.[32] Future growth plans included concentration on what was East Germany and to maintain the existing spread of international store opening. Anders Moberg was quoted as saying, future plans were to 'structure growth, to decentralize more and grow further around the world to respond quickly.'[33]

Exhibit 14.2 *IKEA outlets worldwide, 1993*

Country	Number of stores	Country	Number of stores
Europe			
Austria	3	Italy	4
Belgium	4	Netherlands	4
Czechoslovakia	2	Poland	4
Denmark	3	Sweden	13
France	7	Switzerland	5
Hungary	1	UK	5
Rest of the world			
Australia	7		
Canada	8		
USA	12		
Outlets outside the IKEA Group			
Australia	1	Singapore	1
Hong Kong	4	Spain	3
Iceland	1	The Netherlands	1
Kuwait	1	United Arab Emirates	1
Saudi Arabia	2		

Source: IKEA Facts 1992/93.

Summary

The growth of IKEA in world markets highlights not only the ability of a retail organization to develop internationally despite differences in consumer culture, but also the benefits of careful market entry timing and gradual, as opposed to rapid, market development.

Although the company has had land in Finland for the past twenty years, IKEA has not, as yet, considered the time to be right to establish any stores in this market. A major feature of IKEA's historical development is that of learning by growing with the marketplace, the first store in a country acting as a pilot for further expansion. Decentralization has given the organization the flexibility to develop in this way. This belief in decentralization is an internally driven force linked to the company principles of being a 'socialistic organization'[34] which 'theoretically allows a more flexible response to local market conditions'.[35] A unique feature of organizational development within IKEA has been its ability to retain this structure despite escalating operating scale and competitive pressures across international markets.

Future challenges will face the organization in terms of preventing dilution of the typically Swedish nature of the company's operations, maintaining a centralized sourcing policy as growth occurs in new markets, and broadening the product range as the concept becomes mature in those markets in which the company has traded longest.

Notes

1. K. Travis 'Centralised corporate structure may not be the most effective form for UK retailers to meet the demands of the future', unpublished thesis, Department of Retailing and Marketing, Manchester Metropolitan University, 1993.
2. IKEA, 'The future is filled with opportunities', IKEA internal training handbook, December 1984.
3. *IKEA Facts 1988/89*, IKEA International A/S Strandvej 21 3050, Humblebaek, Denmark.
4. Economic Intelligence Unit, Company profile, IKEA, *Retail Business Quarterly Trade Review*, No. 25, March 1993.
5. 'IKEA logs furniture sales 2.7 times industry average', *Financial Times*, 17 May 1992.
6. 'Daring to be different?', *Retail Week*, 26 March 1993.
7. *Ibid.*
8. *Ibid.*
9. 'Habitat sold for £78m in a new grand design', *Daily Telegraph*, 27 October 1992.
10. Economic Intelligence Unit, *op. cit.*
11. *Marketing*, 8 July 1993.
12. *Marketing Week*, 13 August 1993.
13. *Retail News Letter*, no. 406, October 1993.
14. *Retail News Letter*, no. 367, March 1990.
15. N. Kinch and J. Johansson, *Fallet IKEA in sou 1981*: 43 De Internationella Investeringarnos Effekter Naegra Fallstudier, Liber Stockholm, 1981.
16. 'Re-arranging the Furniture', *International Management*, September 1991.
17. R. Martenson, 'Is standardisation of marketing feasible in culturebound industries? A European case study', *International Marketing Review*, Autumn 1987, pp. 7–17.
18. G. Götberg, 'Franchising in international marketing', in B. Wicksrom, *Marketing at the Gothenburg School of Economics*, BAS, 1989.
19. B.M. Lenfors, 'IKEA Einfallstudium mit dem Schwergewicht auf IKEA's Internationalisierungsstegie und Etablierung in Wien', unpublished paper, University of Lund.
20. *IKEA Facts 1988/89, op. cit.*
21. *Management Europe*, December/January 1991/92.
22. Kinch and Johansson, *op. cit.*
23. T. Levitt, 'The globalization of markets', *Harvard Business Review*, May/June 1983, pp. 92–101.
24. A. Tordjman, 'Internationalism – the route to growth', *Retail and Distribution Management*, March/April 1989.
25. G.S. Yip, P.H. Loewe and M.Y. Yoshino, 'How to take your company to the global market', *Columbia Journal of World Business*, Winter 1988.
26. Kinch and Johansson, *op. cit.*
27. Yip *et al.*, *op. cit.*
28. T. Hout, M.E. Porter and E. Rudden, 'How global companies win out', *Harvard Business Review*, September/October, 1982.
29. 'The Return of the Vikings', *Marketplace*, Spring 1986.
30. *Stores International Award*, Anders Moberg, January 1992.
31. *IKEA Facts 1991/92*, IKEA International A/S Strandrej 21, 3050, Humblebaek, Denmark.
32. *Ibid.*

33.   *Stores International Award*, *op. cit.*
34.   Travis, *op. cit.*
35.   S. Burt, 'Trends in management issues in European Retailing', *International Journal of Retailing* vol. 4, no. 4, 1989.

CASE 15

Carlsberg Ice Beer

Ian Wilson
University of Staffordshire

Radio 5, 20 July 1994, 6 a.m.

PETER ALLEN: Just when you'd got used to widgets, continental lagers and sticking fruit down bottle necks, Britain's brewers have come up with a new trend which they say will be bigger than any of them. It's called ice beer, it's already taken 12 per cent of the beer market in Australia and Canada and this month sees its launch in Britain. Not everyone's raving about it including Britain's best known beer writer, Michael Jackson, who joins me along with a great array of glasses and bottles. Better hand them out while you're talking Michael . . . First of all, what's different about ice beer?

MICHAEL JACKSON: It's frozen during the production procedure, sometimes during fermentation, sometimes during the maturation.

PA: Adrian Childs has suddenly come rushing into the studio so we're clearly going to try this in a second. What do you think of it?

MJ: It's just really the latest gimmick from the big lager brewers to find a way of making beer tasteless.

PA: You didn't approve of shoving fruit down the bottlenecks either, did you? I can see it on your face.

MJ: Well, there are some beers that are supposed to have a slice of lemon in them. A German wheat beer sometimes has a slice of lemon in it, but in the case of some of those very light Mexican lagers that was just a marketing gimmick and really ice beer is a marketing gimmick too, it's . . . there is a genuine process involved, but to what end is rather open to question.

PA: And there's only one way of really being sure about all this. Now, Jane Garvey, despite her demure appearance, has been known to sup the occasional beverage. We'll have a little slurp of it. Hang on a second.

JANE GARVEY: Let's do a big sound effect . . . I think you should aim for the . . . (laughter)

246

PA: I would . . . I would stress that we're only sipping a . . . sipping just the very top of the glass. We've got Torin Douglas here as well and Adrian. What do you think, Jane?

JG: I'd rather have a rum and peppermint, but it's alright.

PA: Torin?

TORIN DOUGLAS: Doesn't taste very different from any other cool lager I think.

PA: Adrian?

ADRIAN CHILDS: I'm glad I haven't paid for it, but . . . no real difference, no.

PA: And so . . . and so to our central guest Michael Jackson, what do you think? I mean, is it going to take off? I suppose it will because these whizzo things tend to just happen and . . .

MJ: Well these . . . these whizzo things tend to last about three years and they tend to be not a nine day wonder but not a nine year wonder either, you know. We had lite beer, we had dry beer and now we have ice beer, it's the latest in that line. There's something missing in the middle of it. When you're . . . on your tongue, it just sort of vanishes somehow. I think what's missing in the middle is a bit of maltiness.

PA: Yeah. Now.

MJ: Doesn't really taste like beer, you know.

PA: Do we have somebody . . . I think we have somebody else I should be speaking to, not sure who it is. Liz Morgan, yes, on the line, Liz.

LIZ MORGAN: Yes. Hello. Good morning.

PA: Hello. Yeah. Not enormously impressed, the general reaction in the studio to all this though.

LM: Maybe it's too early for people to be drinking beer this morning.

MJ: Oh, not me Liz.

PA: Now, Liz is marketing director of Carlsberg/Tetley, which is about to join the throng by launching a Carlsberg ice beer. It's all terrible marketing nonsense, isn't it Liz? I mean we just want a glass of beer, don't we?

LM: Well, not at all. I was pleased to hear Michael saying that it's a genuine process involved, and of the . . . the way it's produced is, as Michael said, is ice crystals are formed in the beer just after production and then those crystals are gently removed and this leaves a sort of distinctive taste and a smoothness which has certainly been recognized and endorsed by the drinkers that we've asked to try Carlsberg Ice.

PA: I just . . . Liz, I'm prepared to give it one more go just to see . . .

LM: That's very good of you.

PA: Everybody here has given it one more go, and . . .

JG: Still don't like it.

PA: I'll be . . . I'll be honest Liz, we're still not convinced. But you . . . just, very seriously, it's going to be big business, is it Liz?

The words of Peter Allen's last question were still ringing in Liz's ears as she drove to the office. It was the sixty-four million dollar question; but it was not the only question. Liz's thoughts returned to the early days of the Ice Beer project – or Project Rapide, as it had been code named at the beginning.

The beginning was in 1991 with the intention to form Carlsberg/Tetley Brewing Ltd as a 50/50 joint venture between the brewing interests of Danish-owned Carlsberg A/S and those of British-owned Allied–Lyons plc. The 1980s had been the decade of pan-European alliances, and the logic of Carlsberg/Tetley as a joint venture in the UK market was clear. Allied had great strengths in ale, with six breweries and a wide brand portfolio including national and regional ales. From a geographical point of view, the company was strongest in the north and Midlands. Allied also had strengths in directly delivered free trade outlets, and a tied estate of some 4,400 pubs (though this would later be reduced as a result of the so-called Beer Orders). By contrast, Carlsberg in the UK was a business based around a single brewery (additional supplies of Carlsberg were brewed under contract by Courage) with distribution generally arranged through third parties, mainly other brewers and wholesalers. However, Carlsberg had a tremendous UK reputation and a worldwide lager strength with over sixty breweries in forty countries, which in the UK was focused solely on the Carlsberg brand and whose largest penetration had been achieved in the south of England.

Product and distribution complementarity was not the only logic behind the venture. Although standing in third place in the overall UK beer market, Allied's market share was well behind the leaders Bass and Courage (Exhibit 15.1). Carlsberg and Tetley combined, however, would produce a third force able to challenge for leadership.

Having been delayed, pending an investigation by the Monopolies and Mergers Commission, Carlsberg and Tetley finally united in January 1993 with a brand portfolio which included the bestselling bitter brand in the UK, Tetley, and a range of lagers which were either owned or brewed under licence. The main lagers were:

- Carlsberg Pilsner, 3.4% ABV (alcohol by volume), the fastest growing major draught standard lager in the UK on trade, supported by the famous 'Probably' campaign.

- Carlsberg Export, 4.7% ABV, number two draught premium lager in the independent trade.

- Carlsberg Special Brew, 9% ABV, the leading superstrength lager in the UK market.

Exhibit 15.1 *Major brewers' shares of total UK beer sales by type of beer and type of outlet*

	Total	By type of beer (%)		By type of outlet[a] (%)		
		Ale	Lager	Tied on-trade	Free on-trade[b]	Off-trade
Allied	13	13	13	15	13	10
Carlsberg	1	0	2	0	2	1
	14	13	15	15	15	11
Bass	22	20	24	22	24	18
Courage/Grand Met	19	17	21	19	18	22
Whitbread	12	13	11	13	11	11
S&N	11	12	9	7	12	14
All national brewers and Carlsberg	78	75	80	75	80	76
All national brewers	77	75	78	76	78	75

[a] The retail beer market can be divided into the on-trade (approximately 80 per cent) and the off- (or take-home) trade. An on-trade outlet is licensed to sell alcohol for consumption on and off the premises. The main on-trade outlets are public houses, of which some are tied to the supply of particular beers through ownership by brewers, some are owned but controlled at arm's length (free on-trade) and others are independent (free trade). Other on-trade outlets include clubs and restaurants. The main off-trade outlets include specialist off-licences (multiples and independents) and multiple and independent grocers.
[b] Includes sales to independents.
Source: Allied/Carlsberg estimates and major brewers.

- Castlemaine XXXX, 3.9% ABV, fastest growing major draught standard in free pubs, award-winning advertising campaign.
- Skol, 3.4% ABV, number two in the off-trade.
- Swan Light, 0.9% ABV, number two of the low alcohol lagers in the UK.
- Lowenbrau, 5.0% ABV, leading German draught premium lager in UK.

Exhibit 15.2 compares the market shares of the top ten on-trade and off-trade brands.

Carlsberg/Tetley now felt that it could claim a leading brand in every sector of the market. However, there was a general feeling that while performance had been solid, it had not been exciting. With the Carlsberg brand itself this had largely been deliberate. Carlsberg had steered clear of radical innovations in the beer market (such as dry beer) in order to avoid diluting its credentials as the custodian of traditional, quality, lager beer values. Nevertheless, management sensed that Carlsberg/Tetley had not had a great story to stir the trade and the public since the launch of Castlemaine XXXX in 1984.

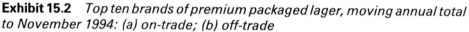

Exhibit 15.2   *Top ten brands of premium packaged lager, moving annual total to November 1994: (a) on-trade; (b) off-trade*

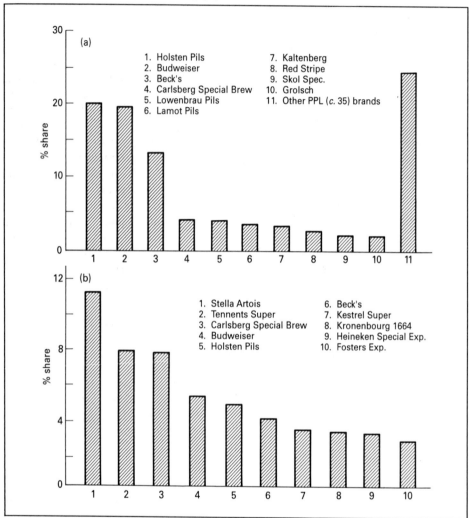

Additionally, it was recognized that the Carlsberg/Tetley presence in the premium packaged lager (PPL) segment was not as strong as desirable. PPL was now equivalent to 10 per cent of the total beer market and growing at a rate of 7 per cent year on year. This contrasted with that premium draught lager sector which accounted for only 5 per cent of the market and was growing at only 1 per cent a year and standard draught lager with 25 per cent of the total market, the largest sector, but declining by 5 per cent year on year. Increasingly, PPL drinkers were looking for an AVB of above 5.0 per cent and were looking for ever-increasing quality and distinctiveness.

The Ice Sector

The ice beer process was developed by Labatt and introduced in Canada in April 1993. The process involves freezing all the beer at $-4°C$ and then gently removing the ice crystals. The result was said to be a 'uniquely balanced smooth tasting beer' and an ABV of 5.6%.

Labatt's were not to be alone in the market for long. Molson introduced its own beer in Canada in 1993 but using a different process. Their beer was 'super-chilled' rather than frozen, the process leading to an ABV of 5.0 per cent and, purportedly, not quite able to replicate the smoothness and balance of the ice beer.

In July 1993, intelligence from Canada suggested that ice beer had rapidly gained as much as 8 per cent of the total beer market, divided equally between Labatt and Molson. However, the impression within the on- and off-trade was that there was a 'definite possibility' that ice beer could be just another short-lived fad, like dry beer. In the short term, however, Labatt's had other worries. In August they filed an injunction against Molson's use of the term 'ice-brewed' and issued the following press release:

> We have a responsibility to our shareholders, to our employees, and to our consumers to put a stop to false and misleading claims by Molson. We are also taking this step to protect the $25 million investment we have made in developing the exclusive ice brewing process which gives us this unique product.
>
> We created the Ice Beer category and Labatt Ice Beer™ is the only legitimate entry. However, in recent weeks Molson has deliberately attempted to create confusion in the minds of consumers by relabelling several conventionally brewed brands as 'ice-brewed'. If it's not Labatt, it's not Ice Brewed™.
>
> Labatt Ice Beer uses exclusive equipment and a proprietary technology developed in the Labatt experimental brewery in London, Ontario. The company has applied for patents on the technology, and is in discussions with brewers around the world regarding potential licensing agreements.
>
> Sharon Paul, executive vice president of public affairs

One such brewer was Carlsberg/Tetley, who already had good trading relationships with Labatt in the UK and had helped to establish Labatt Ice Beer in the on-trade through their extensive distribution network. Carlsberg/Tetley thus had early recognition of the response to Labatt Ice Beer, and results were coming in of launches in other countries. In Australia, Ice Beer from Carlton and United Breweries captured over 10 per cent of the beer market within four months. Share in Canada had, by the end of 1993, risen to 12 per cent of the beer market. In the USA, ice beer had a 4 per cent share. Perhaps most impressive of all was Labatt's sales of two million cans in six months in Japan, making it the leading imported beer there.

The questions facing Carlsberg/Tetley seemed to be:

1. Would ice beer become a long-term sustainable opportunity or would it be a short-term fad?
2. Would the introduction of an ice beer under the Carlsberg brand endanger its position as a serious brewer?
3. Was there room for another ice brew market entrant?
4. What would be the impact on Labatt sales if Carlsberg/Tetley introduced its own brand?
5. If Carlsberg/Tetley did introduce an ice brew, should it use the Labatt process?

The last question was the easiest to answer. Although Carlsberg/Tetley would have to pay royalties to Labatt, they would gain a number of benefits. First, they would be able to offer a 'genuine' ice brew. This would provide one point of differentiation against most competitors as well as preserving Carlsberg's genuine credentials. Secondly, it would maintain and build good relationships with Labatt. Thirdly, the Labatt process could be easily accommodated in Carlsberg/Tetley's Wrexham brewery.

The other Labatt issue was only slightly more problematic. Whilst there would clearly be some element of competition between Carlsberg and Labatt, it was generally felt that Carlsberg brew using the same process would boost the total sector to the benefit of both brewers. A further point on which Carlsberg/Tetley was relatively happy was that there would be sufficient scope for differentiation of Carlsberg from Labatt. Different recipes and ingredients, in addition to the benefits of the Labatt process, would result in product variation. The scope for differentiation through packaging and promotion was also thought to be considerable.

Looking at the third question, American experience suggested that the number of entrants would increase. Within twelve months of Labatt's launching in North America, there were thirty ice brands on the market. Carlsberg/Tetley formed the view that if it could be satisfied on questions 1 and 2, then an early launch in the UK market would give them a measure of protection against followers. Early really meant second.

Debate within Carlsberg/Tetley focused on questions 1 and 2 and associated issues. Whilst some saw ice as just another fad, there was also the possibility, at the other extreme, that, with its perceived quality advantages, the ice brew could develop into a mainstream process. A parallel dichotomy existed in respect of the Carlsberg brand. On the one hand, without a new sub-brand for twenty years, Carlsberg had avoided being associated with gimmicks. On the other hand, without any innovation for twenty years, was the brand in need of some regeneration? Carlsberg/Tetley decided to submit the issues to research. Preliminary research had led Carlsberg/Tetley to the conclusion that ice beer could have strong potential but only if managed carefully, and further, that it could play a role in enhancing the Carlsberg brand credentials with the PPL (premium packaged lager) sector and revitalizing the brand in general – but again, subject to careful handling. Accordingly, further qualitative research was commissioned to increase understanding of the emerging ice beer opportunity within the PPL sector.

Project Rapide

Ten focus groups were held in London and Manchester covering the following drinkers of more than six bottles/pints per week of premium lager:

1. Labatt Ice triallists, aged 20–25;
2. Carlsberg loyalists, aged 25-40;
3. Carlsberg rejectors, aged 18–25;
4. Premium packaged/premium draught lager (PPL/PDL, defined as most often drinkers of Budweiser, Beck's, Molson Dry, Rolling Rock, Oranjeboom, Grolsch, Coors, etc.), aged 18–25 and 25–35.

Discussion topics included drinking behaviour and attitudes, recent innovations, brand imagery, awareness and expectations of the ice beer concept, reactions to Carlsberg Ice Beer and alternative packaging graphics.

Ice triallists had so far tended to be 'serial experimenters' and 'promiscuous' within the PPL category. Research suggested their approval of, if not enthusiasm for, the product's performance. It also appeared that the product story was not well understood and that the product concept of 'balance' had not been grasped. Perceptions of current packaging were not favourable, adding to the problems of visibility cause by limited distribution. Triallists had rarely repeat-purchased. In short, ice beer was not yet established.

Non-ice-triallists showed immediate curiosity as to the reason for the development, but on balance expected it to be more of a sales gimmick than an enhanced product until they tested the product itself. However, they did associate innovation with the PPL sector.

Among respondents in general there was an expectation that an ice beer would emerge from a brewer with one or all of the following characteristics:

1. Record of innovation, PPL credentials, brewing excellence.
2. Affinity with a cold climate.
3. A need to enter the PPL sector.

Respondents' perceptions of brewers and the probability that they would launch an ice beer product are plotted in Exhibit 15.3. Reaction to the notion of Carlsberg introducing an ice beer was generally one of modest surprise but not real resistance. Amongst existing Carlsberg drinkers, 'hard core' loyalists were perplexed by the proposal, whilst those who included Carlsberg within a wider repertoire were more open-minded. Further reflection led to the view that Carlsberg must consider ice

Exhibit 15.3   *Respondents' perceptions of brewers and assessments of the probability that they would launch an ice beer*

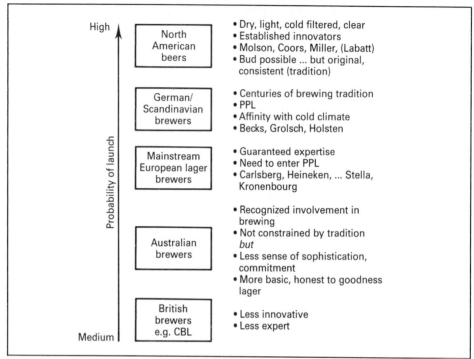

beer to be a genuine innovation in brewing technology because it would not risk its reputation for a 'quick buck'.

Carlsberg/Tetley management felt that Project Rapide research had been sufficiently encouraging to move ahead with further product research and development, and consideration of positioning concepts. It seemed that ice beer could potentially complement the existing Carlsberg range and result in a portfolio that was clearly aimed at distinct types of drinker (and perhaps drinking occasions) and yet remain consistent with Carlsberg's overall desired position as 'the best quality sessionable lager, brewed with experience and expertise'. Liz had pondered the possibilities.

Carlsberg Pilsner brewed for . . .
Carlsberg Export brewed for . . .
Carlsberg Special Brew brewed for . . .
Carlsberg Ice Beer brewed for . . .

Beyond this, the ultimate opportunity lay in the possibility that Carlsberg's association with brewing excellence could bring further endorsement to ice beers, whilst the introduction of ice beer could lead to a rediscovery of Carlsberg. Clearly, the realization of this potential symbiosis depended on how effectively Carlsberg/ Tetley implemented the positioning strategy. The key issues seemed to be:

1. How to identify and describe the target drinkers.
2. How to convey the taste and drinking benefits produced by ice brewing.
3. How to add an appropriate emotional dimension to the functional benefits.
4. How to use a more measured and less brash tone of voice than that used by existing ice brands so as to convey more self-confidence.
5. How to manage the handling process so that Carlsberg values are linked to Ice Beer without the Carlsberg name swamping the identity of Ice Beer.
6. How to package and advertise the product in line with the considerations above.
7. How to price.
8. Where to distribute.

Two further general decisions needed to be addressed:

9. What taste formulation to settle on.
10. How much investment to put behind the launch.

In terms of consumer segmentation, Carlsberg/Tetley managment had been searching more for an appropriate basis than demographics. The pressure to find a solution had hitherto not been so great since the Carlsberg brand, albeit with a leaning towards lighter and older users, had traditionally appealed to a wide range of users. Indeed, research had shown that Carlsberg was second and third choice amongst a wide variety of drinkers.

It was now becoming clear, however, that to achieve preference, more attention needed to be paid to tighter segmentation and to better understanding consumer needs and wants. One approach under consideration, based on Target Group Index (TGI) data, led to the view that 'good time men' was the market of principal interest to Carlsberg, with the possibility that 'good time boys' might be the right target for Carlsberg Ice Beer. Whilst 'good time men' could be considered as 'good time boys' who had grown up, there was also a degree of crossover (Exhibits 15.4 and 15.5). TGI data showed that such profiles applied to above-average consumers of lager from all ages and social grades.

A second approach was based on the degree to which consumers exhibited different degrees of dependence on beer as a vehicle for self-expression (Exhibit 15.6).

With the target consumer in mind, the Carlsberg/Tetley team began to develop a tentative marketing plan for a possible launch fo Carlsberg Ice and its subsequent development. The basic broad proposition which was emerging was 'only Carlsberg achieves the desired balance between the distinctiveness of ice beer and the heritage, authority and confidence of an international brewer's reputation'. Was this strong enough to motivate consumer and trade?

Exhibit 15.4 *Good time men*

What they read
Time Out
Car Week
Loaded
Q
Classic & Sports Car
Mojo
Today

Aspirations
Golf GTi
MG
Convertibles

Newspapers
Guardian
Independent

Good Time Men

What they wear
Timberland
Kickers
Levis

Films
The Crying Game
Much Ado About Nothing
Philadelphia
Unforgiven

Sport
Rugby
Motor racing
Cricket
Snooker
Football

Radio
GLR
JFM
Virgin

TV
Whose Line is it Anyway
Red Dwarf
Absolutely
Northern Exposure
Channel 4 News
South Bank Show
Cutting Edge
American Football

Exhibit 15.5 *Good time boys*

What they read
Vox
GQ
Performance Car
Penthouse
Sky
Viz
90 Minutes

Aspirations
Motorbikes
Jeeps
Harley Davidsons
Porsche

Newspapers
Daily Mirror
The Sun

Good Time Boys

What they wear
Fila
Stussy
Lonsdale
Diesel Jeans
Caterpiller

Films
True Lives
Sliver
Wayne's World

Sport
Football
Horse Racing

Radio
Capital FM
Kiss FM
Faze FM

TV
Big Breakfast
Games Master
Vic Reeve's Big Night Out
Beavis & Butthead
Spitting Image
Men Behaving Badly
Beverly Hills 90210
The Word

Exhibit 15.6 *Use of beer as a vehicle for self-expression*

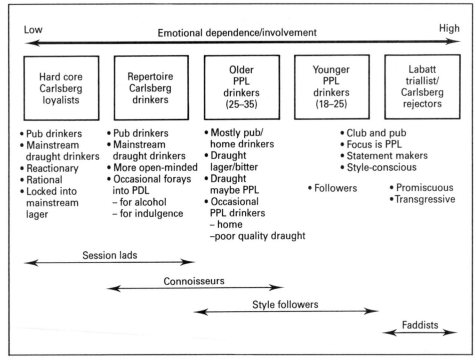

Project Rapide packaging research had shown clear preference for one of the packaging alternatives: a 330 millilitre long-necked amber bottle with screen-printed white and silver graphics. Was it sufficiently distinctive, though, and was the graphic balance between Carlsberg and Ice Beer about right to make it 'clearly Carlsberg but distinctively Ice Beer'?

Initial thoughts on pricing suggested a premium to Labatt Ice. This might help to support a long-term objective to become a mainstream PPL competing with Beck's and Budweiser, but would it make if difficult to secure initial distribution? Maybe not, if distribution were deliberately built slowly, targeting initially only leading-edge brasseries, café bars, wine bars and night clubs.

Meanwhile, additional product research based on refined formulations was looking even more favourable. Of 138 male PPL drinkers aged between 18 and 30, 64 per cent said the beer was better than expected, 82 per cent claimed they would definitely/probably buy and 21 per cent said it was better than their usual brand. Within a fortnight, however, in June, Fosters Ice Beer was launched, making it the second UK ice contender and refocusing attention on Carlsberg's approach to promotional activity. Estimates suggested that a combined total of £7.5 million was being spent on product launch by Fosters and Labatt. Would Carlsberg need to spend similarly to be heard or would Labatt's and Fosters' advertising create sufficient interest for consumers actively to seek out other brands to try?

'Well, the die is cast for the moment,' Liz thought aloud. The trade press was alerted on 4 July and a full briefing of the Carlsberg selling team would take place on 1 August. Support material would be available to the trade from mid-August. Carlsberg Ice Beer had arrived, but as Liz mulled over the decisions taken so far, she realized that the debate was by no means over. The first indications of success or otherwise would not appear until October when distribution, rate of sale, repeat purchase and response to promotional campaigns would be subject to their first evaluation. Had Carlsberg brewed up a hot prospect or would the icy future be a bleak one?